Mark Pimlott

The Public Interior

Jap Sam Books

as Idea and Project

For my sisters

I

II

III

IV

V

VI

Introduction 9

The Garden 16

The Palace 58

The Ruin 96

The Shed 148

The Machine 188

The Network 240

Notes 285
Bibliography 291
Index 294
Image index 297
Colophon 302

Introduction

The interior is fundamental to architecture. Building, in its elemental task of making shelter, protects a space—the interior—from the vagaries of nature, whether inclement weather or predators. Architecture, as distinct from building, communicates that task through its outward and inward appearances, situating and binding its sheltered interior in and to the world. The interior is that space that architecture makes, which is all at once set apart from the world and in its midst. The interior also lies at the root of the settlement, in which a set of interiors and their shelters are set apart from and within the world. The settlement claims a space from the world, within which everything becomes a constituent part of the settlement's interior. In the processes of making of Roman settlements—augury, survey, measure and the cutting of the sulcis, the ritual ploughing of a trench for the foundations of the settlement wall—a space was rendered distinct from the world. That space became an interior set in the world, within which dwellings, monuments, streets and citizens resided, under a range of laws and beliefs. More than a millennium later, Western European empires colonised remote, resource-laden lands: settlements in these new 'hinterlands' at once claimed interiorised domains for their elites and interests, and extended the space of these empires far beyond the spaces defined by their own national boundaries or walled cities. In the United States, the claiming of territories to the west of the east coast colonial settlements followed an abstract, projective method similar to that of the Romans but devised to address the scale of a continent, driving a process that violently wrested these territories from their indigenous occupants; a process that achieved the elimination of space of the other (and the other), and its replacement with a vast and continuous interior.

The interior, regardless of its scale, whether it is that of a dwelling, a temple, a settlement, a city or a continental territory, is informed and shaped by ideas. The interior of the settlement is a space of agreement: in the case of Roman colonial settlements, this could be understood as a set of relations and laws that were consistent with the ideology of Rome. The 'interior' of the United States was shaped by ideology, premised on notions of freedom from authority, individual self-realisation, and divine authority, justifying the banishment and replacement of the other. In our urbanised societies we recognise that the spaces we occupy are those of broad ideological coherence, and despite their internal conflicts and oppositions, they attempt to manage otherness and radiate and aura of agreement, which architecture reinforces. Societies, in order to cohere, promote their agreements as ideology, and as ideas that reflect their sense of themselves and their conceits. These ideas are articulated in cultural expressions and in the representations and arrangements of spaces of our urbanised environment, and projected onto the spaces that we share and experience, regardless of our feeling of identification, enfranchisement or empowerment as citizens. These ideas appear in architecture and in the great variety of those interiors that we take to be public: those within which we consider ourselves to be free individuals, and where we see ourselves among others; those within which we are conscious of our place in society and in the world.

Throughout this book, I will refer to these spaces as 'public interiors'. The term requires some clarification, as many take it to denote publicly owned and fully accessible interiors, discrete and distinct from their contexts. Public interiors as I shall discuss them are those spaces taken to be public, even though they may be privately owned and operated,[1] imposing restrictions upon or determining behaviour, calibrating performance, or shaping relations to authority, others and the world. For example, many people perceive the sheltered streets of a shopping mall as a public interior, despite the fact that its internal streets are likely to be owned and operated by a development corporation or management group. What the shopping mall presents to its visitors is the impression that they occupy a realm which they temporarily 'own', one in which they can behave as though they are in public, with caveats: that their behaviour conforms to reasonable limits that are somehow implicit in their atmosphere, appearances and organisation, and made explicit by security agents when it is deemed that those limits have been transgressed. Despite this, the shopping mall, like the museum—which may indeed be a truly public building—is habitually regarded as a public interior. The public interior realm as it is perceived is in fact in the control of a variety of agents, some serving the public interest more generously than others.

As one surveys the public interiors that we occupy regularly, it is evident that they have a great impact on the shaping of public life and the public's sense of its capacities and liberties. This should be of concern to all those involved in the design of cities and the dispersed urban condition that dominates Western experience, and architects in particular. Those interiors that can be thought of as formative and representative of the society we make include spaces of sociability, of entertainment, of display, of consumption, of contemplation, of looking, of listening, of learning, of representation, of worship, of work, of care, and inevitably, of control. It is clear that the public interior as we recognise it—beyond the cathedral, the bazaar or the market—has emerged in modernity, and has appeared in all its variety in response to the emergence of the modern state with its specialised organisation of functions and its increasingly enfranchised populations. It has been enriched specifically in response to the phenomenon of the metropolis. Public interiors have been charged with a variety of tasks within their development, among them, to represent populations, often through representing the interests of a ruling class and inculcating the public with its ideological principles, proposed as values to be assumed by all; to create environments that provide images for societies' dream image of themselves; to shape behaviour and performance; to create environments for social interaction, and in some cases, to make means available for social engagement and action.

'Public interiors' can also include spaces that are highly specialised or even restrictive in their uses. Although we may have had the good fortune not have direct experience of the prison or the hospital, their designs have influenced interior environments that seem to be accessible, free and open. In effect, these restrictive interiors have been models for those that purport to be their opposite. Within this notion of the influential model, whether positive or negative, lies the purpose of this book, its origins, and to some degree its method.

The book is an elaborated transcript of a series of lectures that were delivered to students in the first year of a two-year Masters diploma course in architecture at Delft University of Technology, in the Chair of 'The Architecture of the Interior', and presented between Autumn 2013 and Autumn 2015. The series was intended to offer fundamental references and models to students who would approach architectural design in their studies from the specific perspective of the interior, consistent with the remit of the Chair in this period, which held that the interior was an architectural subject, integral to the very thinking and making of architecture. This diverged from prevailing views regarding the subject of 'Interior Architecture', which have seen it as a distinct discipline, whose education and developing theoretical bases are closely allied to a discourse that regards the interior as an outward projection from the human body toward a preexisting architectural body, and is more connected to psychology than architecture and its territories.[2] For us, it followed that fundamental discussions of the interior would not defer to discussions of the body, clothing, or the occupation and lining of a given architectural shell; rather, they would follow the story of architecture, and inevitably, narratives concerning its origins and ideas that have been inscribed in its realisations and in material culture. The lecture course, 'Fundamentals: Lectures in the Culture of the Public Interior', was preceded by an analytical course, 'Tools and Methods of Analysis for Design', in which key exemplars—drawn from the many planned to be discussed in the lectures—were examined from a series of perspectives, from the organisation and representations of the buildings themselves to the various contexts in which they and the buildings appeared, so that students might come closer to their contemporary appearances, receptions, readings and meanings. The object of this first course was to prepare students for the complexities surrounding the consideration of architecture, and to make them familiar with the thematic or conceptual frameworks in which works were placed within the lecture series. Both courses were addressed to students as architectural designers—rather than historians—in the making.

The question of how one might frame a series of lectures about the public interior in ways that might be engaging as matters of design for architectural designers was central to forming the subjects of the lectures, which are repeated in the chapters of this book. Various treatments seemed possible: one could present public interiors in terms of building types, in the manner of Pevsner; or on the basis of their character, as interiors of sociability, display, or control; or one could place them within a conceptual or thematic framework, in which certain narrative or organising principles—concerns of design—could be shown to run across various types and characteristics. This last path seemed to be the most promising, in that it offered ways of discussing many different kinds of buildings across different historical periods and the themes that ran through them; that they used, evoked and shared expressions with other cultural practices. As a designer myself, it seemed that in the act of looking, one invariably called upon the knowledge of other things one had seen in to understand what one was looking at; similarly, in designing, one also drew upon a very large and varied range of references of direct or oblique relevance. In short, one used one's knowledge of material culture—the ideas of a culture inscribed in what it makes—to interpret what one saw, and crucially, to go about designing something. The lectures would propose cultural material—interiors, in this case—on the basis of themes that seemed to be latent in their appearances, expressions, representations and organisation. In my view, six themes seemed to resonate within the vast canon of public interiors throughout history: the Garden, the Palace, the Ruin, the Shed, the Machine and the Network. These were not arrived at scientifically, but through an admittedly subjective impulse. Within their arrangement, there was an implicit trajectory that began at the Idea of the Beginning, and followed the development of the character of the space of architecture: from the first interior realm (the story of the Garden, isolated from the world until the Fall); to the most perfect, artificial and extensive interior (the Palace and its world of rooms); inward reflection about origins and human failings (the Ruin); to the simple shelter that protected all activities (the Shed); to the sophisticated device that interiorised and regulated complex operations (the Machine); to the great, extensive interior that attended the patterns of wandering and human gathering (the Network). The first themes might be associated with eras of narrative, allusion, representation and contemplation, while the latter themes might lie comfortably within modernity and its tendencies toward rationalisation and instrumentality. It was clear that all of the themes have been drawn upon and have characterised the public interior over many centuries, and have maintained both their relevance and usefulness regardless of their historical context.

The method used to consider public interiors in this book, although dependent upon material and historical fact, espouses that of interpretive analysis, which at its extreme enters the realm of radical subjectivity. The book does not pretend to be scientific: its target groups are neither historians nor academics, but rather those whose creative work relies upon their interpretation of the world and the traditions of their discipline and its practice: it is a book for designers, and for designers in the making. As I was devising the lecture series, it occurred to me that I was drawing upon models of presentation that had a profound impact on my early attraction for material culture, my way of looking, and my way of thinking about architectural design. These were Kenneth Clark's television series *Civilisation*, made for the BBC and broadcast in the spring of 1969, which he described as a 'personal view' rather than a history of the achievements of Western culture; Robert Venturi's nearly contemporary *Complexity and Contradiction in Architecture*, written in 1962 and published as a set of papers by the Museum of Modern Art in New York in 1966, which always struck me as having the character of illustrated lectures through which its author offered highly subjective—and provocative—readings of architecture and its specific concerns as an artistic discipline; and John Berger's 1972 BBC television series *Ways of Seeing*, which reinforced my natural tendency towards looking, and to ask what I saw when I looked at something. Clark's series stimulated me to look and think; Venturi's book stimulated me to look and make; Berger's series stimulated me to look and describe. I thought that I might attempt to charge architecture students similarly, to look, think, make and describe.

In my own descriptions, I have tried to maintain the original tone of the lectures in these chapters; though inevitably, notes for lectures, which one expands upon naturally at a podium, have had to be corralled into a form. In this case, the six lectures have assumed the form of six lecture-like essays, which are nearly as amply illustrated as the lectures themselves. The delivery of the lectures, and the writing of these chapters that has followed them, has benefitted from observations provided by students, who made consistently insightful presentations in the seminars that followed each session.

I would like to acknowledge the many people who made the lecture series and this book possible. The lecture series was supported from the outset as a tool for educating young architects by the former professor of the Chair of Interiors, Buildings and Cities, Tony Fretton, who retired before the series began. Our discussions as friends, designers and colleagues going back many years have made their way into these pages. The idea of transforming the series into a book was raised by Susanne Pietsch, Leontine de Wit and Jurjen Zeinstra, my colleagues at TU Delft, who saw the Fundamentals lecture course, in combination with a course in which works were critically analysed, as central to the programme of educating architects with specific attention to the interior. The making of the book has inevitably meant a temporary absence as a teacher in the Chair, and I wish to thank Professors Dick van Gameren and Tom Avermaete, and the professor of my Chair, Daniel Rosbottom for their support. The lectures benefitted from the input of the tutors of the first, analytical part of the Fundamentals course and by their work thereafter: first by Susanne Pietsch, Birgitte Louise Hansen and Eireen Schreurs, and subsequently by Catherine Visser, Jules Schoonman, Elsbeth Ronner and Sereh Mandias. Their advice and criticism informed and sustained me throughout the ongoing development of the lectures, which was enormously helpful and encouraging. I wish to thank the students of the course, whose work and attentions to selected exemplary projects, and their insightful contributions in presentations and discussions, constantly helped clarify my thinking through the course.

With regard to the text, I am especially grateful to Jurjen Zeinstra for his careful reading of the manuscript and his thoughtful and sympathetic comments, corrections and clarifications. With regard to images, the work of student assistants has been essential to the book's realisation: Caspar Frenken was quietly supportive through his sustained practice of slipping relevant material in front of me at incisive moments. Kristian Spasov tenaciously and tirelessly sought out the myriad illustrations for this book and permissions for their reproduction, a complex task that warrants my special gratitude. He has been a true and valued colleague throughout. The Chair of Interiors Buildings Cities at TU Delft has generously funded reproduction rights for many of the images herein, and I wish to thank the many holders of the rights of these images for their use. I would particularly like to thank the photographers, artists and architects who have courteously granted the reproduction of their images freely or at very discounted rates, especially Marius Grootveld, Thomas Struth, Tim Street-Porter, Michael Dennis, Adam Caruso, Hélène Binet, Charles Tashima and Nelson Garrido.

The production of *The Public Interior as Idea and Project* would not have been possible without the generous and substantial financial support of the Creative Industries Fund NL, who committed themselves to the project with a grant in the autumn of 2014. I am grateful to my publisher, Eleonoor Jap Sam of Jap Sam Books, who has maintained faith in the project from the outset, and has, as ever (this is our third book), mixed support, patience and appropriate doses of urgency throughout. The book's elegant and fluent design is the work of Studio Joost Grootens, in particular Joost Grootens and Silke Koeck, to whom I am yet again grateful: the studio designed my books *Without and within* (episode publishers, 2007) and *In passing* (Jap Sam Books, 2010). Finally, I am indebted to several long-suffering and dear friends who have encouraged, supported and tolerated me for the duration of this project.

Mark Pimlott
The Hague, September 2016

I
THE GARDEN

Architecture and the interior share the same origins. Both are in the World and set apart from it. The story of the interior begins as the story of architecture begins: in 'nature', a world yet to be addressed or altered by Man. Nature appears in our histories of representation in two guises: as Paradise, the Garden in which harmony between Man, the creatures and Nature is bound to a Creator; and as a hostile wilderness, a hinterland into which Man is cast out, to make his own way, his own shelter. I wish to consider this Garden—the imagined site of Man's beginning, set within the world and apart from it; an interior that contains everything—as it is imprinted upon the story of the interior, and particularly, those interior realms shared by many, who, within, become conscious of themselves and others, and their relations to each other, to their place in the world and to authority. I will refer to these realms as public interiors.

I will refer to the architecture of public interiors that draws upon the idea or dream of the Garden to establish its identity. The Garden, as Paradise, is an ideal and impossible condition, a representation of the entirety of Creation. The reality of nature is turbulent and violent, a never-ending cycle of birth, life and survival, and death, yet Nature as it is idealised and represented in the Garden is benign, beautiful, bountiful, boundless, and out of time: a perfect condition that has been lost and is certainly irretrievable. By invoking the Garden as a theme, architecture is invested with the role of recovering this condition, which is achieved by creating an interior that is complete in itself, distinct and protected from the hostile world without: an ideal or idyll that is fabricated, contained, controlled, and, in its entirety, a representation or a dream.

In some interiors, one is asked to indulge in that dream, and submit to a narrative that suggests our immersion in an environment that invokes, through its imagery and relations, a Paradise that is under our control. The baroque garden, the eighteenth-century city, the burgeoning nineteenth-century metropolis and the twentieth-century regionally-dispersed city alike have all embraced the idea of the Garden as a way of legitimating their projects and soothing their disruptive effects. One has encountered this idea along the tops of decommissioned fortifications; on *grands boulevards* or *allées* leading from town centres to sylvan outskirts; in parks that viewed nature as a picture or suggested that they were fragments of the natural world as found; and in interiors, such as glasshouses, winter gardens, exhibitions buildings, department stores, grand hotels, offices, shopping malls and people's palaces that conserved a 'bounty' of greenery, artefacts and people together, under glass. Through pictorial, decorative and architectural devices designed to evoke the effects of the Garden, a mastery over the World could be imagined. The Garden has been employed to inspire and console the occupants of the interior, and deployed as the ultimate tool in the justification of the human project of settlement. For the architect of the interior, it is important to know how the Garden has been called upon and transformed so as to bring about an architecture and situations for consciousness that are infused with its idea; it is important to know what the Garden is or has been and what is characteristic of it in order to understand that it may be evoked in the present.

THE IMAGE OF THE GARDEN

Our image of that idealised condition of Paradise—the Garden of Creation, the biblical Garden of Eden—is illustrated in Persian carpets, illuminated manuscripts, and in images, such as paintings by Jan Bruegel the Younger and Jan Bruegel the Elder, which show this Paradise on Earth to be full, resplendent with trees, fruits, flowers, animals and, crucially, Man: everything is there, in harmony, and its *original condition*. The 'everythingness' of the Garden represents the completeness of Creation on Earth, its perfect state, its almost incomprehensible variety of living things. The abundance of Creation—depicted in these paintings with such abandon, and yet so inadequately—perpetually inspires our wonder, curiosity and our pursuit of knowledge in philosophy, the natural sciences, physics, poetry and art. It has also inspired or excited our desire for control.

① 01

The Garden is the Biblical Eden and it is Paradise, proposed as the original place of Man; the site of his state of grace, and from where Man is cast out. Through this Fall, the Garden, Eden, Paradise, is the site that is remembered, and will be someday returned to. In many early maps, Eden and the four rivers that run from and through it are placed at the centre of the World. This Paradise was contained, a walled garden. The roots of the word Paradise are from the Avestan (Iran) language: *pairi* (around) and *daêza* (make, form, build (a wall)), meaning a bounded or enclosed space, a walled enclosure, wherein a wall surrounds the garden and separates the garden within from the world without.[1] The Trees of Life and Knowledge stood and grew in the Garden of Eden, rendering it the original site of knowledge and language and names.[2] Adam and Eve could eat the bounty that was offered them without having to compete with the beasts that they lived with; they did not have to kill or eat the beasts, nor did the beasts threaten them. Adam and Eve were expelled from Eden as punishment for partaking of the forbidden fruit of the Tree of Knowledge, cast out because they acquired consciousness of themselves as naked (the animals were naked, but untroubled by it) and an awareness of themselves as distinct, a knowledge that was the exclusive province of God beforehand. Banished by God, they were obliged thereafter to 'delve and weave', to make clothes and shelter, to plough fields. These burdens were the same as those associated with the making of the first settlements, through which history—in that it could be recorded—began: crops were sewn; clothing and shelters were woven, the foundations for the walls of settlements were bedded in ploughed earth.[3] Rent from a condition of oneness with animals, and an embodied truth of existence, people were obliged to begin, and realise another way of being, of sustenance, of difference; they were forced to construct a present and reach back to truth, to stories of their embodied knowledge.

Paradise was thus lost, and was rendered a condition to which a return has been longed for, in life, rather than consummated after death. The lost original state of being that the Garden has represented is one of the recurrent motifs of the interior, which other gardens, either literal or phenomenal, are bound to recall. To have any hope of recovering the Garden and the state of happiness it offers, it must be re-created and therefore 'reconstructed', thus rendering the theme of the Garden and its recovery both powerful and abiding in culture, the architecture of

① 01

the city and its interiors. Its name, its typical components, its deep characteristics, and even its atmospheres have been used to make projects vivid to those who will experience or occupy them, and it can continue to do so today.

RETURN TO THE GARDEN

It is a commonplace to observe that natural forms are represented in architecture, and not just within classical architecture and speculations attendant upon its origins. We see them in the architecture of ancient Egypt, in the abstracted architecture of Mesopotamia, and in the flourishing of Islamic architecture throughout Asia Minor, northern Africa and Al-Andaluz. The Garden is represented in the configurations and decoration of Gothic architecture: the forms of Gothic churches reiterate the forms of the forest, a sacred wood, such as in Sankt Maria auf dem Sande (Kościół Najświętszej Marii Panny na Piasku), in Wrocław (1226; 1342–1362); it is an image that is played back in Marinus Boezem's growing *Groene Kathedraal* in Almere (1978), modelled on Reims Cathedral, which seems to suggest that in the Gothic, the Garden is constantly invoked as a condition that resides in our spirit and is indelible.

In thoughts about correct approaches to the practice of architecture, a return to its origins and its original conditions have been inevitable, and just as inevitably, fraught with speculation. Those original conditions were nevertheless inscribed in the first acts towards the construction of shelter, faced with exposure to the world. In re-imagining the origins of architecture, imagery associated with this moment, its urgency and its agony was called upon. The 'myth' surrounding this moment, and speculation upon the condition of architecture and the interior effected therein, was very much at the centre of Western fictions regarding the origins of architecture, as illustrated by the famous frontispiece of Abbé Marc-Antoine Laugier's (1713–1769) *Essai sur l'architecture* (1753), which depicted the first primitive shelter or hut. The setting for this proto-architecture was a primaeval wood, from which constituent elements of a seminal architecture, such as columns, beams, rafters and roof, were coaxed, hewn and formed. They were transformed, and aspects of them were inscribed in the construction to which an attendant goddess pointed, and furthermore set against analogous elements formed as the constituent parts of classical architecture, and scattered at her feet.

The significance of Laugier's fictive, primitive shelter resided in his assertion that figures of nature were transformed and thus embodied in the forms of pagan, classical architecture. This was reiterated in studies made by William Chambers that attempted to demonstrate the elements of classical architecture were translations of archaic timber construction that came to be the petrified representations of the first classical orders. This was seen again in the illustrations to Claude Perrault's translation of Vitruvius (1684)[4], regarding the origin of the Corinthian order according to the architect and sculptor Callimachus, which showed an acanthus plant growing under and then around a basket weighed down by a stone slab, creating a pattern which was then represented in stone in the capital of the Corinthian order. Furthermore, Laugier considered the city to be a natural environment, whose character was aligned with that of a park, with its incidents, winding ways and clearings, responding to the chaotic state of the eighteenth-century city, which stood in contrast to ideas of naturalistic composition of the Baroque city.[5] All suggested

① 03

that the constructed dwelling, or the first instance of architecture and the interior, was inseparable from this condition of a Paradise lost,[6] and that it was bound to recall it, or retell it as an origin myth in its overall form or its constituent elements, thus compelling a return to the Garden, despite the impossibility of return. As the Garden was remembered in speculations upon the making of the first shelter and dwellings, the idea of a return to the Garden has been central to the fictions that surround the origins of architecture, and the interior.

KNOWN AND UNKNOWN

Western universities emerged from the meeting of studies of the ideas embedded in Christian theology with those that were re-discovered in texts of the ancient world; the study of Divinity met the study of Greek philosophy. In speculations surrounding the origins of Western architecture, stories of Edenic beginnings confronted those of an original world within ancient theistic traditions. The encounter with ruins of ancient Rome in the story of architecture—reinforced in the late eighteenth century with studies of those of ancient Greece, as we will see in a later chapter—added another layer of significance to the Garden. The Garden central to bearings within the ancient world was embodied in Arcady: pagan, rustic the realm of the unknown, unknowable, or original Man. Arcady in Peloponessus was a real place; yet it was also a fictional realm that represented the fecundity of Nature; its inhabitants were considered to be original people or *autochthons*, grown from the Earth, and

① 05

① 06

24

older than the Moon.⁷ Arcady furthermore was the home of Pan, a cloven-footed, music-playing satyr whose name signified 'everything': Pan was thus the keeper of knowledge. The word *panic* also derives from Pan, the figure who was responsible for terror (and woodland noises).⁸ The *autochthon* of Arcady was to be feared because of his/her embodied truth and knowledge, and the corresponding lack of wiles, animal state, and separateness from the World of agreements, customs, conventions, constructions, borders, and language. This fiction, in which the Garden, as Arcady, was cast as the site of knowledge, added to a status already established for it in the Book of Genesis, and reinforced its power and utility as a symbol. The Garden, whether in the guise of Eden or Arcady, also carried a warning: as the site of knowledge and the unknown, it was simultaneously a condition to be feared as much as desired. In Western painting, Arcady at once came to represent pastoral innocence, peace and simplicity (paradisical), and a dark and mysterious realm. The fusion of pastoral and wild Arcady—and its 'everythingness'—yielded a realm in which a place of thought, reflection and study might be found; or a place for solitude or the contemplation of mortality, or for entertainment, or terror. In Nicolas Poussin's two paintings titled *Et in Arcadia Ego* (1627; and 1638)⁹, the sarcophagus that commands the space and attentions of both was placed so to remind the viewer that one's tenure in the world and trappings that come with it are temporal and ephemeral, and that Death awaits all, even in this place Arcadia that is out of the world and out of time; that somehow, as one's beginnings may be found in this hinterland, so one's end shall be, too. Here, the Garden was that realm from where our ancestors came, and where they may still dwell, with greater authenticity and truth than we have managed outside, in the World. In Arcady, one found traces of original people upon which one could devote thought, and through these we could learn something of our essential, forgotten selves. A Garden such as Arcady was the place of knowledge and all things; a place for thought, for retreat¹⁰ from the World; the place of ruins of all that has been known. The Ruin, the ultimate *momento mori* and the subject of a later chapter, has marked the natural decay and consumption of all that we make; the Garden has been an important site for the articulation of the idea of true identity, embodied knowledge and the loss of both.

ⓘ 05

In the sylvan park of the Désert de Retz, outside Paris, built by François Racine de Monville (1772–1784), a theatre was set for visitors wherein architecture featured as a set of relics left from a fictive past, in the process of being reclaimed by nature, and so becoming subjects of contemplation.¹¹ The contents of the Désert de Retz included a 'broken column' (that was, suitably, occupied by a dwelling); a ruined Gothic church; an ice-store in the form of a pyramid; a 'Chinese' house; and notably, a temple to Pan, all returning to the soil of the contrived hinterland or 'desert'. As if to signal to visitors the uncertainty and melancholy portrayed within this theatre of endings, a rocky outcrop at the entrance to the garden was guarded by torch-bearing, cloven-footed *autochthones*: satryrs, relatives of Pan. The Désert de Retz staged a fantasy, common to earlier gardens in Europe that borrowed from Oriental precedents—particularly from China—to create fantastic scenes that mingled nature and architecture. Bomarzo, near Viterbo, (Pier Francesco Orsini, 1560s) featured collapsing buildings, improbable monuments and a population of monsters, in the form of ogres and giants, all contrived to create unease, fright and

ⓘ 06

① 07

astonishment. William Shakespeare's play *A Midsummer Night's Dream* (1600) and its fantastic denizens come from this 'other' world; and gardens designed in this spirit were places for deception, subterfuge, licentiousness, and—always lurking in the shadows—violence. Baroque and Mannerist gardens[12] were sites of excitement and titillation, devised for entertainment and pleasure. In London's Vauxhall Pleasure Gardens (1661–1859), several social classes could promenade, listen to music (Georg Friedrich Händel's, among others) and experience the *frisson* of romantic encounter under cover of disguise. Among the tree-lined paths were works of exotic architecture, such as a Turkish bath, and other pavilions in the *Chinoiserie* style, derived from interpretations of Chinese garden architecture. The Vauxhall Pleasure Gardens would later serve as a model for Cedric Price's unbuilt Fun Palace (1964), a 'zone' of earthy delights. All of these Gardens indulge in a kind of delirium that comes with the release from responsibilities in the World: as Man was cast out of the Garden, obligation, toil, hardship and pain became his burden, so a return to a fantasy of the Garden—consistent through Bomarzo, Vauxhall, Tivoli in Copenhagen, and the Fun Palace—implies that all the shocks and natural heartaches of the World are replaced with pleasure; with ludic entertainments, titillations, excitements, and even the thrill of panic or terror. These kinds of Gardens had their roots in Arcady, whose hinterlands contained all things, fusing the unknown with essential truths. Primordial, fundamental and fantastic things happened there, quite unlike the burdensome facts and pacts of the human yet all-too-well-known World.

One notes how frequently the control of the hinterland, the wilderness, or nature visibly demonstrated the exercise of power, and thereby victory over the unknown and the unknowable autochthone or other. This too was an aspect of the Baroque: a desire for order inspired by the order within nature, that can be heard in its contrapuntal music, and seen in monumental gardens such as at Versailles (1664–1789), or at Vaux-le-Vicomte (1658–1661). In its gardens, designed

① 07

① 08

① 09

① 08

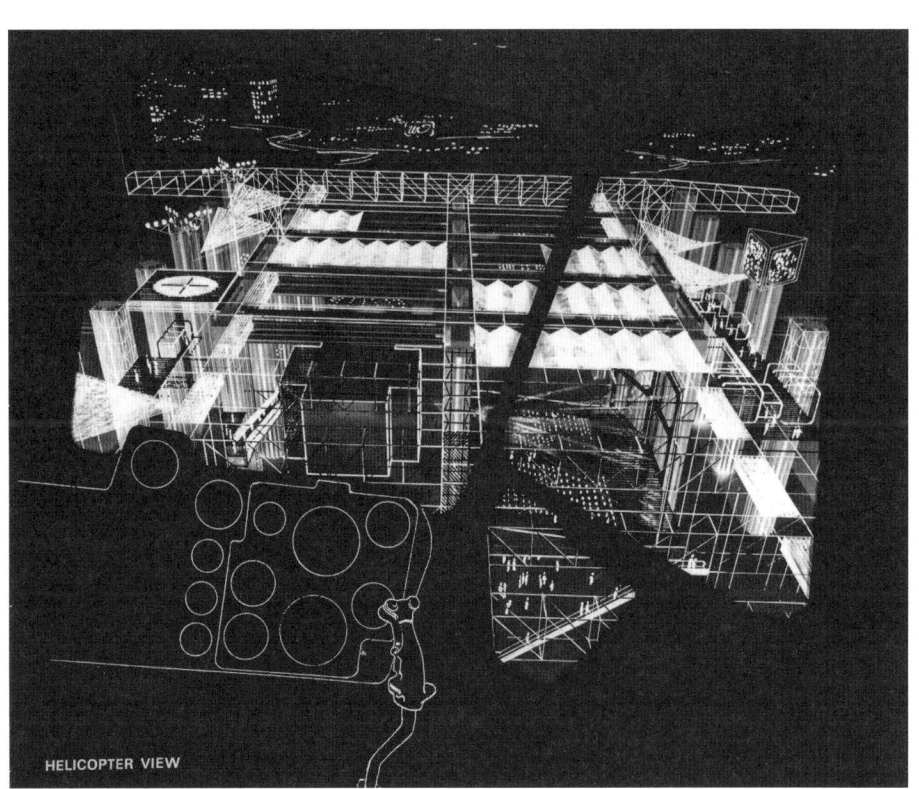
① 09

THE GARDEN

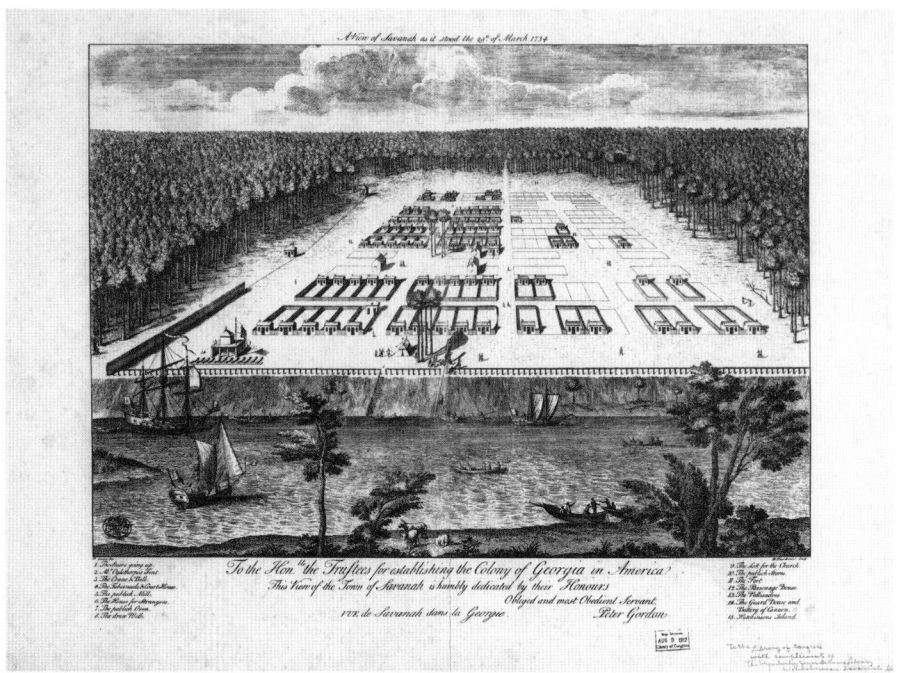

10

11

by André Le Nôtre (1613–1700), nature in the form of a wood was cast as inchoate disorder, which was called to order, overwhelmed by geometrically arranged figures opposed to it: incisions of clearings, paths and boulevards, pools and fountains. These gardens were projections of will that replaced the dangerous or unpredictable aspects of the hinterland (or the local nature that played its part) with measurable achievements, miracles and entertainments. These acts were small versions of the very real clearings that would be made shortly thereafter in the establishment of colonial settlements in the Americas and the East Indies, in which the space of real autochthones—rather than mythical denizens—was cleared for European occupation and rule. The image of the clearing for the settlement of Savannah, Georgia (1735) was emblematic:[13] control was confined to a clearing at the edge of a vast, unknown hinterland spreading in all directions, with the other, danger and panic therein. The 'dialogue' between the space of the known and the unknown could be interpreted as a play—as in the design of the Baroque garden—or a conflict between projective authority and the indigenous other. It was play that characterised the effects of Baroque architecture, and in particular, its late flowering, the Rococo. The Hall of Mirrors of Amalienburg at Nymphenburg Palace (1734–39)[14] near Munich, proposed itself as a garden of the imagination, and featured decoration based on forms of nature that were represented, gilded and reflected in its many mirrors, and furthermore intermingled with the foliage of the park outside. One could imagine an interior that itself 'imagined' a garden; in this case, a transformative garden in which one might play.[15] It is an example to which we will return in the next chapter.

① 10

THE PICTURESQUE

The designed garden was a potent site for contemplation of the world, one's place in it, and the conceit of one's dominion over it. Altogether lighter interpretations of what transpired at Retz—effectively summarized by Poussin's Arcadia—could be found in England, in estates such as Castle Howard (1699–1811), designed by John Vanbrugh (1664–1726) and Nicholas Hawksmoor (1661–1736); Stowe, whose gardens (1741–1751) were designed by Lancelot 'Capability' Brown (1716–1783), and in eighteenth-century estate gardens that represented the Picturesque, particularly to the designs of Humphry Repton (1752–1818). The Picturesque style related managed landscapes—often involving enormous earthworks and diversions of rivers—to country houses under the regimen of pictorial composition. Its manner was translated effortlessly into painting, and specifically 'landscape portraits'.[16] The Picturesque's chief advocate, the surveyor, landscape gardener and designer Humphry Repton, used a method of before and after 'visualisations' of his garden designs for clients—a new prosperous class—in portfolios or 'Red Books' that showed the landscape of the entire estate conforming to gentle control. These country estates were effectively private parks, designed for the visual enjoyment of their owners. The features of the landscapes, reshaped under Repton's design at enormous expense, were complemented by the insertion of architectural fragments that were meant to be appreciated from a distance, as though elements of a picture. Houses (such as Blaise Castle, with its castle 'folly' (1798)) sat within the delineated ground of a designed garden, which was set in contrast to a contrived pastoral setting that surrounded it. The landscape garden and the house were bound together in one fiction, with architecture (and its owner-occupant) asserting dominion over the landscape, which was rendered as natural and as Arcadian—replete with follies or 'ruins'—as possible.

These architectural follies, interwoven with a fictive landscape, were captivating and evocative, and the variety and ambitions of such structures were developed and extended, notably, by the scholarly neo-classical architect William Chambers (1723–1796). Kew Gardens (1749–1773) contained an extraordinary variety of structures designed by Chambers,[17] among them a ten-story Chinese pagoda and a ruined arch. Considered altogether, the menagerie of follies were articulations of an international language of the designed landscape park. The imagery of this Garden architecture could conjure up ideas of exotic 'elsewheres', substitutes for Paradise. The architecture of the house at Sezincote, designed by Samuel Pepys Cockerell (1805), and its landscape designed by Humphry Repton were representative: the house proposed exotic architectural forms, derived from elsewhere, in this case, colonised India, and was offered itself as a work of 'garden' architecture, a Picturesque folly. In Repton's park, structures were of uncertain, yet exotic pedigree, and furthermore contrived to effect the illusion of being consumed by vines and plants, thereby suggesting their origins in deep time, and a place that had always been occupied. This naturally represented the authority and dominion of the house's owner, which, in this fantasy, extended beyond the confines of the immediate landscape to encompass faraway places, and beyond the confines of the present, to command the past. These gardens, over and above their inscribed fantasy of the rule of space, time and others, indicated a correlating desire to take command of origins, and their authority.

ⓘ 11

THE ESSENCE OF NATURE

Another thread to our consideration of the Garden concerns its capacity, as the original home of Man, regardless of its cultural context, to be the site of Man's emancipation, of his delivery from the inequities and vanities of the World. The awareness of the authority of origins in Modernity was indebted to Enlightenment consciousness, and to the essayist Jean-Jacques Rousseau (1712–1778), who had written about the social contract and the rights of man,[18] had seen that nature, and specifically, the act of dwelling in nature, would bring about an appreciation of the essential aspects of life. Doing so, one could be 'out of the world', closer to an original self and therefore, free. Rousseau inspired a reading of nature (one that might be aligned with Arcady) that reinforced its power, and its status as a place or a state of mind to which one might return. Rousseau's last years were spent on the estate of Ermenonville, whose gardens were transformed by René de Girardin (1766). When he died, his body was laid there, on a small, treed island in a classical sarcophagus, a central figure in a wood, reminiscent of Poussin's *Et in Arcadia Ego* paintings. His body was later exhumed and moved to the crypt of the Panthéon in Paris, where the wooden sarcophagus was, aptly, in the form of a primitive hut or temple, with columns in form of tree trunks, laced with vines. A hand emerged from the door, holding a torch, the light of Reason. The return to nature was characterised as a return to an original or honest state: if not to Paradise or Arcady, then some

ⓘ 12

12

13

14

worldly place that could be experienced, thereby transforming and re-forming Man. Some inspired by Rousseau came very close, such as the American writer Henry Thoreau. His *Walden, or Life in the Woods* (1854) described a retreat from the world, which was as much a declaration of personal independence as a seeking out of an original spirit, which would be rediscovered through walking, and a sustained and daily contact with nature.[19]

13

The reconstruction of an 'original condition' of a garden in the semblance of Eden or Arcadia involved a complex of ideas about nature's innate characteristics, its aspects, and its lessons. This re-imagined Garden was a field of projections, fancies and fictions that came to the fore of European cultural life at a time that coincided with the Enlightenment and the onset of Modernity: that time when mysteries were being steadily dispelled by empirical analysis, and the idea of the enfranchised individual, as opposed to a feudal subject, was being brought to life and broadly articulated. This re-appraisal of the possibilities for Man as an agent of his own destiny was concurrent with the rise of the philosophy of science, the flowering of the study of the natural sciences, and, of course, with advances in technology that yielded, ultimately, new structures, new spaces, and the new metropolis.

GLASS-HOUSES

The rise of *bourgeois* culture in Northern Europe in the eighteenth and nineteenth centuries was driven by colonialism, and the subjugation, exploitation and removal of resources of faraway lands by force. Tales of adventure cast these lands in the role of Paradise and inspired the emulation of their exotic environments at 'home'; and so as a bi-product of colonial dominion, the acquisition of natural trophies—plants and animals—led to their accommodation in representative structures whose technology would sustain them. Exotic plants became visible in domestic and public environments: they signified the reach of Empire (Britain, France, Portugal, Spain,

15

ⓘ 16

the Netherlands, Belgium), and represented fragments of Paradise brought home. Of those Paradises elsewhere, the others who occupied them were 'primitives' living in unspoiled environments as close to the original condition as could hope to be found. Their 'discovery' implied their rescue by Culture, and their colonisation served to incorporate and 'redeem' them. The recovered fragments of Paradise could be sustained in artificial environments. These constructions were built at various sizes for various situations: from little glass caskets that could sit on a table containing a variety of diminutive plants, to larger structures such as conservatories and glasshouses added to or set within the grounds of a house; and finally even more elaborate and spacious structures—winter gardens and glass 'people's palaces'—for public enjoyment. The interiors of country houses, urban villas and gentlemen's clubs furthermore started to accumulate and feature exotic plants that could survive cooler temperatures, such as rubber plants and ferns. In Britain, such plants were intended to evoke the colonies of Africa, or India. In the Netherlands, one was familiar with, until quite recently, little hotel lobbies and cafés filled with plants that evoked memories of the splendour of Indonesia, Curaçao, the Antilles or Suriname.

The private and public collection of exotic plants became common, and came to be accommodated in highly engineered structures that were suitable for mass-production.[20] The private estate of Chatsworth was home to several experiments (such as the Conservation Wall and the Great Stove (1836–1840), by Joseph Paxton (1803–1865) who transpired to be a great innovator in the construction and technology of glasshouses, selling glass house kits, from which he made a considerable fortune, much like the even more popular innovator John Claudius Loudon (1783–1843), the designer of the glasshouses at the Birmingham Botanical Gardens, and the Derby Arboretum (1840), the first dedicated public park in England.[21] The Palm House at Kew (1844–1848), designed by the iron-founder and engineer Richard Turner (1798–1881) and the architect Decimus Burton (1800–1881), was a development of both the form and technology of Paxton's Great Stove. In addition to its extension of iron and glass technology, it expressed most completely the idea that a fragment of Paradise could be possessed. It was, all at once, a statement regarding power and knowledge: the

ⓘ 14

stewardship of Paradise abroad and its sustenance at home indicated a nation's (and its culture's) potency, and signified that the legitimacy of its entire colonial project. The Great Stove and the Palm House represented this through delicate constructions of glass and iron that could accommodate and sustain environments that were impossible, offering the image and experience of a captive, interiorised Eden.

Such glasshouses soon moved away from structures dedicated exclusively to plants to those that included exhibitions, diversions and entertainments—Winter Gardens or *jardins d'hiver*—which enjoyed enormous popularity in European cities.[22] The Jardin d'Hiver in Paris designed by Hippolyte Meyndier (1847) contained 'ballroom, café, reading room and paintings along the high glass walls'.[23] The building, along the Champs Elysées, inspired Paxton, who inflated its design among others in his project for the Crystal Palace.

ENVIRONMENTS UNDER GLASS

The development of the arcades or *passages* of Paris preceded, paralleled and ultimately followed the development of these monumental glasshouses. Johann Friedrich Geist, in his fundamental study *Passagen*,[24] described the arcades as derived from the bazaars of Asia Minor and the Middle East (which we will touch upon in later chapters); but the principle of making little shopping streets that connected other busy streets depended on their distinctiveness from 'normal' streets, and this was achieved by harmonising their architectural expression, with identical façades lining both sides, paving their floors with tile, mosaic or terrazzo, and finally, placing them under glass. A 'perfect' interior architecture was sustained under glazed roofs, which, due to their double layering, offered 'studio' lighting conditions for the interior. The arcaded space, as an architectural device, was derived from a structural interpretation of a *pergola*: an open frame made to train climbing flowering or fruiting plants, thereby evoking a natural bower, and inducing rest and pleasure. It is reminiscent of the impulse contained within the image of the primitive hut provided by Laugier. The first of these arcades appeared at the end of the eighteenth century in Paris, and developed in London and then all over Europe, particularly in Northern European metropolitan centres, right through the nineteenth century, assuming monumental scale following the singular event of the construction of the Crystal Palace.

ⓘ 15

The Crystal Palace was both a public glasshouse in the manner of a *jardin d'hiver* and a hypertrophied arcade, inflating and conflating the characteristics of both. As a building meant to accommodate the Great Exposition of 1851 in London's Hyde Park, the first of the international expositions that were so important in the nineteenth and twentieth centuries, it was conceived by its designer Joseph Paxton as a great shelter that could be erected very quickly, assembled by mass-produced components of iron and glass. Paxton was originally a gardener whose work at Chatsworth acquainted him with the inter-relation of environmental, structural and glass technologies and their techniques. The Crystal Palace was arrived at in response to a situation in which all other competition designs by architects were too monumental, too costly and unlikely of being realised in the time available. Paxton proposed a simple structure of mass-produced components, consistent with contemporary developments in glass house technology, which, when assembled, would present a singular image to the Park, and an extensive, voluminous and

ⓘ 16

17–18

⊙ 19

luminous interior. Like the glasshouses and the arcades, the Crystal Palace was not considered a work of architecture; rather, it was a feat of technology, whose huge structure—some 564 metres long and 39 metres high—placed it among other engineered structures—largely sheds for locomotives—that made their presence felt increasingly in major European urban cities, particularly London and Paris. Alongside the development of large-span structures for railway stations and markets, the great vault of the Crystal Palace became a motif for the large-scale public interior and representative of the scale of ambition typical of the international metropolis. The interior hosted a vast display of products of art, craft and industry from all over the world, and primarily the British Empire. Held at the moment of the Empire's greatest extent, it was natural that the national ambition of imperial pretension would loom large in the impression felt by its visitors. Goods inside were bathed in natural light, in an interior so large that it could be thought of as a kind of exterior. Indeed, the interior contained a great tree from the park, undisturbed: it was simply incorporated, inferring that Hyde Park itself had joined the exhibits in the building. The interior at once contained the landscape of the park and was continuous with it, sheltering artefacts from every part of the world and preserving them in its great glass case, in the manner of a conservatory for exotic plants. The interior became an *everywhere*, obviating the need, as far as representative space was concerned, for any other kind of provision. It was the ideal public interior, whose power derived from being more than an interior, but an *environment* that projected its continuity with its symbolic pastoral setting. At this time, a Royal decree rendered all Royal Parks—as well as the gated estates of London—open. The freedom of the streets and the making of public space in the form of parks had a dramatic effect on the ordinary Londoner's access to and experience of the city: the shared realm was suddenly and dramatically expanded. The Crystal Palace was emblematic of this emancipation. Its aesthetic, derived from the techniques of conserving exotic plants, yielded an industrially produced and potentially endless architecture that included the park and showed it to be representative of a much more extensive condition, one that fused interiority and liberation. Its interior furthermore legitimated the colonial

⊙ 17–18

project so that dreams of uncontaminated, original Garden in the possession of imperial masters could flourish in the minds of a city-bound public.

The attractiveness of the idea of placing the world under glass, thereby creating a condition of apparent freedom—a feeling of liberation from streets and buildings, traffic, pollution and inclement weather—was not lost on Paxton, who shortly after the success of the Crystal Palace proposed a development for a giant passage or arcade to wind around London in a continuous ring, crowned with a glazed vault in the style and at the scale of the Crystal Palace. The construction of the Great Victorian Way (1855) would have involved the appropriation of urban properties on an unprecedented scale (Haussmann was only beginning his work in Paris under Louis Napoléon III), creating a glazed boulevard lined with several stories of shops, offices and apartments on both sides: a complete, self-referential urban structure. A megastructure *avant la lettre*, the project is important to us because of its imagery: a perfect public interior was imagined, that rendered all other developments redundant. As an urban version of the Crystal Palace that preceded it, it bore the same promise of arcadian emancipation, and its suggestion that urban conditions might be remedied through fundamentally anti-urban means. The strategy of moving the Crystal Palace to the city was one of redeeming the city through the way of the glasshouse: by preserving or cultivating the best aspects of urban life under glass.

The Crystal Palace, and perhaps Paxton's project for the Great Victorian Way, acted as inspiration for the passages or arcades of European cities to grow to great proportions, embracing the benefits of large-scale interiorisation. The Galleria Vittorio Emanuele II (1865–77) in Milan, designed by Giuseppe Mengoni (1829–1877), was an urban infrastructural project cut through a portion of the city's medieval historical centre, connecting its core to the greater network of streets beyond it, and effectively serving as the new core of a re-configured historical centre. The area immediately north of the Duomo was rendered 'rational' and ideal, with a gridded plan, and the Galleria, in this context, was proposed as a perfect junction of streets protected under glazed, Crystal Palace-like vaults. The buildings that formed the crossing benefitted from protection from the elements, and so could be elegantly decorated; the pavement was similarly dressed in refined patterns of mosaic and *terrazzo*. The sheltered street achieved more than the accommodation of shoppers and *flâneurs*: it provided the city with an image of itself that would resist change, an environment that would be preserved in perpetuity under glass. Through the portals of its ideal streets, one could see the Duomo and its piazza, representing the city's spiritual foundation, and the Piazza della Scala, representing its cultural aspirations and its lived modernity. The idealised environment proposed by the Galleria suggested that the city could resist the ravages of time, and that it and the city it 'viewed' were at once at the centre of the world and 'everywhere'.

The Great Victorian Way, as realised through the Galleria, seems to have a place at the centre of Ebenezer Howard's idea for a Garden City, proposed some fifty years later, in his manifesto *Garden Cities of To-morrow* (1901). Howard, in his bid to reform processes and patterns of urbanisation, suggested a dispersed structure for cities that would merge the resources and benefits of the city with those of nature and the agricultural landscape, and in which a matrix of small- to medium-sized towns would be embedded in and evenly distributed across the (English) countryside.

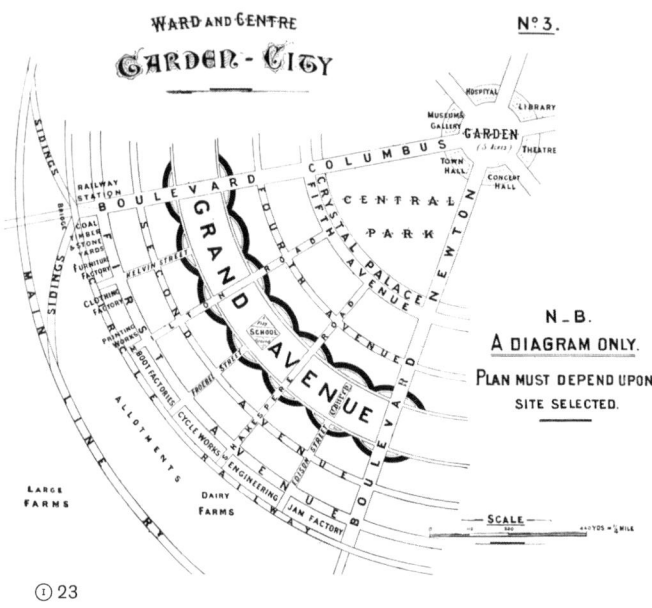

23

Each of these towns was to be connected by rail, for the movement of goods. The towns were otherwise self-sustaining, their circular plans formed of concentric bands of buildings, parks and gardens. The core of the Garden City was to be a natural void: a (not unconsciously named) Central Park ringed by a torus-shaped Crystal Palace, in which citizens could stroll in an endless promenade. Howard had proposed an antidote to the metropolis, at whose heart was a figure associated with the metropolis, revealing the Arcadian dream at its heart. The image presented to citizens would thereby return the monumental arcade to its Arcadian roots through a constantly orbiting view of the park trapped within the arcade, convincing citizens that the dispersed city at once contained and conserved a fragment of the Garden.

23

GARDENS OF GLASS AND IRON

Consistent with the suggestions of Laugier and others, Eden could be invoked through the very materials that constituted architecture. Two museums dedicated to the study and exposition of the breadth of Creation did so explicitly: the Museum of Natural History in Oxford (1861), designed by Thomas Newenham Deane (1828–1899) and Benjamin Woodward (1816–1861),[25] and the Museum of Natural History in London (1867), designed by Alfred Waterhouse (1830–1905). Both buildings bristled with sculptures of flora and fauna representing of the fruits of Creation. The fabric of Deane and Woodward's building suggested that it was a product of both Man and nature. Its stone exterior was decorated with carvings by the Irish sculptors James and John O'Shea and Edward Whelan, and bound to the Gothic tradition: although it was not a church, it was funded and constructed as though a demonstration of a divine project, articulating in its *architecture parlante* the splendour of its subject and its studies. The interior was dominated by a glazed interior courtyard, which featured cast iron columns wrought in motifs that drew the Gothic closer to its sylvan roots, resembling a bower confined by a trellis-like enclosure, all in iron. The Museum of Natural History in London seemed to use a similar language. The museum was one of many in the Exhibition Road in Kensington that were the legacy of Prince Albert's ideas for the Great Exhibition of 1851. Its terracotta façades, in

24–25

ⓘ 24

Neo-Romanesque style, ran continuously through the interior of the building, and were decorated with cast figures of plants and animals (extant and pre-historic), inferring that the entire construction both hosted and was being consumed by the abundance of Creation. Its central representative space was a glazed courtyard whose supporting structure of open-web iron beams was designed to evoke a pergola wound with vines. The iron-work of both museums was in parallel with the lyrical structural innovations of Louis Auguste Boileau in France, who was designing department stores—to which we will return—and iron churches, the latter explicit about the relationship between Gothic form and its natural inspiration. As we have seen, the sacred wood summoned by the Gothic was at once biblical and mythical.

The capacity of iron structures to suggest the natural and effortless spans of trees and their branches made them useful in both utilitarian and representative interiors. The reading room of the Bibliothèque nationale de France (1868), designed by Henri Labrouste (1801–1875) was a walled chamber confining a nest of domes supported on attenuated iron columns. The structure left an impression that the ⓘ 26 columns appeared to be restraining the domes from taking to the air, rather than supporting their weight. This suggested that the interior was to be regarded as a sheltered exterior, which was reinforced by the decoration of the room: in the space above the screen of bookshelves that lined the room and below the span of the domes, panels were painted with scenes of treetops in a forest. The occupant of the room—a reader or a scholar—was asked to consider sitting and reading in a clearing in a wood, defined by the screens of books and sheltered by the domed canopies tied to the earth. Again, the wood was invoked as that realm where both knowledge and the unknown resided, which one could interpret as being either Eden or Arcady. It matters little which: the interior's design articulated a condition or cultural situation that its readers would have understood.

The general public also understood the inferences of such iron and glass structures. The great department stores or *grands magasins* of Paris assumed the lessons of the Crystal Palace directly, emulating its light, visibility, transparency and invitation to free movement and free access to objects of desire. Au Bon Marché, a *grand magasin* founded by Aristide Boucicault (1810–1877) in 1852, and given its definitive form in the structure designed by Louis-Auguste Boileau (1812–1896) and the engineer Gustave Eiffel (1832–1923) in 1876, offered interior courtyards of iron and glass that were directly inspired by the Crystal Palace, and put to commercial use.[26] Customers were offered grand vistas, the spectacle of seeing others filling the space and crossing it along delicate *passarelles*, and the pleasure of seeing bountiful arrays of consumer goods, in displays reminiscent of the most extravagant markets. Prices of all items were on view for all customers to see—a democracy of consumption—and diversions were arranged for their entertainment. Everything was visible and open to experience; one could simply wander and look within an interior that evoked, through the planting and distractions of its glazed *serre*, a garden of earthly delights. Indeed, Emile Zola recognised this character in his novel *Au Bonheur des Dames* (1883), which placed Au Bon Marché (under another guise) at its heart. Fittingly, its first translated title was *The Ladies' Paradise*.[27] In the novel, the department store was the social condenser *par excellence*, pressing together the shop girls of the suburbs arriving by train at Gare du Nord and the *bourgeoise* ladies from the districts around the Opéra nearby. At Au Bon Marché, architecture had become invisible, and idealised as nature; its space was an environment and its interior a garden, reinforcing the visitor's experience of pleasure and indulgence.

The message of the Crystal Palace was passed on to other building types that might be regarded as elements of infrastructure for an international metropolitan lifestyle. Grand Hotels used the courtyards of their city blocks for light-filled interior salons, with glazed ceilings, dotted with exotic plants—a strategy, incidentally, that saw itself applied to vast country houses of the late nineteenth century, notably in England, France and the United States. The Palm Court of the Ritz Hotel in London (1906), designed by Charles Mewès and Arthur Joseph Davis, did not seem particularly arcadian or Edenic, yet it evoked the figure of a tamed garden, a figure that was increasingly associated with metropolitan public interiors. The Ritz was built in the 'Haussmannian' style: a fragment of visibly metropolitan Paris immediately adjacent to Green Park and close to Buckingham Palace that echoed the ambition of Edwardian London to be a metropolis in the continental mode.[28] By inference,

25

26

ⓘ 27

its Palm Court was part of that bucolic infrastructure of parks and gardens that represented the benign aspect of London's metropolitanism amidst its chaos.

URBAN PARKS

In late nineteenth-century Paris—the metropolis created by Haussmann—the appearances of buildings and streets conveyed the message that one occupied a considered, rational, designed interior. Outward appearances were, like the city's infrastructure, institutions and equipment, contrived to achieve a vast range of predictable and interrelated effects, performances and behaviours. And, like those rooms that had accommodated fictions of the Garden in order to lay claims to knowledge or freedom, the interior of the metropolis accommodated images of the Garden in the form of designed parks to establish authority over the natural world and the natural impulses of its citizens. Parks were part of the urban infrastructure of leisure, and constituted public 'interiors' within the body of the metropolis whose imagery was crafted in studied contrast to that of the city's buildings and pavements. In London and Paris, parks were conceived in the image of managed nature and incorporated into the self-image of each city. The presence of fragments of an idealised, bucolic, pre-urban or 'original' world made the project of the city that much more palatable.

London's Hyde Park, a Royal Park turned public, offered itself in the image of the English countryside, complete with grazing sheep; London's Hampstead Heath was presented as found landscape;[29] the Bois de Boulogne and Bois de Vincennes in Paris were offered as vast hunting grounds. Jean-Charles Alphand (1817–1891) designed these last two and the Parc les Buttes-Chaumont (1867), reworking a barren hill that had been used for dumping, quarrying and hangings in an exotic manner. Its stump was made to look like a fantastic mountain, adorned with a classical temple and a waterfall, while the rest of the park featured *faux*-ancient lodges, suggesting that the park was in fact a storied landscape in existence long before the arrival of the city. In such parks, images of nature were crafted that were subsumed in the identity of the metropolis; the parks appealed to the broad public, and as we have seen in London with the opening of the Royal Parks, were used by all classes. The parks were bound to the city, popular public 'interiors' of those cities that took care to institute them, that offered important contrasting images to their frequently chaotic built environments.

In the United States, Frederick Law Olmsted planned many urban parks, managing existing topographies into natural infrastructures for their cities, including Boston, Chicago, Louisville, Milwaukee, Montreal, Niagara Falls, Oakland, Rochester, Tarrytown, and, of course New York, where he designed several parks. Central Park (1858–1873, with Calvert Vaux) was the most celebrated, occupying a substantial rectangular figure in the city's gridded plan. City commissioners established Manhattan's grid in 1811, leaving a void for a future park, which, after being secured in a different form in 1853, was extended to its present dimensions in 1873.[30] Olmstead worked with, modified and amplified the existing Manhattan island landscape to create a naturalistic realm that combined pastoral zones with those resembling original, untouched terrain.[31] Conceived in the most fervent period of enthusiasm for the Yosemite-driven, Deity-sanctioned American project, Central Park brought an image of Eden to the city that produced considerable monetary value for properties erected around its perimeter, a phenomenon that was taken advantage of in other designs by Olmsted. Olmsted's attachment to the power of the untouched American landscape had begun while manager of the Mariposa Mines in California, adjacent to Yosemite Valley. He campaigned to have its still-isolated landscape protected, and thereafter was involved in urban planning that integrated nature, its image and environments into cities and their outlying suburbs. Yosemite was renowned from the moment of its 'discovery'—transmitted by the photographs of Carleton Watkins[32]—as the seat of an American Eden. The very existence of Yosemite was used as a sign, by advocates of the ideology of Manifest Destiny—an ideology positing that white, European Americans had the God-given duty to settle the frontier and supplant indigenous peoples—to legitimate the American 'project' of establishing dominion and control over the vast American continental territory (known as the 'interior') and all its occupants. Central Park occupied the centre of the island of Manhattan; from within, the city all around it could be seen in all its splendour. Central Park was a public interior in which the city's citizens saw their own endeavours reflected in the urban fabric, and saw themselves both as citizens and as the inheritors of Eden. The Park was as significant a model as the Crystal Palace before it. Although it was not a literal interior, it worked as such, with the city's buildings serving as its enclosure.

① 28

① 29

Olmsted's parks were taken to be fragments of the United States' great continental Garden, at once working elements of natural infrastructure for urban settlements, and reminders of the charged character of the continental interior. The work of Olmsted proved to have a lasting effect on ideas driving the growth of American suburbia.[33] The evocation of Eden, in America at least, continued to be a powerful force in shaping the image and representational motifs of the dispersed city in the second half of the twentieth century, yielding perceptions of the landscape, the city and its interiors that in turn produced new kinds of interiors, including the experience of territory as interior, that have been exported worldwide and with which we in Europe have become familiar.

THE GARDEN, SUBURBIA AND THE CITY

An important characteristic of American urbanisation in the twentieth century continued to be its stated bond with the American territory, which was interiorised.[34] It was considered a realm that had been tamed, claimed, mythologised, pictured and represented in myriad forms. Following the end of the Second World War, motorways—known as parkways—drove through that fabled continental interior and offered the possibility of easy occupation. The bending, winding roads, lyrical and naturalistic, connected cities to dormitory suburbs—the American Paradise—in which the presence of Eden might seem quite close.[35] In execution, however, Eden was parcelled out into individual lots, the front, back and side yards of mass-produced tract housing; sold in real estate brochures; promised in easy access to credit for the purchase of property, automobiles and consumer durable goods, and pictured in magazine advertising, television and films. The American interior was revealed to an exploding suburban population in exodus from the cities as a common cultural experience. The American city was now a dispersed entity, its form spread over a network containing fragments of working parts, its urbanity surrendered to a completely opposite paradigm. The suburban dweller's public interior was the indoor shopping centre—the shopping mall—which, beginning as an interior town square in Victor Gruen's (1903–1980) design for the Southdale Center (1956), eventually adopted the forms and allusion of the arcade—the idealised, interior street—and the Crystal Palace. The shopping malls of the 1970s embraced the possibilities of accommodating natural displays and becoming 'environments'.[36] The Houston Galleria (developer Gerald D. Hines, 1970) borrowed its name and image from the Galleria Vittorio Emanuele II in Milan, and fused aspects of that imagery with event spaces like those of the Rockefeller Center Plaza in New York. The Eaton Centre in Toronto designed by Eberhard Zeidler with Bregman and Hamann (1977) also proposed itself as a huge, construction-set Milanese *galleria*. The Galleria/Crystal Palace reference guaranteed in these developments that everything could occur inside their spaces. Each larger shopping mall promised an experience that, if it was extensive or grand enough, could become an *environment*, sustained under glass, the activities and entertainments accommodated within becoming increasingly exotic. Tropical forests, swimming pools and skating rinks were found in the giant vaulting glasshouses of the West Edmonton Mall designed by Maurice Sutherland (1986), and promised a multitude of environments and *experiences*. These extensive, enclosed realms, perceived by their visitors as public interiors, existed in an

① 31

① 32

THE GARDEN

33

① 34

expanded and distended urban condition; their indoor Edens purported to redeem the banal manifestations of their cities' loose forms and the corresponding loss of urbanity and shared civic space.

In order to compensate for that loss, a result of urban depopulation, mismanagement, economic and racial inequity and the blight and strife that went with it, urban centres in the United States turned to the suburbs—and particularly the suburban mall—for their new 'public interiors'.[37] The compelling anti-urbanism and Edenic escapism of suburbia embodied in the malls was adopted for the purpose of their revival, and perceived as an antidote to the many failures of the metropolitan idea as it stood at the time. Victor Gruen had attempted the 'mallification' of smaller American cities in the 1950s and 1960s, pedestrianising streets and situating planting, furniture, signage and directories in a manner reminiscent of interior shopping centres,[38] but it was the indoor mall that inspired downtown office building atria, which presented themselves not only as spaces for employees, but public interiors for the use and diversion of the general public. City planning laws provided incentives for developers to make public spaces, either plazas or atria, in exchange for building more office space on urban cites. The atrium of Hugh Stubbins's Citicorp Building in New York (1977)—an office building—served a 'plaza', a church, and an occasional farmers' market. The décor of its plant-filled interior evoked the casual and reassuring spaces of suburban malls, in which one felt free. This promise was many stages removed from that offered by the Crystal Palace, yet still depended upon on its legacy. ① 33

Perhaps the most radical re-appraisal of what purpose should be served by the atrium of an urban office building was offered by the Ford Foundation Building in New York (1969), designed by Kevin Roche (b 1922) and John Dinkeloo (1918–1981). Built for the benevolent foundation of the Ford Motor Company, it proposed a vast interior garden, its height that of the entire building, through which the public could pass in order to cut through and across local topography (the site straddled a slope) ① 34 between East Forty-second and Forty-third Streets. Pedestrians could linger for a while in what appeared to be at once an empty office building and an enclosed, glazed and maintained environment filled with trees, intended by its designer

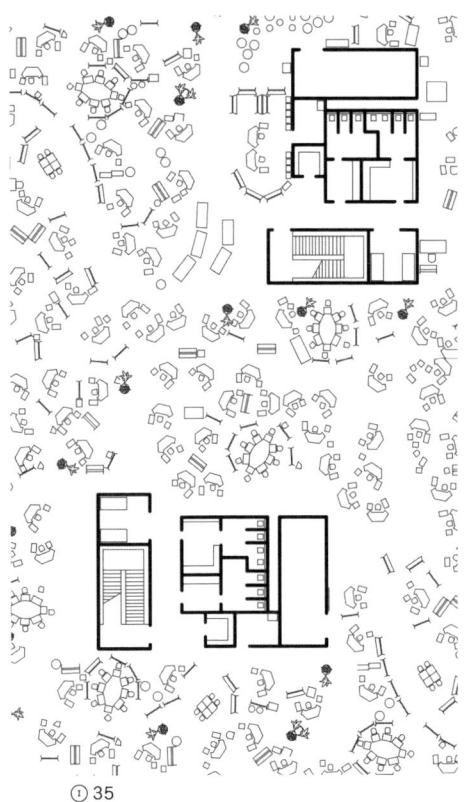

① 35

Dan Kiley (1912–2004) to be an ecosystem emulating the temperate climate that would have dominated the region before the arrival of Europeans. Offices were arranged around the garden on two sides, looking into it, while people passing through the atrium could look at the offices and those working within. Some offices were quite intimately related to the verdant scene, and in fact, the offices—designed for executives of the organisation in the manner of private studies, with desk and lounge—assumed the form of glass pavilions, arranged in relation to each other on each floor as though neighbouring bungalows in a suburban close. With the Ford Foundation—which Kevin Roche described as a kind of antidote to the paucity of public space in American cities[39]—one saw a compromise between the suburban idea of the public realm and the business operations that dominated American cities at the expense of the public space, offered in the form of a public interior directly related to the street. The atrium of the Ford Foundation was not particularly urban, nor was it suburban, yet its image was based on the idea of a contained pre-urban fragment, representative of the indigenous *hinterlands*—much like the fiction of Olmsted's Central Park—an Edenic garden that might be regarded as significant to the city and the suburb alike. It happened to be precisely the same image that had served the nineteenth-century city in crisis—the burgeoning metropolis—so well.

The Ford Foundation proposed an entirely different paradigm for the place of office work, one that was green, and consciously Edenic, at least in the American framing of that term. The 'greening' of the office environment seemed allied to an understanding that the place of work existed in a larger environmental system than the urban centre, and that the city and its array of representative spaces were in fact dispersed, widely distributed across and through a landscape.

36

37

THE GARDEN

① 38

① 39

At the same time as Roche and Dinkeloo were arriving at an image and atmosphere that elided characteristics of the city and the suburb, offices continued to move out from city centres to the suburbs, reinforcing the tendency towards dispersal and diffusion. This was echoed in the new treatment of the office interior as a 'landscape'. We have regarded the office interior as a public interior[40] because the office effectively operates as a 'society' that requires certain forms of behaviour from its worker-citizens in order to achieve its desired levels of efficiency and performance. Bürolandschaft, or 'office landscape', a concept developed by the German design agency Quickborner from its foundation in 1956, was promoted as an innovative study in the organisational planning of 'office environments', the implementation of which was geared to effecting maximum performance at the level of both the individual and the group. Design considerations incorporated the arrangements of furniture within offices, working hierarchies, the ergonomics of furniture and the definition of supporting equipment and building services.[41] Despite the rigour of Quickborner's findings, the imagery of Bürolandschaft was managed so that workers would have the impression that they were sustained within an informal working 'landscape', one which would appear at first sight 'chaotic', with apparently loose rather than constrictive arrangements of furniture and meeting areas, in open plans, dotted with potted plants, that, consistent with its naturalistic image, was 'natural' and easy to understand and use. The casual arrangements were in fact condensed representations of managerial hierarchies, with plants providing the impression of informality. This superficial gesture was effective, and has continued to be deployed in the contemporary workplace. It was honoured in the office environment of Norman Foster and Partners' Willis Faber Dumas Building in Ipswich (1978), to which we will return in a later chapter, and appeared as a motif in the Rolex Study Centre in Lausanne, designed by Kazuyo Sejima and Ryue Nishizawa of SANAA (2010). The interior's undulating topography, rising and falling in sympathy with the mountainous scenery of Lac Léman, was designed to promote the interaction of students, its forms suggesting both informality and a corresponding freedom.

  These new arrangements have not, however, constituted a new reality. They have been but friendly presentations—in the guise of a redemptive Garden—of total environments that have encompassed the place of work, the home and the place of consumption, portrayed all together and presented as benign 'paradises', extensive public interiors that obliterate conflict and disagreement. This state of affairs, in which a fiction is offered as a norm, was illustrated in the critique of Andrea Branzi (b 1938) and his Florentine associates in Archizoom, in their project for 'No-Stop City' (1969–1972), which described a continuous environment of office, home and landscape, populated with naked people (LSD-enlightened new autochthones), animals, office equipment and consumer goods, all under one illuminated and air-conditioned ceiling of infinite dimensions. The critique's relevance persists. The illusions that continue to suggest that the continuous and ideologically determined interior we occupy is paradisical have not yet been dispelled by the all too evident realities, inequalities, conflicts of ideologies and vested interests that have framed and attempted to dictate our collective experience. The everlasting reliance on the Garden, used as an offering that promises emancipation and ensures obedience, demonstrates its perpetual currency.

ⓘ 01
The Earthly Paradise.
Jan Bruegel the
Younger, 1620.
Prado, Madrid
© Public domain
Source: Museo
del Prado, Madrid
https://www.
museuodelprado.es/
coleccion/obra-de-
arte/el-paraiso-
terrenal/7ae065e3-
b653-8e36-
bb7d06efeb5d

ⓘ 02
*Essai sur l'architec-
ture* (frontispiece).
Marc-Antoine
Laugier, 1755.
Jacques Aliamet,
engraving; Charles
Eisen, artist.
© Public domain.
Source: http://www.
promolengo.com/
materialegno/04/
abitarre-albero-
il-bosco-il-legno

ⓘ 03
Primitive huts, from
William Chambers,
*Treatise on Civil
Architecture*, 1759
© Public domain.
Source:
www.archive.org

ⓘ 04
*The origin of the
Corinthian order,*
from Claude Perrault,
L'Architecture de
Vitruve, 1684.
Metropolitan
Museum of Art, New
York 41.100.388.
Source: www.
metmuseum.org

ⓘ 05
Et in Arcadia Ego.
Nicolas Poussin,
c 1638. Musée du
Louvre, Paris.
© Public domain.
Source: https://
commons.wikimedia.
org/wiki/File:
Nicolas_Poussin_-_
Et_in_Arcadia_ego_
(deuxième_version)
jpg

ⓘ 06
Le Désert de
Retz, Chambourcy,
1772–1784. Photo
© Michael Kenna,
courtesy Michael
Kenna

ⓘ 07
Bomarzo, il Sacro
Bosco. Monster in
the garden of Pier
Francesco Orsini.
Photo Herbert
List. 5497265
© Hollandse
Hoogte. Source:
Magnum Photos

ⓘ 08
*View of Vauxhall
Gardens,* London
(Maurer view).
Victoria and Albert
Museum, London
W.27BB-1947
© Victorial and
Albert Museum

ⓘ 09
Fun Palace,
Helicopter view,
Cedric Price,
c 1964.
Photographic
reproduction on
Masonite board,
102 × 122 cm.
Centre Canadien
d'architecture/
Canadian Centre
for Architecture
DR1995:0188:521
© Cedric Price
fonds Source: CCA

ⓘ 10
*A view of Savannah
as it stood the 29th
of March 1734.*
Peter Gordon,
delineator. Library
of Congress,
Washington
DC 97683565
© Library of
Congress,
Geography and
Map Division

ⓘ 11
*View of the
Wilderness at Kew,*
William Marlow,
1763. Metropolitan
Museum of Art, New
York 25.19.43
© Metropolitan
Museum of Art.
Source: www.
metmuseum.org

ⓘ 12
The tomb of Jean-
Jacques Rousseau,
Panthéon, Paris.
J.-G. Soufflot. Photo
© CNMHS/
SPADEM Photo
Caroline Rose

ⓘ 13
Henry Thoreau's
cabin, near Walden
Pond. Photo © flickr
user: Sarah Pants.
Source: https://www.
flickr.com/photos/
sarapants/11072
76322/sizes/l

ⓘ 14
Great Conservatory,
or Great Stove at
Chatsworth House.
Joseph Paxton,
1835. Photo © and
source: Devonshire
Collection, Chats-
worth Reproduced
by permission
of Chatsworth
Settlement Trustees

ⓘ 15
La Galérie
d'Orléans, Jardins
du Palais-Royal,
Paris Pierre-
François-Léonard
Fontaine, 1829.
Demolished. Photo
Albert Harlingue
RV-607322
© Albert Harlingue/
Roger Viollet.
Source: www.
parisenimages.fr

ⓘ 16
Crystal Palace,
Hyde Park, London.
Sir Joseph Paxton,
1851. Joseph Nash;
Robert Haghe.
The British Library,
London 068608-
Cup.652.c.33
volume 2, plate 1
© and source:
The British Library
Board

ⓘ 17
Crystal Palace,
Hyde Park, London.
Transept. Sir Joseph
Paxton, 1851.
From *Dickenson's
Comprehensive
Pictures of the
Great Exhibition*
1851 (1854).
Joseph Nash;
Robert Haghe.
The British Library
068678-Cup.
652.c.33 Volume 2,
frontispiece © and
source: The British
Library Board

ⓘ 18
Crystal Palace.
Hyde Park, London.
Transept. Sir Joseph
Paxton, 1851.
Interior view, 1851.
Photograph John
Nash © Victoria and
Albert Museum,
London

ⓘ 19
Joseph Paxton,
*The Great Victorian
Way,* London, 1855.
© Victoria and
Albert Museum,
London

ⓘ 20–22
Galleria Vittorio
Emanuele II, Milan.
Giuseppe Mengoni,
1861–1877.
Photo © Marius
Grootveld.
Source: Marius
Grootveld

ⓘ 23
Diagram of Garden
City. Plate 2 from
*Garden Cities
Of To-morrow,*
Ebenezer Howard,
1902. © Public
domain. Source:
https://commons.
wikimedia.org/wiki/
File:Garden_Cities_
of_Tomorrow,_
No._2.jpg

ⓘ 24
Oxford Museum
of Natural History,
Oxford. Deane and
Woodward, 1860.
The Courtauld
Institute of Art,
London 188214.
© and source: The
Courtauld Institute
of Art, London

ⓘ 25
Natural History Museum, London. Alfred Waterhouse, 1867–1881. Photo Charles Latham. Natural History Museum 024107 © and source: Natural History Museum, London

ⓘ 26
Bibliothèque nationale, Paris. Reading room. Henri Labrouste, 1854–1875. Photo © Georges Fessy

ⓘ 27
Au Bon Marché, (interior photographed c 1900). Archives Moisant-Savey, photograph Albert Chevojon (1865–1925). Wikipedia Commons

ⓘ 28
Central Park, New York. Frederick Law Olmsted and Calvert Vaux, 1865. Photo © Geoffrey James Centre Canadien d'architecture/Canadian Centre for Architecture PH1992:0119. Source: CCA

ⓘ 29
Yosemite, *First view of the valley*, 1866. Photo Carleton Watkins. J. Paul Getty Museum, Los Angeles 85.XM.11.1 © Digital image courtesy of the Getty's Open Content Programme. Source: The J. Paul Getty Trust

ⓘ 30
Aerial view of a complex of Long Island highways that provide access to New York City, c 1946. Photographer unknown © Public domain. Source: https://commons.wikimedia.org/wiki/File:Aerial_view_of_a_complex_of_Long_Island_highways_that_provide_access_to_New_York_City,_ca._1946_-_NARA_-_518064.jpg

ⓘ 31
Los Angeles Sprawl, 1954. Photo William A. Garnett. Estate of William A. Garnett 2000.32.19 © Estate of William A. Garnett. Source: The J. Paul Getty Trust

ⓘ 32
Southdale Center, Edina MN, interior. Victor Gruen, 1956. Photographer unknown. © and source: Minnesota Historical Society

ⓘ 33
Citicorp Building, New York. Atrium. Hugh Stubbins Associates, 1978. Photo © Norman McGrath. Source: HAS

ⓘ 34
Ford Foundation, New York. Interior. Roche and Dinkeloo, 1968. Photo © and source: Mark Pimlott

ⓘ 35
Bürolandschaft, typical plan. Quickborner, 1950s. Drawing © Julia Hegenwald, Martine Duijvis, Giulia Principi. Source: Mark Pimlott

ⓘ 36
Interior, Osram building, Munich. Walter Henn, 1963. Photographer unknown. Source: Mark Pimlott

ⓘ 37
Willis Faber Dumas building, Ipswich. Foster Associates, 1978. Photo © Tim Street-Porter. Source: Norman Foster and Partners

ⓘ 38
Rolex Learning Centre, Lausanne. SANAA, 2010. Photo © Hisao Suzuki

ⓘ 39
No-Stop City. Archizoom, 1970. © Andrea Branzi and Archizoom

THE GARDEN

II
THE PALACE

When the word interior is mentioned, one naturally tends to think immediately of a room, probably a room one is most familiar with. It might be a modest room; it is most likely to be so. When it is proposed that one might think of a room that is much grander than our own, more perfect in every respect, we might think of one, and would possibly go on to imagine a series of such rooms: a sequence of different, special rooms of various sizes that carry on in succession. One might dwell upon a complex organisation of such rooms, combined horizontally and vertically to form an elaborate, exceptional house that could be used for anything that one dreamed of: a house that would offer rooms of every possible purpose and appearance. The special house would accommodate many: family, friends, guests, strangers: an ever-changing flow of people passing from one room to the next.[1] Visitors would be in wonder at the variety and spaciousness of the rooms, their proportions and beauty, their features and appointments, and the apparent endlessness of their succession. One might become excited at the prospect of even being in such a house, and feel privileged to be there, whether on one's own, in the company of a select few, or among a throng of others. One, however, would never feel a sense of belonging: one would always feel like a visitor, an interloper or even an intruder, whose presence was dependent upon the behest of the host, whose authority or power would be palpable, inscribed in the architecture of this exceptional residence, this palace.

The role of the palace has been to embody and represent the power, significance or authority of its host, regardless of whether that power has been ascribed to an individual, a family or a political body. The palace is relieved of the task of other functions, and so accommodates visitors and displays itself to them, delivering its messages and eliciting compliance with them. The functions it contains are, by nature, representational or ceremonial. A palace is indeed a scaffold for representation and ceremony: an empty, perfect vessel.

The interior that assumes the guise of the palace suggests an order or hierarchy between 'owner' and 'visitor'; it transforms its itinerant occupants through its spatial characteristics and representational systems, either humbling or ennobling them. The palace effects this transformation through illusion, built into its organisation, its construction, and its imagery.

Because of its power, the palace as a phenomenon and a theme used by designers has been central to the development of the public interior. In an age in which palaces no longer seem to be central figures in the representative frameworks of our society, the palace remains potent as an idea, or theme, in the design of public interior. The development of the palace as a building type has fuelled the development of the palace as a theme. As a building type, the palace has been particularly sensitive to historical conditions, which have affected the public's perceptions of its address and its meaning. As an idea or theme however, the palace has retained a kind of currency: its motifs have been applied a variety of building types in order to effect certain responses, buildings and interiors that are not palaces that have used aspects of the palace—as a theme—to transform the perceptions of their visitors through a borrowed idea of *aura*. The palace, as a representative type, demands that it is read, and interpreted. Its interiors, dominated by representation, have been dedicated to suggestion and designed to engage and influence their visitors' behaviour.

(II) 01

The palace (as a type), a relatively rare phenomenon in the world of building, has represented the power—real or projected—of the 'ruler', through its organisation and its appearances, articulated through buildings of exemplary aspect with splendid interiors. As well as looking at some real palaces, and buildings and interiors that have aspired to the condition of the real palace, we shall look at projects whose interiors have exploited the palace as an idea or theme, and have proposed frameworks onto which representations with messages about power have been appended.

MOTIFS OF THE PALACE, AS A TYPE

The Winter Palace, now part of the Hermitage Museum in St Petersburg (Francesco Bartolomeo Rastrelli and others, late 1730s-1837) was the central protagonists of the film *Russian Ark* (2002).[2] The film unfolds through a continuous moving shot, which begins with the view of a throng of visitors arriving at a vestibule, then becoming conscious of the palace's great interior on the steps of a grand staircase: a voluminous, vertically-oriented space where their movement is articulated, given an august, regimented pace, and checked. Here, the visitors have the opportunity to take account of where they are and the magnificence of the gilded décor all around

(II) 01-04

⑪ 02–04

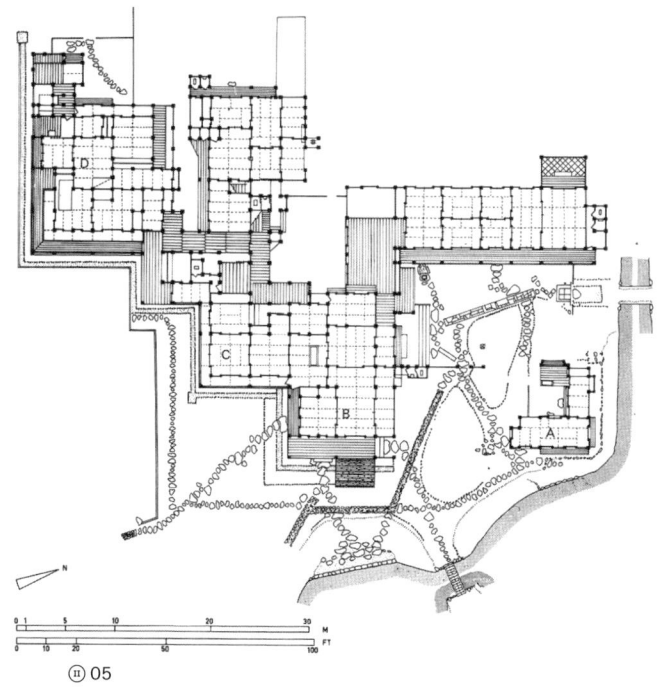

(II) 05

them; they look at each other, dressed (decorated) specifically for their visit; and gather a sense of themselves, in relation to others, to the space they temporarily occupy, and crucially to the 'ruler' of the Palace. Arriving at the top of the stair, they are then followed as they enter and pass through a sequence of rooms, each magnificent, each different, each, without any apparent 'function' other than to receive visitors who will either walk, or stand, or watch, or listen, or dance. The film offers the palace as a living framework, imagining its occupation at various historical moments, and the viewer follows the narrator and guide moving through the scenes, along with the crowds and the historical residents, from room to room. One who walks through the palace in its present guise as museum, alongside throngs of tourists and art lovers, inevitably experiences vestiges of the past and the lives lived within the palace that are evoked by its rooms, and furthermore feels bound to imagine a former, hypothetical 'self' as a privileged guest of the 'ruler', and so, is correspondingly transformed.

The Katsura Imperial Villa in Kyoto (Kobori Enshu and others, in stages between 1615–1663) was a special villa, whose refined uses, ceremonies and architectural character caused it to be called a palace. It cannot really be said to be a public interior. Although one can visit its gardens, the villa is unoccupied and inaccessible to visitors. Our knowledge of its interiors in the West arrived through the accounts of the European architects Bruno Taut and Walter Gropius; and through the efforts of the Japanese architect Kenzo Tange to 'recover' the Villa for architectural discourse, in the service of a specifically Japanese argument for Modernist architecture, and more precisely, for the aims of his own practice. To this end, he commissioned a set of photographs by Yasuhiro Ishimoto (1960) for the book *Katsura: Tradition and Creation in Japanese Architecture* (1960). Tange consolidated a particularly Japanese Modernism through his reading of the villa, building on the observations made by Bruno Taut, who was welcomed in 1933, and reinforced by Walter Gropius in 1954.

(II) 05–08

⑪ 06–07

THE PALACE

They saw qualities in its appearances, construction and spaces, especially in the oldest part of the villa, which reflected their own views on architecture: for them, it was a work of *ur*-Modernism. Ishimoto, in line with Tange's argument for a Japanese Modernist architecture that established its lineage through this revered source, photographed the villa in ways that elided its appearances with those of orthodox Modernist aesthetics, cropping out those aspects of its appearance that did not fit. (In 1983, Ishimoto photographed the house again, revealing completely different characteristics.)[3] I wish to concentrate on those characteristics suggested by Ishimoto's first photographs, the 'emptiness' of the villa's rooms, their relations to each other, and to the designed landscape.

The villa was designed for very exclusive use in the seventeenth century as a country house, designed for living and for specific forms of entertainments relating to its designed landscape garden, to be enjoyed at particular times and seasons of the year. The entertainments had a lyrical or literary quality, attached to readings of Murasaki Shikubu's epic *Tale of Genji* (c 1007). It is a perfect, mysterious monument. The villa is a fusion of buildings, the result of several constructions added over three generations of the Toshihito Imperial family. The contiguous cluster of villas consisting of the *Koshoin* (Old Shoin), *Chushoin* (Middle Shoin),[4] *Gakkinoma* (Music Pavilion), and *Shingoten* (New Goten) (1641–1647), is organised in a staggered, retreating formation oriented in relation to the carefully designed landscape garden. The uses of the rooms were inferred by the sequence of their encounter, with the most important rooms the 'deepest' in the sequence, and the most private rooms, for eating and sleeping, being the most withdrawn. The sequence of spaces followed a passage through the layers of rooms, upon the principle of *Oku*: a penetration of layers along a route.[5] The dimensions of rooms were determined by the arrangement of *tatami* floor mats.

The principles of their layout developed over the course of the villa's construction. In the oldest portion of the villa, the *Koshoin*, the rooms were separated by opaque *fusuma* screens, which slid apart to reveal the next. When opened, there was a suggestion of a limitless succession of cells. Even the first, small house achieved this impression, which was augmented by the constructions that followed.

The precise purpose of each room is open to interpretation,[6] but inferred by their decorative arrangements—in wallpapers, in niches or *tokonama* for the display of hung scrolls or flower decorations, and the making of tea—and their constructional nuances. All effectively operated as rooms for the tea ceremony, an indication of the *Koshoin*'s origin as a tea pavilion. Uses were occasionally given overt form: a room for cooking contained a very beautifully designed hearth; while the Imperial Dais in the *Shingoten* was furnished with an elaborate set of shelves made of many exotic woods, a kind of register of the Imperial presence.

The most important rooms of the villa were all closest to the light, and, when the translucent *shoji* were open, attentions of guests and host alike are turned to the garden. The relation to the garden was paramount and adjusted to the seasons: one special incident was concentrated on a bamboo-floored balcony for viewing the Moon in mid-Autumn. The garden formed a kind of interior itself, with incidents and scenes contrived for visual delight and aesthetic stimulation, aligned with the seasons, readings and tea ceremonies in the several pavilions distributed throughout: the villa looked upon this landscape suggested by in very precise ways, and therefore upon a world charged with meaning.

The photographs reinforce the image of the villa as a shell, or a sequence of connected, multivalent cells, each bearing subtle representations of significance. The movement through them, and into the depths of the villa, was meaningful. Bruno Taut described it in a way that echoes the essence of the idea of the palace: 'The entire arrangement, from whichever side one might care to look at, always followed elastically in all its divisions the purpose which each one of the parts as well as the whole had to accomplish, the aim being that of common and normal utility, or the necessity of dignified representation, or that of lofty, philosophical spirituality. And the great mystery was that all three purposes had been united into a whole and that their boundaries had been effaced.'[7] The views and movement from room to room resembled patterns within the great homes and palaces in the West, from the fifteenth through the nineteenth century. It was the character of movement from room to room that revealed the idea of the palace and its infrastructure for various orders of social interaction between guests and occupants.

The Katsura Imperial Villa appealed to the Modern architect largely because of the character and atmosphere created by Yasuhiro's photographs, which offered the villa as a model of a spatial idea and a sublime figure of abstract composition. Although the period of Modernist dogma has faded, its call for a kind of transparency has not. The elevating of the Katsura Villa as a model—of expression and of spatial arrangement (horizontal, continuous, connective, cellular)—enabled its transposition or projection onto other tasks, examples of which we shall encounter later. Furthermore, it offered the prospect of indeterminacy—wherein the functions of rooms were not necessarily prescribed and appeared to be interchangeable—that has abided with Modernism and the Palace (as a theme) alike.

(II) 12–13

PALACES AND POWER

The Palazzo Ducale in Urbino was a complex of buildings that formed most of the public spaces of the city centre, dominating views of the city from the western countryside and representing the power of its warrior-ruler, the renowned and cultured Federico III da Montefeltro. Its buildings, dating from 1470, were designed by a series of architects, including Maso di Bartolomeo, Luciano Laurana, Francesco di Giorgio Martini and possibly Donato Bramante. Appearing from the landscape like a fortification decorated by a tower of aediculae around the Duke's private apartment, within its walls it assumed the image of a city, and in turn offered the city itself a street, and a piazza defined by a fine façade of brick and dressed stone. One passed through this façade to a sequence of refined spaces, the first a four-level courtyard—or *cortile*—with a correct and elegant arrangement of classical orders (attributed to Laurana). From one corner or

(II) 09–13

67   THE PALACE

14

the *cortile*, one ascended a broad, shallow ramp for men and horses, to a *piano nobile* suite of simple, well-proportioned grand rooms, bare, save for their door casings marked with Federico's initials; windows (facing the corridor around the courtyard, with seats ensconced in their deep reveals); and monumental chimneypieces, all of which were executed in the most sophisticated detail in white stone. These rooms were rather similar, and one may have been impressed, passing from room to room, of the magnitude—or endlessness—of the interior and the authority that it represented. The sequence ultimately terminated in the Duke's private chambers, whose features erupted into complex arrangements as they collided with the façade, concluding with the *intarsio*-panelled private study or *Studiolo*. This tiny room's marquetry, whose panels were all rendered in perspective, depicted artefacts that represented Federico's erudition in the arts and sciences, and muses that inspired his knowledge of science, astronomy, mathematics, geometry, military arts, charity, dance and poetry. The *Studiolo* placed the Duke at its centre, as the engine of the room's depictions and the elaboration of the entire complex.

Although the buildings in Urbino represented the authority of an individual who both ruled and embodied the state, the power inscribed in the fabric of a palace could also be that of a political class or body. The vast rooms of the Palazzo Ducale in Venice (1340–1565, but begun on its site as early as the eleventh century), represented the power of the city-state and its idea of itself. It was a building that called representatives of the city to it, apparently 'containing' the Basilica of San Marco in its main courtyard and accommodating all the operations of state: its chambers of representatives, its treasury, its archives, its judiciary and their courtrooms, and its prison. The expansiveness of the building, embodied in a great sequence of elaborately appointed rooms, one leading to the next, was impressive and representative of the reach and authority of the city-state. The Palazzo as a

14

(II) 15

representation of the city's idea of itself was expressed most clearly in the *Sala del Maggior Consiglio* (Great Council Hall). The room was vast, over 1,300 square metres, an interior *campo* designed to accommodate over one thousand representatives.[8] A ceiling encrusted with paintings spanned its entirety without columns, and acted as its canopy. The whole complex and its puzzle-like arrangement of rooms was encased and represented outwardly in a façade of identical expression to the *piazzetta*, the lagoon, and its citizens: its delicate double arcade supporting a shimmering and inscrutable box of pink and white marble.

The imposing Würzburg palace—modestly called the *Residenz*—was commissioned by Prince-Bishop Johann Philipp Franz von Schönborn, and designed by the architect Balthasar Neumann, and completed in two stages (1720–44; 1780). The whole was notable for its imposing presence, and its suite of grand rooms on the *piano nobile*. Yet the most important room and most representative of our consideration of the palace as a theme was the Hall and its staircase, conceived as a courtyard, in which the symmetrical stair rose to a single broad landing and then split into two returning runs, surrounded by a balcony on all sides. Looking up as one ascended, the suggestion of the courtyard became clear. Its four façades surmounted by a cast of painted characters drawn from reality and allegory, all

(II) 15

16

returned one's gaze from over the cornice. Among them was the painter himself, the Venetian Giovanni Baptista Tiepolo; the architect Balthasar Neumann; and of course, the client, Archbishop Schönbrunn. The continents were all there in attendance too, each in their appropriate attire, with a retinue of men and beasts. The staircase is of particular interest to us, because it presented a vast allegory of the whole world, intended to overwhelm visitors, and impress upon them the eminence of the sponsor of the entire scene, the Prince-Bishop: not a ruler, but a powerful individual who wished to express his power. The characters all around, with their heads in the clouds, were witnesses to that power, with its visitors humbled. The fiction at the heart of this palace was that the sponsor had authority over all, and this hall was both the centre of that authority of the world itself. The idea that an interior could be at the centre of the world became important to projections within public interiors thereafter, and frequently part of their imagery.

There is a degree of indeterminacy in the assignment of function in the palace, and the uses of rooms are frequently provisional, fluid, or interchangeable. Within its many iterations over history, there have been rooms that carried or evoked the promise of transformation of their visitors and 'owners', such as the *Salon des Miroirs* at Versailles; the Silver Room at Amalienburg; and the *Sala dei Giganti* at the Palazzo del Te in Mantova. These were rooms for diversion and fantasy, over and above any uses they might accommodate. With the application of decoration, painting, or extraordinary materials, one was asked to consider their environments as 'other realities' that would transport one 'elsewhere'. These rooms invited other sorts of engagement from the visitor or the sponsor, who, immersed in the spaces, could suspend belief and become the author of the room's proposed fictions. In these rooms, the palace as a scene of transformation became particularly clear, and thus its capacity as a symbol and tool in the representation, construction and exercise of power.

The Silver Room in the Amalienburg lodge of the Schloß Nymphenburg near Munich, designed by François de Cuvilliés, with carvings by Joseph Baptist Zimmermann and Joachim Dietrich and built between 1734–1739, was decorated

ⓘⓘ 17

with forms of nature, in the Rococo style. The Rococo was a sensibility that added
to, and elaborated on those already germane to architecture, searching for the
beauty of the natural through the sinuous line, the pleasures to be found in it, and,
in the words of the art historian Kenneth Clark, 'the pursuit of happiness'.[9] The oval
form of the Silver Room, decorated with gilded foliage, transformed nature's forms,
visible through its windows, into silver. At the end of the day, in the dying light of
the sun, this foliage, all at play for the benefit of its sponsors, was transformed into
gold. The occupant (the Holy Roman Emperor Charles VII) was at the centre of the
room and so became the agent of its transformation. Nature was at his command,
and he was cast an alchemist[10] at the centre of the world, with the greatest power
one could have, which could be taken for a representation of the power of his office.

ⓘⓘ 16

THE PALACE, FROM TYPE TO THEME

Changing historical circumstances alter the meanings and readings of all things.
In much of Western Europe, changes within the context of Modernity—the transformation from feudal society to a civic society—saw changes to the distribution
and representation of power, from the hands of nobles, dynastic monarchies and
feudal lords toward emergent governing classes and to private citizens who were
increasingly enfranchised. As structures of power were modified, so were the artefacts that symbolised them. The palace did not disappear, but became adopted for
different purposes and adapted to different uses: a relic of another time and idea

71 THE PALACE

18

of political structure, the palace came to be occupied by or reinvented by newly formed representative institutions that used the idea of it as a device to represent new orders and new ideas, effectively emptying it out and recasting its role. As the palace was assumed within new political orders in the service of a more broadly enfranchised society, its symbolism was used to represent that society and its members, their ambitions and their ideas.

Therefore, the Palace changed as its ownership or 'master' changed (a demand of society, as it transformed itself): its representations lost their link to rulers, but remained as representations, with some residue of their currency. 'New' palaces were made to accommodate institutions rather than rulers, which retained the obligation to be representative, and these new palaces bore with them all the memories of the palaces that preceded them. They would be obliged to represent something else: not the authority of the individual ruler, but the achievements of the new political or social order, represented by new political, cultural and social institutions.

The construction of the Altes Museum—originally the Königliches Museum— in Berlin, designed by Karl Friedrich Schinkel (1823–1830) for the art collection of Friedrich Wilhelm III marked an important moment: the idea of the Palace as a repository of symbols was, newly made, transformed into a repository of things: things that were stored, removed from the economy of use and displayed for the edification of a new *bourgeoisie*. The historian Alois Hirt had urged Frederick the Great to allow the works of art in his palace to be made public and shown in a specially built museum, 'for public instruction and the noblest enjoyment'.[11] The palace as an idea was used to inform the design of a new civic institution, and cast as a house of representation dedicated to representations. Schinkel's neoclassical design for the Museum design presented itself as a *stoa* to the city—a place for discourse poised over it—and from within its colonnade and its vestibule, Berlin was presented to visitors as a scene viewed from a stage or *Belvedere*. The first floor vestibule offered a view in which representative buildings set around the *Lustgarten* were proposed as a sort of Acropolis, dedicated to political (Königliche Schloß), military (Zeughaus) and spiritual authority (Dom). The greater context of these was

17–20

(II) 19–20

conceived as a sort of landscape, within which buildings were artfully distributed, as in the Picturesque tradition.[12] The Museum represented the authority of knowledge and culture embodied in science and art. As a storehouse of values, it presented itself as a representation, and relied on artificiality in its expression: its architectural elements were among the first to be mass-produced,[13] and there was a severe quality in their repetition, particularly in the façade facing the *Lustgarten*. Within, the building provided images of a palace in spaces redolent of artifice. The central rotunda took this artifice to an extreme: its architectural motifs combined to offer visitors the effect of occupying a representation of an interior, with the Pantheon in Rome serving as its model. Lines painted over architectural profiles suggested their re-presentation, creating the atmosphere of theatre, wherein the building pictured itself, acknowledging the artificiality of its proposition. This artifice was consistent with ongoing themes in Schinkel's work, both in painting, and in his designs for sets for the opera at the *Schauspielhaus*.[14] The Altes Museum, alongside the creation of other public museum buildings, offered a new sort of palace to the city's infrastructure of monuments, transforming the palace as a type into a palace as an idea, a representative public building with public interiors.

PALACES AS METROPOLITAN INFRASTRUCTURE
Public palaces with programmes similar to the Altes Museum proliferated in European cities in the nineteenth century. The public palace was a figure deployed within rapidly growing cities—often exploiting the new spaces provided by the demolition of urban fortifications and the exploitation of land immediately beyond their *glacis*—to resolve problems of imagery regarding new institutions and their representational character. The palace was furthermore used as a motif or theme in the representation or accommodation of the metropolitan elite. The Reform Club, in Pall Mall, London, was a gentleman's club, designed by Charles Barry (1841), which assumed the form of a Renaissance *palazzo*, its external appearance modelled on the Palazzo Farnese in Rome (Antonio da Sangallo (1511–1527) and Michelangelo Buonarotti (1541)). The Reform Club stood in a street of such clubs that were built right into the twentieth century in the St James district.[15] The club building was a potent symbol of a particular class, protected from outsiders (notably women) to conduct gentlemanly discourse in private. Within the Reform Club, one ascended a grand stair to a top-lit courtyard, ringed by galleries around which, on the *piano nobile*, the various club rooms were distributed. The rooms were accorded notional functions—'withdrawing', reading, smoking, dining—yet carried recognisable images associated with stately procession, assembly and homeliness, with bedrooms for members staying in London after dinner. The Club was modeled on a 'special house'.

(II) 21

The Reform Club was very much a monument to a ruling elite in a class-riven society. In continental Europe, those buildings that were proposed as public palaces were useful symbols for a new and broader *bourgeoisie*, representing its ambitions and its authority. In Amsterdam, the Rijksmuseum, designed by Pierre Cuypers (1885), was built as one of a number of monumental buildings devised to ring the city, forming a new institutional infrastructure along the line of the city's decommissioned and dismantled fortifications. The Rijksmuseum was proposed as a metropolitan palace, a distorted château in a Netherlandish-Mannerist style

(II) 22–23

THE PALACE

⑾ 22–23

that closely resembled Cuypers's design for Centraal Station (with A. L. van Gendt, 1889), and Adriaan Willem Weissmann's Stedelijk Museum (1895). Other palaces built as cultural infrastructure in Amsterdam in that period were A. L. van Gendt's Concertgebouw (1886), to which Cuypers had acted as client advisor. These constructions seemed to demonstrate that the imagery of cultural and transport infrastructure was best delivered in a consistent form for ease of communication to the public. The Paleis voor Volksvlijt, also on the ring at Frederiksplein, was designed by Cornelis Outshoorn (1864) and modelled on London's Crystal Palace (1851), both of which we will return to shortly.

The palace motif was also adopted by grand hotels, which emerged in the late nineteenth century in response to expanded travel of the *haute bourgeoisie* to metropolitan centres and resorts, which extended metropolitan life into the natural settings of mountains, lakes and seafronts. The interiors of such hotels, such as the Ritz in London (Mewès and Davis, 1910), conflated the playful experience of the resort with the luxuries one might expect to enjoy in a palace.

POPULAR PALACES AND THE POWER OF INDETERMINACY AND TRANSPARENCY
The Crystal Palace, London, built as the representative building of the Great Exhibition of 1851—the head of the broad and permanent infrastructure of institutions built along Exhibition Road in South Kensington—was called a Palace, which is significant in itself: it was the first in a long line of 'People's Palaces' built in western Europe that gave priority to an idea of transparency, or an extreme measure of indeterminacy to convey the ambition of universality and popular access. The Crystal Palace reappears several times in these chapters because of its ambiguity—its imagery seems to touch many areas of knowledge and experience— and its suggestive power. Its outward form was rendered in glass, open to sight; and the building viewed both itself and its parkland setting. In essence a monumental conservatory, the Crystal Palace was conceived as a framework to be claimed by its visitors, very much as the park in which it was set was 'handed over' to the public by decree, through which Crown lands were made universally accessible, in line with the opening of London's urban estates. The essentially private streets and squares of the gated developments that characterised much of the West End, Mayfair and Bloomsbury were thrown open. The Palace as a type was effectively opened to the public in the context of that decree, representing a notional transfer of ownership, that offered the building as a palace for the general public, one that was part and parcel of a newly emancipated setting and condition, and that possessed all that was within and around it. The building was capacious enough to contain both the park and the public in its open, indeterminate architecture. In the apparently indeterminable dimensions of its interior, the Crystal Palace epitomised the transformation of the city's perceived space. The building excited public engagement: people could promenade within, seeing themselves reflected in the faces of others and in the fruits of the efforts of their nation, to which they could claim to have created. The goods displayed within the Crystal Palace were 'possessed' by its visitors, whose visual consumption of them was transformed into a kind of enfranchisement. Visitors became 'owners' of the artefacts and 'rulers' of the Palace; and it is this effect that caused the Crystal Palace to be adopted by

(II) 24

the department store or *grand magasin* as a preferred format of enclosure for the public interior and disclosure within it.

The Crystal Palace became representative of the idea of a People's Palace, alongside the growing number of buildings in iron and glass—often filled with exotic plants—that came to be used as places of leisure and entertainment, such as the Jardin d'Hiver in Paris (1848).[16] When used for the display of goods, such constructions would be taken as palaces of consumption. We have seen how the Crystal Palace appeared as a central device in Ebenezer Howard's projected Garden Cities as a continuous arcade (1901); it also re-appeared as versions of itself in Europe and the United States; in parks, such as Madrid's Parque de El Retiro as the Palacio de Cristal, designed by Ricardo Velásquez Bosco (1887), and in city centres, as part of the array of urban equipment—like the museum-palace—seen as necessary to the articulation of the idea of a modern city, a metropolis. The form of the Paleis voor Volksvlijt (1864) in Amsterdam evoked the Crystal Palace; set on one side of the Frederiksplein, it was an important figure, a monument for expanding city with metropolitan desires. Until its destruction by fire in 1922, it was the central figure of a development for a whole city block and cast in the role of a vehicle of transformation of the city's basic organisation. Its vast interior was dedicated to exhibitions and to noble musical entertainments provided by its own orchestra, amplified by a great organ. The Paleis voor Volksvlijt stood at the head of an entirely new urban model: the glass monument facing the city advertised an urban block of housing arranged around three sides of an internal garden, with a commercial arcade all around rendering the whole an elaborate public interior.

It was as a palace of consumption that the Crystal Palace initially became most useful. The great department stores of European metropolitan centres offered themselves as such palaces, thriving on transparency and an 'emptiness' (they were storehouses) that was filled with the bounty of consumer goods and its attendant spectacle. Indeed the abundance and splendour of these goods and entertainments, now representative of the wealth of the emerging middle class, echoed the worldly accumulation and culture of pleasure associated with the palaces of the nobility. We recall that the *grand magasin* Au Bon Marché (1853; 1874) was directly inspired by its owner's visit to the Crystal Palace. Aristide Boucicault made it a popular palace filled with people, a bounty of freely accessible goods, and entertainments. Along with its fully glazed courtyard, the circulation within the store contained set pieces, such as visible grand staircases climbing sinuously to *passarelles* above in the manner of an imaginary palace for the stately movement of people, who could see the throngs of shoppers as they were seen. These effects were also deployed in Charles Garnier's Palais de l'Opéra (1875), in which the *bourgeoisie* could witness themselves consuming the most representative metropolitan cultural productions and creating metropolitan culture in the process. Au Bon Marché served as a model for *grands magasins* to follow throughout large urban centres in continental Europe, and then the United States. The *grand magasin* Galeries Lafayette was designed by Georges Chedanne (1907) and Ferdinand Chanut (1912), and located near both the Opéra and Gare Saint-Lazaire. The store grew block by block; the boulevard Haussmann premises featured a central, glazed, courtyard that Chanut wished to evoke an oriental bazaar. This interior had, in fact, both the aura of a

(ii) 25

(ii) 26

ⓘ 24

ⓘ 25

26

jardin d'hiver and a grand court of royal patronage, with heraldic motifs (crests of the French *départements*) and a grand staircase (removed in 1974 for more retail space). Parisian and American department stores exchanged ideas about display and store architecture throughout the late nineteenth century; the innovations of Parisian entrepreneurs were not lost on their American counterparts.

The Marshall Field Department Store in Chicago, named after its proprietor and designed by Daniel Burnham (1888) made itself a very public version of its first store, the accurately named Marshall Field Warehouse Building designed by Henry Hobson Richardson: a fiercely rusticated Florentine palazzo on the outside, accommodating a 'rack of shelves' for mass-produced clothing within. Burnham's department store had entirely different qualities, opposite to the warehouse in many ways: although a functional building on the outside, it had all the trappings of a popular palace within, superimposed on the open frame of the interior. It featured a decorated courtyard, lit from above by a stained glass lay-light, evocative of the arcades and the *jardin d'hiver*-type internal halls of the grander country houses of American millionaires; a grand staircase, galleries, and entertainments, such as orchestras that would encourage consumers to spend their entire day there.[17]

HOUSES AND PALACES OF THE PEOPLE

Department stores imitating the effects of the Crystal Palace were proposed by their promoters as people's palaces, but given that these were enticements devised for people to consume goods, what could a real people's palace be? The transparent, 'empty' and indeterminate Crystal Palace can be regarded as an ideal representative public building (though it was an exhibition building and temporary) in an age when a far greater number of people became aware of or assumed political enfranchisement. The building came to represent that broader but still by no means universal public. There were consciously constructed 'palaces of the people', without ulterior purposes, built in the late nineteenth and early twentieth centuries, which were either sponsored by philanthropists to represent the working class in society, or generated directly by working people, to act as agents for

Ⅱ 27–28

THE PALACE

them and their emerging idea of themselves within society in collective facilities in which consciousness would be raised through education and meeting, and culture would be 'made'.[18] These were products of workers' movements emerging simultaneously in Britain and continental Europe, and later in the Soviet Union, from which emerged, as part of the programme of the complete transformation of society, workers' clubs and other 'social condensors'.[19] The idea that a palace should be considered something for the benefit of the common populace rather than the exclusive domain of an elite yielded the idea of *Maisons du peuple*, as centres of activities of the working citizen.

In the Maison du Peuple in Brussels, designed by Victor Horta (1899), industrial imagery of the city and a notion of 'transparency' indebted to the new palaces of the metropolis were fused. Horta arrived at an order of realism whose effects yielded an industrial palace, whose public rooms' character evoked the street, the factory and the urban shed. The imagery of the station—the representative figure of space for the masses of the nineteenth-century metropolis—served the design of the internal, ground floor *grand café* and the first floor auditorium or 'orchestra'. Here, the image of an industrial hall was offered as a figure just as representative, iconic and fantastic as the classical courtyard within Balthasar Neumann's Residenz in Munich. And so the industrial hall was adopted and adapted to be put to another service—emancipation—in the making of a working man's version of a 'people's palace'.

Some forty years later, the Maison du Peuple in Paris's suburb of Clichy, designed by Marcel Lods, Eugène Beaudouin, and Jean Prouvé (1938) was a building intended for a wide range of uses for a working class part of the city: a 'facility' that would change in order to accommodate them. Hence the upper hall, which was voluminous, with the character of an aircraft hangar or a factory, could be partitioned in a variety of ways through sliding and folding partitions. The roof could even be slid open to the sky, to allow the liberation of interior activities right down to the ground floor: the spaces on the ground floor, largely used for a market, were low, but this space could be opened to the great hall above (and to the sky beyond that). The building had the capacity to achieve the quality of complete emptiness, which seemed implicit in the design of both the external façade and interior partitions. These were made of panels of glass and metal that emulated panelling for aircraft that were equivalent and multivalent. The spirit of the building was consistent, regardless of how it was arranged and how its interior 'form' was changed.

⓪ 27–28

The people's palace in the role of a *Maison du Peuple* was a factory whose imagery was subverted, transformed and put to new uses and new work. Twenty years later still, the Fun Palace project for London's East End, commissioned by the theatre director Joan Littlewood and designed by Cedric Price (1961–1964), took this idea on at a very grand scale: the users of the building would be able to do anything they wanted within the framework of a very adaptable structure, with roofs and components that could appear, move or disappear in response to need. The naming of it as a palace suggested its bounty of possibilities. For Price, the Fun Palace was 'primarily a workshop or university of the streets', or 'a short-term toy' (in the manner of the popular 'Meccano' set); therefore, 'the self-participatory element of the activities must extend to a degree of control by the users of their physical environment'.[20]

⓪ 29–30

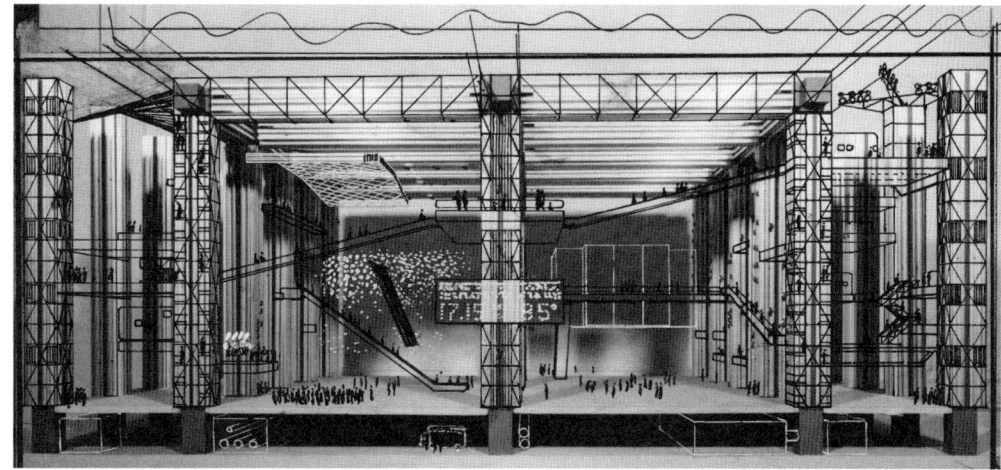

(II) 29–30

Furthermore, many different types of activity would be available to users simultaneously, offering them something Cedric Price called 'inter-accessibility' which enhanced freedom of choice for users and the possibility of new activities created from fluid conditions. Large-scale and large-participation activities dominated the central 'nave' of the structure, while its 'aisles' were available for smaller-scale activities that could also service the former. The form of the interior would be continually modified. In the service of users' freedom, Price developed choice-making survey forms that concerned a wide and unorthodox range of possible activities. With the cyberneticist Gordon Pask—who was interested in how people learned from the various forms of information in their environments—they designed a little decision-making machine,[21] suggesting the best arrangement of the total system for its accessibility to the public of all classes. Although it was to be built in the working-class East End, its allusion to the eighteenth-century Vauxhall Pleasure Gardens, which mixed social classes and offered the possibility of self-invention, was clear. The Fun Palace was indeterminate and empty, and these two characteristics return us to our view regarding the palace as a theme articulated from the outset: the palace is a scaffold for representations. Shorn of the obvious

(ii) 31

(ii) 31–34

representations of palaces for ruling classes both without and within, as well as those many devices that maintained the notion of procession through (representative) space, the palace for the people described by *maisons du peuple* and the Fun Palace was reduced to an open frame through which people could move and upon which representations could be suspended, changed and moved.

An open framework or scaffold eliciting the movement, actions and representations of the public informed the design of the Centre Georges Pompidou in Paris (1977), by Renzo Piano (b 1937) and Richard Rogers (b 1933), and indirectly, that of the institution that preceded it, the Kulturhuset in Stockholm, by Peter Celsing (1966–1974), a building described as 'the shop window of the Welfare Society'.²² The Centre Pompidou proposed itself as a rack of large-span shelves, capable of accommodating any order of cultural activity or event, and in its imagery suggesting that it was a vast factory or rig, it appeared to offer to change its form to do so. The Kulturhuset presented itself as a broad, open stack of concrete balconies suspended from a wall that terminated the main axis of the new modern district of the city, upon which activities were highly visible. Both exploited large clearing in their urban fabrics to symbolise the centrality of both the public and culture, and the public's role in making culture every day; in both cases, it was suggested that these spaces were continuous with their interiors. In both, furthermore, one saw registers of the theme of the palace as a container of significant cells, whose transparency proclaimed unlimited availability. The Kulturhuset faced the busy and central Sergels Torg, a sunken square connected to metro system and regional rail lines. Within, a spiral staircase commanded processions of users through the building's open floor plates, set at varying heights, all of which looked onto the activity of the public square below. The Centre Pompidou and Kulturhuset shared a central, driving figure in common: the curator Pontus Hultén (1924–2006) had been the director of the Moderna Museet in Stockholm during the development

⑪ 32–34

⑪ 35

⑪ 36

and shaping of the Kulturhuset project, and became the first director of the Centre Georges Pompidou, framing the terms of the brief presented to architects for the international competition held in 1971. His radical and liberating ideas about expanding the role and work of the museum had gone on to be critical and central for the conceptualisation of the Kulturhuset. Hultén, first at the Moderna Museet and then as director of the Kulturhuset, thought of the museum as a house or place where culture was made, and wished to involve all of society in the act of 'making culture', since this is fact what people did, unconsciously. He became the director of Centre Pompidou in 1973, and his ambitions were extended in its construction. Its open floors, their free space enabled by their wide-span structures, could accommodate any kind of internal arrangement, inviting constant change and constant re-interpretation, in the manner of a multi-level Fun Palace. The building's services and lifts were attached to its long 'rear' elevation, facing Rue Beaubourg. Its front face was turned to the new amphitheatre-like public *place* that sloped towards it and its broad phalanx of entrances. The *place* was continuous with the interior of the sunken ground floor, which expressed itself both as an industrial hall and living room for the city. The façade, despite its industrial image, was rendered palatial due to its representational staircase—a continuous run of connected escalators—being suspended from its structural frame. This at once enabled the logic of the free floors of the massive structure to be free of interruption, and the moving public to see itself consuming and making culture, as in the *grands magasins* and the Palais de l'Opéra. Subsequent modifications to the building imposed a conservative ethos on its fabric: a conventional suite of galleries ('*enfin, une vraie musée*') were installed to the designs of Gae Aulenti in 1984; internal staircases were added on several floors; and its openness was reduced to a one-metre wide space between internal walls and the façade.[23]

All of these factory-like palaces featured a promise of phenomenal transparency and a concomitant complete flexibility, wherein the 'palace' as name or motif suggested a carapace or scaffold that could be claimed for any desired purpose as long as it 'produced' culture. The transparency, multivalency or emptiness of these palaces was directed toward ultimate utility: anything could be accommodated or projected within, where not only could everything be seen, simultaneously; there was also opportunity or provision of free movement from space to space (or within open space), and from 'cell' to 'cell' through space. The palace—as a theme—became a public interior in which culture was housed and produced—indicating its truly representative origins—and a locus of complete indeterminacy. It was also seen as the ultimate site of social contact, connectivity and interaction. The Fun Palace's indeterminate design, using a regular structure as infrastructure, permitted indeterminacy to be, in itself, representative. This established a normative condition that was explicitly referred to in the renovation of the Palais de Tokyo in Paris, designed by Anne Lacaton and Jean-Philippe Vassal (2001; 2012). This new Palace—its name derived from that of the existing building, one of a collection of exhibition structures erected for the *Exposition Internationale des arts et techniques dans la vie moderne* in 1937, of which it occupied one half—was re-created as a centre for contemporary art by its curators Nicolas Bourriaud and Jérome Sans in the spirit of Pontus Hultén: *une centre de création*. In its grand and theatrically contrived ruinous interiors, it set forth an atmosphere of ease, anarchy and relaxation (a direct echo of the aims of the Fun Palace, however, as a spectacle without the possibility of change), and proposed itself as yet another palace of the people, addressed to a public who had learned, over forty years of exposure to the theme, to understand its signs. It is a project to which we will return in a later chapter.

A RETURN TO TYPE

The Royal Festival Hall in London (1951), built for the Festival of Britain, a centennial celebration of the Great Exhibition as a 'tonic to the nation', was primarily a concert hall for classical music. Its design kept very much to the script of a palace as a sequence of representative spaces in which people were conscious of themselves and their relations to others. Designed by a collaborative led by Leslie Martin and Peter Moro, it was the Festival's 'legacy' building, and like the Exhibition Road legacy of 1851, the Festival Hall eventually found itself at the centre of a cluster of cultural buildings on the Thames that comprise the South Bank Centre. Within, people move across broad staircases and wide concourses, all appointed in luxurious treatments of wood, brass, glass and carpeting on a variety of levels, organised to provide the maximum number of views of different spaces and others moving in and between them. Broad indoor terraces used as lounges afforded panoramic views of the Thames, inviting people to sit and rest whether they were attending a concert, a tea dance or doing nothing at all. The interior's other surfaces were white and openly Modernist, decorated in the style of the immediate post-war years, indebted both to Le Corbusier and British interpretations of the sweet and light precedents of the new architecture of Sweden, that evoked domesticity and a political outlook of social welfare and social democracy that post-War Britain felt it shared.[24]

The Festival Hall drew on palatial tropes: the grand staircases wrapping around the concert hall and the proliferation of landings, balconies and terraces appended to them were singular features of its interior, prolonging anticipation of the spectacle within, reminiscent of the theatrical staircases preceding the great sequence of rooms in the Winter Palace in St Petersburg and the Residenz in Munich. An image of engagement—much like these and even the experience provided by the Centre Pompidou's suspended escalators—was evident in the Festival Hall's staircases, where the real-life performance of movement, interaction and play occurred. The performance and the self-regarding theatricality of the Festival Hall led to its characterisation as a 'people's palace', and its popular moniker.

PALACE AS MEDIUM WITH A MESSAGE

In the twentieth century, the idea of the palace acquired broad usefulness, particularly in the service of political regimes in which 'the people' were cast as central figures in the representation of power and ideology. The infrastructure of underground Metro stations in the Soviet Union (and instituted by Josef Stalin) were designed as 'people's palaces' and elaborated in neoclassical and latter-day roccoco styles.[25] In Moscow (1932–1935), station concourses, such as Konsomolskaya or Prospekt Mira became great halls for the metropolitan collective on the move. Chandeliers illuminated their spaces as though features of palaces of an ideal (and borrowed) age,

37–38

⓿ 39

while patriotic scenes rendered in mosaic situated the commuting public in the midst of an all-embracing and distinctly Soviet world. Cities of the Soviet Union were abundantly equipped with such Palaces for different aspects of socialist life: sports palaces, cinema palaces, youth palaces and culture palaces, to name but a few. Unlike the twentieth-century palaces in the West we have discussed, Soviet citizens did not assume the controls of the state machinery; rather, their participation, as genuine as may have been, was transformed into the décor of the spectacle of the State. After Stalin's death, these palaces were designed within a Modernist idiom, either openly expressive in the manner of a residual constructivism, or in a functionalist style based on a reductive neoclassisicm.

In the Soviet Union's satellites, the palace motif was followed similarly. The Palast der Republiek, Berlin, designed by the Kollektiv der Bauakademie der DDR, under the direction of Heinz Graffunde (1976) was an enormous megastructure, with large spans springing from giant concrete cores, a structure intended to accommodate all manner of activities representing the life and idea of the German

Ⓘ 40–41

THE PALACE

Democratic Republic. The halls for parliament and political congresses offices were certainly central to its design, but it outwardly offered itself as a palace, containing ample and well-appointed facilities for entertainment, leisure, and a variety of social and cultural gatherings. The building was organised so that these two worlds—the political and the social—were interwoven as they may have been in palaces of pre-modernity, and so embedded politicians within its structure, who could survey the citizen-visitors: a real time version of that surveillance the Stasi conducted in secret in all aspects of life 'on the outside'. All the functions of the Palast der Republik were housed under one shelter, in the manner of the Fun Palace project—albeit more severe—on whose influence on the architects one can only speculate. Despite its outward monumentality, there was a high degree of flexibility afforded by the structure: the congress halls could be cleared and adapted to very different uses, such as a grand dining room or a festival stage. The interior was one within which an image of DDR culture was displayed, and an idea of its making was played out, fantastic and distinct from mundane, quotidian experience. Residual palace motifs were distributed over and through the building's structural framework: a monumental hall, a grand staircase, sequences of vast spaces of indeterminate use, and myriad decorative effects, including handsome monogrammed service in glass and porcelain. The palace's materials were quite distinct from and more luxurious than those typically afforded within DDR construction: within, marble and decorative glass, and ceilings featuring constellations of crystalline globes suggested fantasy,[26] while without, a crystalline and rose-tinted mirrored Modernism—with the State's authorisation literally affixed to it—was presented to Berlin and to the whole world.[27] The Palast der Republik was a container of ideological messages that were to be absorbed by its captive public and reflected in its obeisance and obedience. These messages were projected through interiors of exceptional material and spatial characteristics that represented and embodied the outlook, authority and power of the regime. In order to work, the interior relied on 'emptiness': a multitude of rooms without apparently fixed or predetermined use, that gave the unsettling and potentially liberating impression of indeterminacy, were augmented by a sequence of spaces that achieved the effect of endlessness, and its accompanying disorientation. With space ordered into significant rather than operational sequences, the idea of procession was imprinted upon its visitors. Elements that articulated the ownership or possession of the regime were at the centre of the palace, affecting the visitors' consciousness of its power and their relation to it. The indeterminate nature of the Palast spoke of that power; it was, like all palaces, a receptacle—a storehouse—of value and values.

We have seen how the emptiness of the palace has been translated into the phenomenon of transparency, and that transparency—every bit as much as emptiness—can be representative of the values of a society, whether it is an autocracy, a liberal *bourgeois* state, a social democracy or an authoritarian regime posing as a democratic republic. The life of the Palast der Republik in its original form was but thirteen years. The collapse of the German Democratic Republic's regime and the fall of the Berlin Wall in 1989 discredited the Palast and all its apparati. Following the Palast's closure (ostensibly for the removal of asbestos), It was determined in 1993 that it was to be demolished, and for years, it performed a role as a space

⑪ 42

for cultural happenings, passed through a completely different cultural filter. Its dressings of marble and its halls of political assembly were stripped away, and the building assumed the character of a ruin, whose emptiness was quite real, and allied with its new transparency of access and use. In this guise, it became closer to the idea of the Fun Palace that had seemed to serve as a model for its original construction; its spaces were open to interpretation and re-configuration, and to the possibilities of assuming multiple identities. Perhaps this emptied-out form, this shell capable of transformation and assumption of any idea projected upon it by its authors—in this case, the great, emancipated public of a unified Germany—was closest to the spirit or idea of the Palace. Nevertheless, the building was regarded as an outdated relic, too closely associated with the collapsed regime and its ideology, and demolished in 2006.

⓫ 01
Winter Palace, St Petersburg. Francesco Bartolomeo Rastrelli and others, late 1730s–1837. Photo © and source: Mark Pimlott

⓫ 02–04
Winter Palace, St Petersburg. Francesco Bartolomeo Rastrelli and others, late 1730s–1837. Photo © and source: Marius Grootveld

⓫ 05
Katsura Imperial Villa, Kyoto. 1640s. Source: http://25.media.tumblr.com/tumblr_ma4etqQNg21rww1nyo1_1280.jpg

⓫ 06
The New Palace and Lawn, seen from the Middle Shoin, Katsura Imperial Villa, Kyoto (1953). Photo Yasuhiro Ishimoto. Centre Canadien d'Architecture/Canadian Centre for Architecture PH1986:0205 © Kochi Prefecture. Source: CCA

⓫ 07
View of the Moon-viewing platform, the pond and the garden, showing he Second Room of the Old Shoin in the foreground, Katsura Imperial Villa, Kyoto (1953). Photo Yasuhiro Ishimoto. Centre Canadien d'Architecture/Canadian Centre for Architecture PH1986:0199 © Kochi Prefecture. Source: CCA

⓫ 08
Interior view of the Old Shoin, showing the Second Room in the foreground and the First Room and the Spear Room in the background, Katsura Imperial Villa, Kyoto (1953). Photo Yasuhiro Ishimoto. Centre Canadien d'Architecture/Canadian Centre for Architecture PH1986:0203 © Kochi Prefecture. Source: CCA

⓫ 09–12
Palazzo Ducale, Urbino. Maso di Bartolomeo, Luciano Laurana, Francesco di Giorgio Martini, c 1470. Photo © and source: Marius Grootveld

⓫ 13
Palazzo Ducale, Urbino. *Studiolo*, c 1470. Photo © and source: Mark Pimlott

⓫ 14
Palazzo Ducale, Venezia. Photo © and source: Mark Pimlott

⓫ 15
Residenz, Wurzburg. Balthasar Neumann, 1720–44; 1780. Photographer unknown. © Web Gallery of Art. Source: http://www.wga.hu/html_m/t/tiepolo/gianbatt/5wurzbur/2stair1.html

⓫ 16
Silver Room, Amalienburg lodge, Schloß Nymphenburg, Munich. François de Cuvilliés, 1734–1739. Photo Flickr user: barnyz © CC BY-NC-ND 2.0. Source: https://www.flickr.com/photos/75487768@N04/7061205899

⓫ 17
Altes Museum, Berlin. Karl Friedrich Schinkel, 1824. Photo © and source: Mark Pimlott

⓫ 18
Altes Museum, Berlin. Karl Friedrich Schinkel, 1824. View on the Lustgarten, from the Altes Museum (1850). Michael Carl Gregorovius, delineator. © Public domain. Source: https://commons.wikimedia.org/wiki/File:Michael_Carl_Gregorovius_(attr)_Blick_vom_Alten_Museum_auf_den_Lustgarten.jpg

⓫ 19–20
Altes Museum, Berlin. Karl Friedrich Schinkel, 1824. View of the Rotunda. Photo © and source: Mark Pimlott

⓫ 21
Reform Club, London. Charles Barry, 1841. Photo Flickr user: Phil Guest © CC BY-SA 2.0 Source: https://www.flickr.com/photos/philip-rosie/15435568855/in/photolist-bHMzRF-pvZjRv-pevaTe-peu-6UX-pvGVe8-FTfEvb-jGkHi4-buSPiq-Gg5fM3-buSP71-Fo6pgt-4Wi3SF-GacSdw/

⓫ 22–23
Rijksmuseum, Amsterdam. Pierre Cuypers, 1885 Photo © and source: Marius Grootveld

⓫ 24
Nash's views of the Crystal Palace. The Inauguration, 1851. Victoria and Albert Museum, London. Joseph Nash E.604-1949 © and source: Victoria and Albert Museum, London

⓫ 25
The main staircase of the grand magasin Au Bon Marché, rue de Sèvre, Paris. H.-A. Boileau and Gustave Eiffel, 1868. Michel-Charles Fichot, engraving. 5495755 91 © Hollandse Hoogte. Source: Roger Viollet

⓫ 26
Galeries Lafayette, Paris. Georges Chedanne, Ferdinand Fanut, 1912. Photo © and source: Mark Pimlott

⓫ 27
Maison du Peuple, Paris-Clichy. Beaudouin, Lods, Prouvé, 1930. RIBA30841 © and source: Architectural Press Archive/RIBA Collections

⓫ 28
Maison du Peuple, Paris-Clichy. Interior. Beaudouin, Lods, Prouvé, 1930. Photo © Steffen Haug. Source: https://www.flickr.com/photos/86088109@N00/484241775

⓫ 29
Fun Palace. Interior perspective, Cedric Price, 1964. Centre Canadien d'Architecture/Canadian Centre for Architecture DR1995:0188:518 © Cedric Price fonds. Source: CCA

⓫ 30
Fun Palace. Perspective, Lea River site, Cedric Price 1961–1965. Centre Canadien d'Architecture/Canadian Centre for Architecture DR1995:0188:522 © Cedric Price fonds. Source: CCA

⓫ 31–34
Kulturhuset, Stockholm. Peter Celsing, 1978. Photo © and source: Marius Grootveld

(II) 35
Centre Georges Pompidou, Paris. Piano and Rogers, 1977. Photo © and source: Mark Pimlott

(II) 36
Palais de Tokyo, Paris. Lacaton et Vassal, 2001. Photo © Philippe Ruault. Source: Lacaton et Vassal architectes

(II) 37–38
Royal Festival Hall, London. Sir Leslie Martin, Peter Moro et al, 1951. Photo © and source: Marius Grootveld

(II) 39
Konsomolskya Metro station, Moscow. Photo © and source: Marius Grootveld

(II) 40
Palast der Republik, Berlin, 1976. Heinz Graffunde; Kollektiv der Bauakademie der DDR. Photographer unknown (Post card). Source: Mark Pimlott

(II) 41
Palast der Republik, Berlin, 1976. First big youth dance night. Heinz Graffunde; Kollektiv der Bauakademie der DDR. Photo Jürgen Sindermann 183-R0706-417 © and source: Bundesarchiv

(II) 42
Palast der Republik, Berlin, 1976. Eleventh Party Convention of the SED, 1986. Heinz Graffunde; Kollektiv der Bauakademie der DDR. Photo Klaus Franke 183-1986-0417-414 © and source: Bundesarchiv

III
THE RUIN

We occupy the places of others who have gone before us; those who we have never known, those we have forgotten, and those who we half-remember. Walter Benjamin, in his *Arcades Project* (1927–1939),[1] sifted through the hand-me-downs and cast-offs of the nineteenth-century *bourgeoisie* sold in the faded arcades of early twentieth-century Paris and regarded them as though they were the relics of distant civilisations. In his study, in which the arcades constituted an archaeological site, he was able to develop a history of the material culture of the nineteenth-century metropolis. The consciousness of the past, and our identification with its ruins has been an ongoing theme of architecture and the visual arts since the Renaissance. From the onset of Modernity, and its convulsive transformation of the world as it had been known, ruins have persistently held a poetic potency. Ruins contain the remnants of the ideas and ambitions of the past; and, regardless of the intensity of their intent, those ideas are appreciated in their evident decay, being reclaimed by nature, collapsing back into the earth from which they had sprung.[2] The ruin has been regarded as beautiful precisely because it holds the germ of what was, representing the passing of all things, and the portent of our own demise and disappearance, an eloquent reminder of our own mortality.[3] What endures in the ruin is its uncanniness; it seems to stand for an attack on the sanctity of our constructions, and our bodies. When the fabric of the present is devastated, a people's sense of itself is defiled, and it is almost unbearable: for example, the Second World War ruins of Ouradour-sur-Glane are retained as a monument to this pain; the burnt-out remains of Dresden, particularly as viewed from the skies from which its destruction was wrought, still evoke horror.[4] Recently, images of the destroyed streets of Beirut, Sarajevo and Aleppo figure in our imagination alongside those of the ruins of the World Trade Center in New York. Our feelings extend to the ruins of ruins. The destruction of the Buddhas of Bamiyan, as that of Palmyra's temples of Baalshamin and Bel, its triumphal arch and funerary monuments reacquainted us with the horror of desecration, and provoked revulsion such as that attendant on images of the mutilation of the human figure. As much as the ruin has prompted contemplation of the demise, decay and degeneration of all things, it has been a spur to the imagination for interpretation, for construction and re-construction.

The ruin is a figure that did not arise in cultural discourse until there was consciousness of the incompleteness of the present. Before this consciousness, ruins did not 'appear': relics of previous civilisations and historical periods were simply residual matter that were ignored, used, or otherwise incorporated into everyday life. Ruins were plundered for materials, occupied, and built upon. However, at some point, their residue became visible for what they were, and entered consciousness as significant and worthy of attention. When it became clear that the ruined constructions of those previous societies and civilisations, such as the Greeks and the Romans, were indeed important, it became legitimate to attend to them, contemplate them, and speculate on what might be done in relation to their legacy. These ruins could be subjects of reflection; they could be re-made; they could become the material of fancy, or nightmare, or inspiration. And in their re-making, the greatness of previous civilisations could be borrowed and re-lived.

(Ⅲ) 02-03

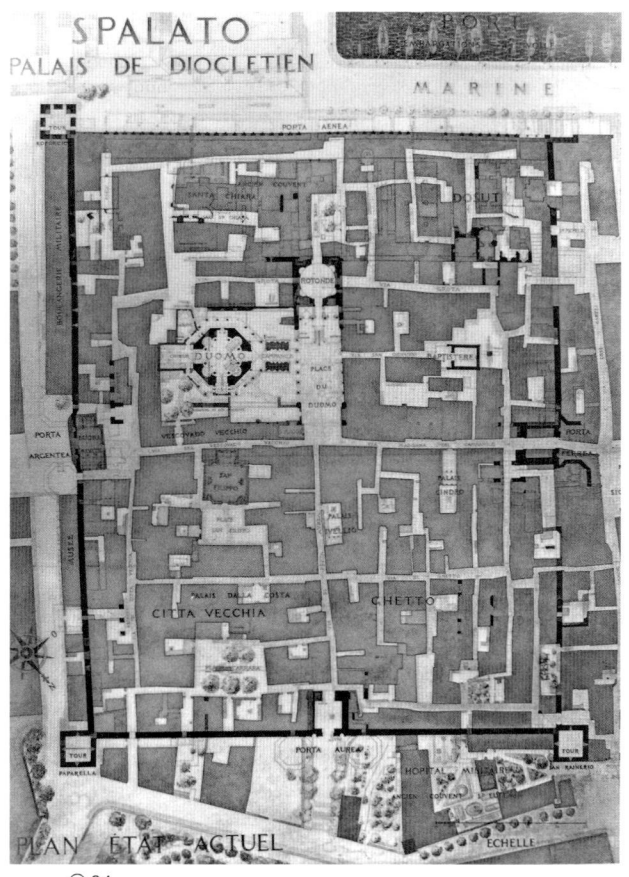

⓷ 04

The fanciful reconstruction was a preoccupation of nineteenth-century eclecticism, particularly of the Gothic in England and Germany; but it was characteristic of the Renaissance as a project of recovery, too, and after, from the Baroque through neo-classical periods as a project of 'theatre'. The invocations and borrowings of the burgeoning nineteenth-century metropolis continued this stage-setting tradition. The ruin, revived, represented both the narcissistic confidence of its revivalists, and the anxiety of inauthenticity attendant upon the historical period of its revival: in short, it served as a constant reminder of the crisis of Modernity.

All this might seem to us as though concerns of another world, and of another time, long past. Yet the Ruin remains present and potent within our architectural culture. I wish to ask where we might find the evocation of things past in the present, and particularly within public interiors, and whether the Ruin indeed informs the concerns, or play, of contemporary practice; and if so, what its relevance might be.

The Ruin, that broken relic of the past, has inspired and reproached successive generations, who have turned to it for redemption. In the chapter 'The Garden', we saw how the story of the primitive hut legitimated the very idea of architecture that represented its own construction and its origins, suggesting that architecture (the most elevated form of building) was rooted in an original nature. The Ruin, similarly, had provoked contemplation of those times when Man was supposedly closer to origins, and to stories about original truths. The return to the Ancients

⑪ 05-06

signified a compulsion to find the essence or the basis for action in the present, despite its very altered conditions, and marked, through the evidence of artefacts their societies bequeathed, a return to the roots of culture. The Ruin, or fantasies around ruins, suggested origins and the contemplation of fundamental things.

There seems to have been a series of stages to the realisation that ruins had the capacity to guide the making of architecture and painting. It is important to remember that much of that was built and written of ancient Greece and Rome was lost through the Middle Ages; what was retained came through those very few texts that were saved both in form and spirit by an exclusive set of readers and translators. The language of the Ancients, contained in texts of philosophy, mathematics and poetry, was preserved in ancient libraries, both secular and monastic: and in these private libraries, their transcription into Latin was pursued. The meeting of Greek and Roman philosophy, science and literature and Christian theology yielded the intellectual inquiry that brought about the first universities. In contrast, the forms of its architecture were essentially lost, either literally amidst the jumble of other constructions—such as in the case of Diocletian's Palace (305) in Split, Dalmatia—or in ruins; or barely present as mere echoes in the doggerel forms of building that ultimately developed into architecture of its own considerable sophistication and expression in the Romanesque and Gothic styles.

(III) 04

RECOVERY OF THE ANCIENTS

It was not until the fourteenth century that a sustained attention to the architecture of the ancients was attempted, and the next until it was finally given form—as a recovery of the Roman re-invention of the architecture of Greece—first, by Filippo Brunelleschi (1377–1446), and fully, by Leon Baptista Alberti (1404–1472). As we have noted, what was known of the architecture of the ancients was found in ruins: scraps and fragments buried in the ground and submerged in subsequent constructions, remnants of the architecture of Rome and her colonies, and fragments of others.[5] To 'decode' the structures of ancient Rome, there was, crucially and critically, a text: Marcus Vitruvius Pollio's (c 80–70BC–c 15BC) treatise on Architecture, *De Architectura* written some time between 46 and 30 BC, and rediscovered in Florence in 1414. Leon Baptista Albert, in wanting to make the text available to contemporary readers, was obliged to almost re-write it.[6] Alberti's re-writing, therefore, was a way of reconciling his own direct studies of the ruins of Rome with Vitruvius's texts. The act of re-writing was one of cultural recovery and a search for new life for the principles embodied in the texts—particularly concerning those of order and proportion—and those embodied in Roman ruins themselves: a re-birth. Alberti's thesis on building *De re aedificatoria* (1452)[7] acquainted architects with the principles of architecture embodied in the forms, proportions and organisation of the architecture of ancient Rome, and introduced them to the essence of Vitruvius's lessons. Thereafter, knowledge of Vitruvius was key to an architect's fundamental and complete education and working knowledge, and through Alberti's agency, immediately considered indispensable. Consequently, the ruins of Rome would be inscribed in Renaissance architecture; Alberti gave those ruins new pertinence and new life.

The ruins recovered and revived by Alberti spoke of a harmonious approach to the issues of construction and its representation at a great number of scales.

Alberti wrote, and built, and these two activities were intertwined; his buildings were demonstrations derived from his research. The façade of the Palazzo Rucellai, in Florence (1446–1451) was a summary of his discoveries of the relation of the classical Orders applied, almost pictorially, to a surface of represented stones; the Tempio Malatestiano, in Rimini, (1447) was made in the form of a temple, articulated through the classical orders; a sepulchre for the Rucellai family in the church of San Pancrazio, Florence (1467) was yet another refined and pictorial reinterpretation of a classical ideal. The reach of Alberti's considerations was great and his views influential. He was consultant for the design of the Piazza at Pienza (1459),[8] which established a spatial ideal echoed in the paintings of ideal cities by Laurana and Piero della Francesca.[9] The façades of the churches of Santa Maria Novella in Florence (1470), and in Mantova, Sant' Andrea (1471) and San Sebastiano (unfinished, begun 1458) established compositional norms for completely new conditions based on his interpretations of Vitruvius, as demonstrations to be taken up by other architects.[10]

Alberti attempted to establish an architectural orthodoxy, inscribed within an idea of a whole society's expression (his concept or theory of 'historia') in harmony across the arts that was rooted in those of ancient Rome. Writing in his thesis on painting *De pictura* (1435), Alberti referred to a balance or harmony of animate and inanimate elements that appealed to all eyes. The legacy of Rome was the material to be studied: its images, its text and its ruins. Through the brief period of academic recovery and pictorial and built revival—the Renaissance (the 're-birth')—the ruin was given new life through its address of contemporary problems and tasks (architecture and painting among them) and a unified presence across the arts. This recovery of the idea of the Ancients through the lessons contained within their artefacts was a project that would hold the architectural imagination until the arrival of a-historical Modernism.

ⅲ 08

ⅲ 09

ACADEMICISM

Following Alberti's example (and putting aside for now the development of Mannerism and the Baroque), architects felt obliged to follow the example and study of the ancients: Vitruvius's treatise found itself consistently inscribed in the architect's education. Architects placed their knowledge of Vitruvius in the foreground; built demonstrations were evidence of their skill. Rather than constituting a restriction of architectural expression, this academicism inspired invention in composition, inevitably based on interpretation of ancient models. Furthermore, it legitimated the increasingly confident expression of the church, city states and powerful individuals alike, demonstrating their authority over their own time and that of the past. The most inventive architect of the sixteenth century—Andrea Palladio—was also the most public regarding his erudition and his genius for re-interpretation. Palladio (1508–1580) studied Roman architecture from 1554, and wrote his conclusive four volume *I quattro libri dell'architettura* in 1570. It would be regarded as a 'bible' of classical architecture and used by virtually all the important architects, internationally, for the next 250 years. A demonstration of Palladio's confident handling of the legacy of Roman architecture was the design of the Villa Almerico Capra, or Villa Rotonda near Vicenza (1571), where he proposed an almost cubic country house positioned on a hill, high above its possessions, with each of its four faces fronted by a classical temple, resting on a basement plinth filled with spaces for services. Each temple was in fact a portico, framing views all around of the land from the house. The house borrowed the sacred form of the temple front and transformed it into a sign of the landowner's power, visible from every part of his property: an example of Palladio's 'play' with Rome and the inheritance of 'classicism'.[11]

That play could express itself in mere appearances, in the extended façade of the Basilica (1549, completed 1614), for example, or the etiolated temple façade of the Palazzo Chiericati (1550, completed 1680), both in Vicenza. His design for the church Il Redentore, on the Giudecca in Venice (1577–1592) took into account that it would be mostly viewed from a distance, across the lagoon, and so its dome hovered over a façade featuring what appeared to be a concatenation of overlapping temples, a forum of temples condensed into a shallow plane. His design for the Teatro Olimpico in Vicenza, (1580–85), proposed the revival of an ancient Roman theatre, the auditorium surrounded by a colonnade, the ceiling painted to resemble the sky in a completely convincing illusion. From the auditorium, the audience looked onto a Roman-format stage, a broad façade with the appearance of a set of triumphal gates. This element, designed by Vincenzo Scamozzi, appeared to carry on to great depths through a *trompe l'œil* effect, extended by interior streets, whose forms, manipulated in keeping with the rules of perspective, were manifestly false, artificial and appropriately theatrical.

The academicism of the sixteenth century led to an ever-increasing interest in the ruins of the ancient world: they came to be considered, effectively, modern, or at least as direct inspiration for contemporary developments in the arts. The popular vehicle for this interest—for the privileged economic or social class at least—was the Grand Tour, a pastime that was popular from about 1550 until the age of rail transport in the 1850s.

(iii) 10

THE GRAND TOUR

Taking the Grand Tour was a significant episode in the life of a young English man of means (training to be a man of influence in maturity) to see the ruins of the Ancient World, and of Rome in particular, for education and acculturation, in order to mix and flourish in good society. They were an essential part of the education of a young aspirant, regardless whether he had a taste for architecture and culture or not. Culture, in its recognised art and expressions (including language), was the currency of European good society. Familiarity and confidence in that currency offered a necessary point of contact and access to that society, learned 'on tour' and indispensable at home. One might describe the Grand Tour as obligatory, and therefore, its highlights became elements of the cultural currency one used. The Tour reinforced north-European cultural hegemony. One would trail from Britain through the Low Lands, through Germany and over the Alps into Italy, into the cities of the north, with time spent in Venice, Florence and Rome, with further travel to Naples, likely ending at Paestum; or even onto Sicily and Palermo. One would see exemplary architecture; and ruins in particular. One would meet people of similar or higher social status according to arrangements made; one would listen to music. The Tour was costly, but was an investment that one would expect to recuperate over the course of one's career. The Tour was a kind of promenade across Europe, akin the notion of going for a walk in a landscaped park, to see what was left behind by others who had come before them. A Tour offered erudition, amusement, and entertainment. In the settings of the cities of Old, Mediterranean Europe, ruins were figures that provoked thoughts of the passing of things, of mortality; but as figures of contemplation, ruins were furthermore figures of fantasy, of play. Over

(iii) 10

⑪ 11

⑪ 11

the centuries of the Tour's popularity, the meanings of those artefacts contemplated changed in relation to the changes within the societies of the Tourists themselves, and the Tour therefore changed from a form of entertainment to a form of erudition, then to a form of cultural colonialism, and ultimately, at the onset of Modernity, to a form of Romanticism that remains with us in our own appreciation of ruins today.

Tourists were accompanied on their journeys by guides or *Cicerone*, who were familiar with the itinerary of important buildings to be seen along the way, and the monuments, or more precisely, half-buried ruins of the ancient world. The British architect Inigo Jones (1573–1652) was an early *Cicerone*, whose architecture, such as the Banqueting Hall at Whitehall in London (1619–1649) was the fruit of his studies of ruins, Vitruvius and Palladio. The 'masques' or plays he designed, first for gardens and then the stage (he introduced the proscenium arch to Britain) used ruinous fantasies as settings for 'play' between the present and the antique world, set between garden and palace, the garden being—as we have seen earlier—a place of knowledge, intrigue and deception. The ruin was invoked in performances initially enacted in formal garden settings and then moved to the formal stage. Developments of fantastic scenery and follies in gardens were consistent with those that continued in the theatre. Inigo Jones's masques moved from the Garden to the Stage, and the fantasies of the garden led to the fantastic scenes of the stage, where they could be manipulated before the focused gaze of an audience, through the seventeenth and eighteenth centuries. Hundreds of stage sets for celebrations, and theatre were designed by generations of the family of Ferdinando Galli-Bibiena (some eight of them, over 100 years), many proposing fantastical scenes apparently inspired by the re-imagined ruins drawn by Piranesi, rendering the ruin broadly present in contemporary cultural presentations and spectacles.[12] Jones's gathering up of sources and inspirations was representative of the usefulness of the Grand Tour:

⑪ 12

⒊ 12

⒊ 13

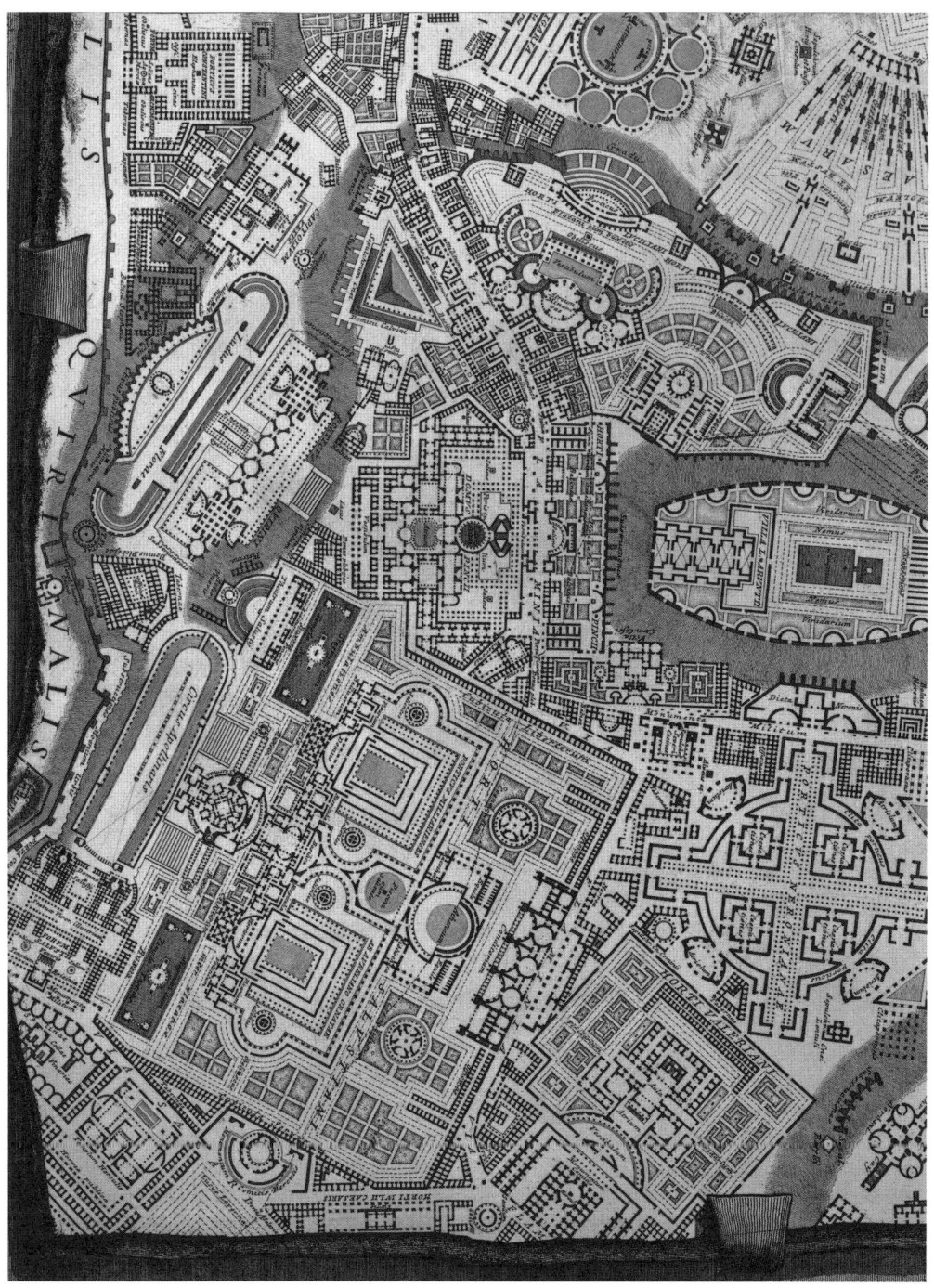

Ⓘ 15

he collected some 300 of Palladio's drawings on his own Tour of 1613–14. The tour smoothed the transfer of information from the ancients to contemporary architects through the agency of Vitruvius, and through Palladio's didactic folios dedicated to both Roman architecture and his own practice. Palladio's *I Quattro Libri dell'architettura* (1570) provided further grounding for architecture in Britain, for example, through its lessons on correct principles of composition, proportion and character. It inspired Colen Campbell's (1676–1729) *Vitruvius Brittanicus* (1715–1725): a British 'bible' of architecture for the guidance of amateurs building country houses, which took Anglicised interpretations of Vitruvius and Palladio as proper foundations for practice.

Grand Tours were ultimately social, academic and romantic, stimuli for genuine study yet also provocations for a taste for the spectacular. Among the prints or books one would take back home, significant among them would be engravings of views of Rome, the famous *vedute*[13] by Giambattista Piranesi (1720–1778). In the eighteenth century, Piranesi was an essential contact or source, and for the aspiring architect in particular. He made engravings of Rome for what he saw it as: a palimpsest, a tablet written upon by successive generations, an urban phenomenon of new constructions built amidst the ruins of the ancient city and inspired by them. He made drawings that investigated the science of Roman construction; he speculated, fantastically, on the architecture of the ancient city as a vast and singular construction in his plan of the Campo Marzio, and he indulged in further speculations on the capacities of the ancient imagination in his series of engravings of prisons, or *Carceri*.[14] The engravings conjured nightmarish visions of a chaotic, wretched antiquity. Furthermore, he developed his own fantasies in various designs for altarpieces, catafalques, braziers and architectural paraphernalia.[15]

Ⓘ 13

Ⓘ 14–15

109   THE RUIN

(iii) 16

GREECE

The Grand Tour eventually incorporated Greece and its ruins. For most on the Grand Tour, Greece was too far away: the few who strayed there before the mid-eighteenth century might have been regarded as explorers rather than tourists. A 're-discovery' of Greece extended the imaginary territory of the Tour, and provided a new dimension to considerations of the past and its authority, which of course affected the authority of the present at that time in describing and resurrecting that past.

In Great Britain, the re-discovery of Greece was signalled by the publication of James Stuart and Nicholas Revett's *The Antiquities of Athens* (1762),[16] a document of the measured surveys and drawings undertaken in their tour of 1761, funded by the Society of Dilletanti. The pair found ruins frequently obscured or buried among other ordinary buildings: artefacts known, preserved or ignored by the locals. The documentation of the ruins were accompanied by the possibility of imagining them re-constructed: first, in drawings and then elsewhere, as pavilions or as reinterpretations, modified as required, in the forms of country houses in England, Wales, Scotland and Ireland. The Temple of the Winds, for example, was re-created in several places, notably in Oxford, as the Radcliffe Observatory; in Dublin; and in Milan, near Sant' Ambrogio.

(iii) 16

(iii) 17

THINKING RUINS

The fanciful reconstruction of a past as inspired by ruins has been seen in the Giardini Bomarzo and the later Désert de Retz. In both cases, ruins were constructed afresh as fakes or follies, provoking contemplations of the past so to inspire speculations on the present, and to legitimate the project of the present by proposing that its roots were in the past, both completing it and providing it with a context of deep time. This tendency to use the past— disconnected and unimpeachable—to establish the foundations for the present was recurrent: it had been seen in the

(iii) 18
(i) 06

17

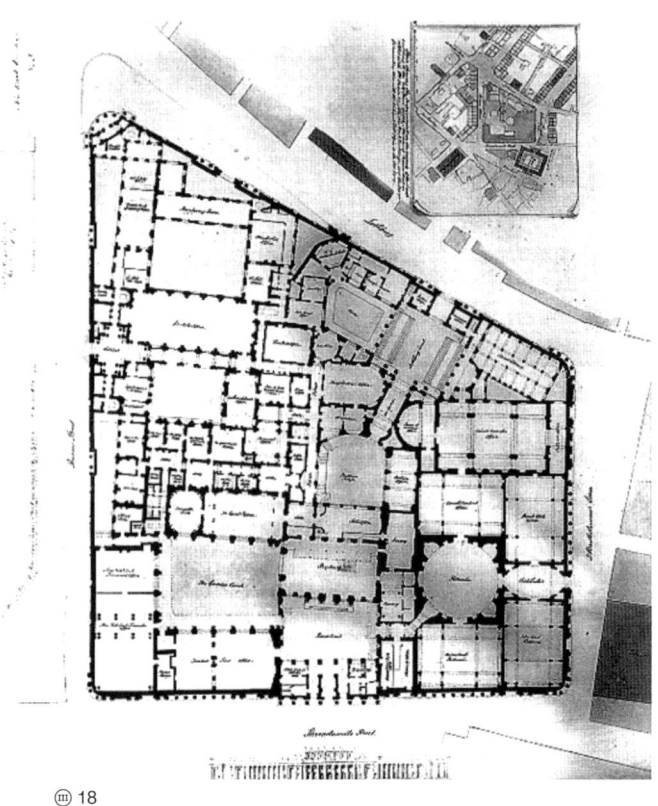

⊚ 18

work of Alberti and Palladio, in the work of British Palladians. William Chambers (1723–1796), for example, concerned himself with legitimating contemporary architectural practice by re-constructing its beginnings through academic speculation: we have seen in his re-construction of the primitive hut in the form of a prototype for the Greek classical temple, which he proposed as a representation of transformed natural resources and the processes of their assembly. This handling of the past, reconstructed from ruins, was a way finding mastery over the present. This kind of reconstruction was of course the basis of architectural theories that would affect architectural practice very deeply for about one hundred and fifty years.

It was against this background of academicism and speculation—composed of fact, conjecture and fantasy—that Sir John Soane (1753–1837), who had undertaken his Grand Tour in 1771, came to his study and inquiry into architecture, his penchant for collecting, and his idiosyncratic architectural propositions.[17] His house at Lincoln's Inn Fields in London was an accumulation of spatial experiments and effects, encrusted with his collection of ancient sculpture and architectural fragments. His architecture, as drawn and painted by his assistant Joseph Gandy (1771–1843),[18] was depicted either under construction or in ruins (often two indistinguishable states) and there is little question that his architecture was both inspired by that ruined architecture he studied directly, or as embroidered by Piranesi, or transposed to Paris in the paintings of Hubert Robert (1733–1808)[19], or by the ruins of Greece as studied and revived by Stuart and Revett.

Soane's Bank of England (1788–1833), in the City of London, was a re-working of the original designs of George Sampson (1732–1734) and Sir Robert Taylor (1765–1788). Soane surrounded the Bank with a wall, containing the entire site in the

19

20

manner of a fortified city. The extensive buildings and their interiors featured an accumulation of effects of Roman architecture, re-combined to create an elaborate pattern of open-air and covered courtyards, and singular rooms for the various banking offices that invoked the monumental spaces of Rome, as experienced in his Grand Tour, and perhaps as depicted by Piranesi—who he met in Rome—in his *Vedute*. Soane complemented his experience of the Tour with reading: he had a copy of Palladio's *I quattro libri* given to him after his Grand Tour; and among the 7,500 other items in his library, a copy of Julien-David Le Roy's *Les Ruines des plus beaux monuments de la Grèce* (1758).[20] The plan can be imagined (it was demolished between 1925–1939 and replaced by the much larger project, still within the walls, designed by Sir Herbert Baker) as a sequence of vaulted and domed enclosures, passageways and courtyards, themselves imagined as scenes replete with architectural relics.[21] It was experienced in sequences of staged scenes, which could be likened at once to scenography (and here, Inigo Jones's *masques* come to mind) and landscape, in the sense that it 're-created' the landscapes of ruins of the Grand Tour. The walk through the Bank's rooms, corridors and courtyards were reminiscent of walks through these same ruins as might be taken on the Tour, an effect that seems most marked in the misplaced and standing fragments of Lothbury Court. The route through the entrance at Lothbury would lead to Lothbury Court, and toward a triumphal arch that was visible to the interior rather than the street; the Court was lined by tribune stairs on both long sides as though to greet the visitor, who would turn left and right to see great porticos: one sheltering an exedra providing entrances to the Consol's Library and Transfer Office, the other, opposite, a screen to an courtyard (the Residence Court), effectively a piece of scenery between the two. One would move from great room to great room, the spaces of each illuminated through a system of clerestory and lantern windows in the walls, vaults and domes. The abundance of daylight provided from windows in the lanterns of pendentive domes and the walls bearing them exaggerated their resemblances to the monumental ruins of Rome from which they were derived. The parallels between Gandy's paintings and Piranesi's fantastic engravings of the ruins of Roman baths and tombs are striking. The Bank as a Ruin, a conceit made all too clear in Gandy's watercolour paintings of the Bank in such a state, viewed both from the ground and the air and openly recalling the sensation of surveying the Roman Forum or encountering the vast remains of the Baths of Caracalla seemed to suggest that the Bank as it was conceived was as great as the monuments that had inspired it; that its remains might be paused over in a thousand years' time, and thought of as the heroic undertakings of a great civilisation. Its construction was contemporary with Percy Bysshe Shelley's poem 'Ozymandias' (1818),[22] which dwelt upon the ephemeral nature and the vanity of all such undertakings.

    This theme of the ruin, and the implied authority of its keeper, was replayed in miniature in Soane's own house in London, which became a museum of his work immediately upon his death. Scenic routes could be followed in its narrow passageways, and through its sequences of rooms and courtyards; each courtyard and several rooms were domed. Spaces were manipulated so that they seemed to be out of doors. The central room, the Dome, was a triple-height courtyard surrounded by galleries that were, in fact, corridors connecting other rooms. The structure, voids

(iii) 19–20

(iii) 21–23

㊂ 22–23

and niches all served as supports to fragments of plaster casts that clung to them in the manner of an structure on the verge of collapse, suggesting the remains of a monument whose substance had largely fallen away. From the *piano nobile* where one arrived, one looked up to the impressive array of relics against the zenithal light of the dome itself, and down into the 'pit' of the cellar one floor below, and its chief attraction, the open, onyx sarcophagus of Seti II. In a painting by Gandy, the fragments have been illuminated by candlelight from below, light forms against a vast and complex penumbra. The deep space of uncertain measure was a motif repeated in the compact, complex forms of the most important rooms of the house: the Living Room featured a mirrored frieze above a lining of bookshelves, suggesting that the rooms existed in a larger 'field', and a similar technique was deployed in the 'handkerchief' dome of the Breakfast Room, apparently suspended over it. Light fell through the lantern above the dome's oculus and all around its edges, suggesting that the room was not solid but a temporary *templum* within a larger, pre-existing, archaic structure. This layering of perceived surfaces was used again and again. Near the Dome was the double-height Painting Room, whose panelled lining could be opened and opened again through a succession of panels supporting William Hogarth's painting cycle *A Rake's Progress* (1732–1733), to reveal that the whole room was but an aedicule suspended within a larger structure within the walls of the house, which then would be perceived suddenly as an exterior, or a courtyard, at whose base—again, the cellar—lay a fictional dwelling: the 'Monk's Parlour'. Other courtyards opened to the sky to suggest that the house occupied the space of another house that preceded it, that it was in fact a ruin built upon other ruins. The fiction of the Monk's Parlour below the Painting Room was part of this narrative, as was the little monument in one courtyard built for one of Mrs Soane's dogs, and the *Pasticcio*, a column of patched together fragments of stone of various historical periods and styles, a fictional construction. The owner and the visitor were both immersed in scenes that proposed ruminations on mortality and time past.

VISIONARY NEO-CLASSICISM AND RUINS

As Soane's constructions were at once fictive and fantastical, there was a tendency in practices at the end of the eighteenth century and the beginning of the nineteenth century—the period of Enlightenment and Revolution—to propose architecture that could be considered as grand as the ruins that inspired it; architecture that would draw itself parallel to and equivalent to those ruins and the magnificence that surrounded them. The core of this fantasy was the transcendence of death and time. This visionary neo-classicism predicated on the idea of the idea of the ruin—particularly the stoic, Greek variety—was evident in the work of the French architects Etienne-Louis Boullée (1728–1799), Claude Ledoux (1736–1806), and the German architect Friedrich Gilly, who was a mentor to Karl Friedrich Schinkel. Boullée took Piranesi's imaginary scenes and transformed them into visions of the ruins of an impossible and monstrous future, products of a heroic future civilisation.[23] That desired civilisation was fictional, but in Boullée's drawings, its ruins were already bequeathed to us. Many of his vast imaginary projects seemed to have been made of pure mass, featureless save for the deep shadows carved into their surfaces. His Project for a Cenotaph for Sir Isaac Newton (1784) was a colossal sphere set in

Ⅲ 24

Ⅲ 25

a tiered plinth ringed with cypresses in the manner of Hadrian's tomb in Rome, its scale difficult to ascertain. Its interior, with Newton's sarcophagus on a raised platform in the centre was dark, save for the light that pierced a constellation-like array of apertures. Another section shows an armillary sphere suspended within its void, an intense light at its centre. Both drawings suggest that the interior—to be visited by masses paying homage—were designed to represent the infinitude of the universe and the power of a civilisation that could dare to create such a monument. Such projects can be imagined to have inspired Adolf Hitler and his architectural cipher Albert Speer's plans for monumental buildings in a new Berlin to make structures—and ultimately ruins—that would honour the Third Reich for a thousand years.[24] These were not projections that evoked associations and connections with times and others who have passed, but projections of totalitarianism into the deep future. They were monuments without any sense of reflection.

Friedrich Gilly's (1772–1800) project for a monument to Frederick the Great in Leipzigerplatz, Berlin (1797)[25] followed from Boullée's example in one important respect: the design appeared to be indifferent to the passage of time, and was proposed as a kind of Acropolis, or a reproduction of that ruined scene that would last forever. In the work of his student Schinkel, however, the ruin was not the figure of a heroic future, but a memory, a scenographic device that 'spoke' through its imagery. As we have noted, Schinkel's Altes Museum frontage was modeled on a Greek *stoa*, a covered porch for the intermingling of citizens. Schinkel revived the *stoa* and presented it as a living image for Berlin re-cast as a contemporary Athens.

Continuing in this spirit of evoking the illusion of the past, Schinkel's Schloß Glieneke at the Charlottenhof, Potsdam (1826), built for Prince Carl of Prussia, was a summer palace that assumed the attributes of a modest ancient villa, with a garden populated with reconstructed historical fragments such as may have been found in the Greek travels of Winckelmann, to act as charming foils. More suggestive still

27–29

30

ⅲ 31

ⅲ 32

were the Roman baths that served as a folly for the nearby Charlottenhof Palace (1834–40) commissioned by Crown-Prince Friedrich Wilhelm (later Friedrich IV of Prussia). The villa assumed aspects of a Roman classical villa, with garden extensions and accompanying architectural devices, while the Baths themselves took on the semblance of a Roman farm, its buildings arranged in a studied casual composition mingled with classical pavilions, pergolas and aediculae. These assemblies were sustained by the idea that they were scenic recreations of ruins to be re-occupied in the present. The play of the ruin as a foil to the present would pre-occupy artists, writers, poets and architects in the nineteenth century, in the context of the destruction and construction of urban and social structures concurrent with industrialisation.

RUINS AT HOME: ROMANTICISM AND NATURALISM

The ruins of Fountains Abbey in Yorkshire, their structures open to the sky and the bucolic landscape all around inspired poets and artists (Joseph Mallard William Turner (1775–1851) among them) in the late-seventeenth and early-nineteenth centuries, who recognised that its ruins were metaphors for the erosion, in their time, of a whole world or civilisation. The power of these ruins—Rievaulx Abbey was also iconic—resided in their abandon, their state of decay, and their evocation of a pre-Tudor England nestled amidst landscapes being radically transformed by industrialisation.[26] The dissolution of abbeys and convents in the sixteenth century under Henry VIII had left these religious complexes standing in fields that eventually consumed them, detaching their sacred stones from their purpose, leaving them to speak of the past, and of the future that would lay waste to everything. They were given additional poignancy by the convulsive changes and devastation going on all around them. The urgency attached to the loss of 'old ways' made the ruins—both ancient and more recent—even more significant: the stones had something to say of both the past and the present. This capacity, the representational function of built material and its place in time, is what John Ruskin (1819–1900) touched on in his *The Stones of Venice* (1851–1853), in which the buildings of the Gothic Venice, in their decay, spoke of the city's former moral and spiritual health, compromised by the arrogance and sensuousness of modern (Renaissance) conceits.

 It was perhaps inevitable that there would be architects who attempted to re-construct narrative aspects into their work, and it was quite suitable that this narrative would be used to illuminate museums of natural history, whose content and form would ultimately illustrate the complacency of the view that held Man as singular and the idea of Biblical time exclusive. Such buildings embodied a consciousness of deep time and its pathos. In the case of Deane and Woodward's Museum of Natural History in Oxford (1854–1860), cast-iron structures of the glazed courtyard sprang from the stone structures decorated by the sculptor James O'Shea. As we have seen, that structure, formed into skeletal gothic arches that evoked natural forms, suggested that the stone from which they had emerged was that of a ruin. The glass roofs trellis-like patterns suggested frameworks through which the iron forms might wind and spread: the new, sprouting—as nature—from the carapace of that which had been. A museum of natural history that illustrated the history of the world without Man and the cycles of development and extinction was bound to provoke ruminations on the ruin of the body and mortality without

(iii) 33

redemption. The display of creatures' skeletons in the *Galeries de paléontologie et de l'anatomie comparée* at the Muséum national d'histoire naturelle in Paris, designed by Ferdinand Dutert (1898)—the architect of the *grand magasin* Galeries Lafayette and the *Palais des machines* at the *Exposition universelle* of 1889)—set out the lines of a history that had proceeded without human involvement, and presented this as a spectacle to the visitor. The skeletons that seemed to march in one direction toward the visitor caused pause and thought upon his or her corporeality, and mortality, in a soon to be realised future. The architectural setting precisely reflected this in its own brittle, skeletal construction of masonry, iron and glass, decorated with the skulls of beasts. It was a structure that bore the signs of its own ruin.

(iii) 31

The design of Pennsylvania Station, in New York, by Charles Follen McKim, William Rutherford Mead and Stanford White (completed in 1910) also relied on the theme of the ruin—in this case, that of buildings and civilisations—and borrowed directly from the remains of monumental Roman architecture, specifically the Baths of Caracalla. The city's commuting citizens were asked to associate themselves with the greatness of ancient Rome evoked by the station's halls, and imagine themselves as contemporary occupants of the future ruins of their own metropolitan civilisation. The great steel and glass sheds behind the masonry concourse and waiting

(iii) 32–33

(III) 34

halls served as a contemporary counterpoint, manifestly of the present, rendering perception of the monumental structures of the halls even more 'ancient'. As in the museums of natural history, the conceit of the ruin, illustrated by the dialogue between masonry and iron or steel provided a fiction that sustained the public imagination and the fantasy of greatness.

A dialogue between masonry and iron was important to the structural and expressive rationalism developed by Eugène Viollet-le-Duc (1814–1879), which, though rational, was also romantic. His *Entretiens sur l'architecture* (1863–72), seen by some as essential to the trajectory of Modern architecture, advocated an orthodoxy wherein masonry was static, and iron was its dynamic, spanning and naturalistic complement. Viollet-le-Duc was one of the first 'restoration' architects, involved in the repair and ultimately the reinterpretation of existing monumental structures, Notre-Dame de Paris and the Château de Pierrefonds—whose 'restoration' was a fantastical reconstruction—the most notable among them. These restorations presented a paradox, given the dialectical nature of his thoughts on structure, that in his practice, the ruin as an index of decay was unacceptable.

REPRISE OF THE GRAND TOUR: THE RUIN IN MODERNITY

The ruin was also a trace, an aspect of architectural fiction informing the work of architects associated with the tendencies of Modernism. The tiny Kärtner Bar, or American Bar (1908) in Vienna, designed by Adolf Loos (1870–1933), offered itself as an impromptu enclosure, nestled in the penumbral depths of a vast virtual temple. Its ceiling of marble coffers, evocative of ancient Rome, was reflected into infinity by mirrors above the wooden screens that separated the bar room from its virtual

(III) 34

(III) 35

setting. The mirrors suggesting vast spaces beyond were indebted to John Soane and his house in Lincoln's Inn Fields in particular. The visitor was invited to read the walls as *Wand*,[27] or partitions of an elemental structure, of the kind described by Gottfried Semper in his *Die vier Elementen der Baukunst* (1851). In Loos's idea, these partitions were the tapestries that formed the walls of the first Temple of Solomon, and hence elements of ancient architecture.[28] The scene offered by Loos was played out in a framework that suggested deep time (and civilisation, an ongoing preoccupation of the architect who railed against Vienna's parochialism). Loos's design proposed a noble fiction for drinkers to dwell upon as they slipped into unconsciousness.

In the Stockholm City Library (1925), Erik Gunnar Asplund evoked an ancient order of uncertain provenance, mixing classical and Egyptian motifs, which revealed itself through a penumbral interior, its deeply cut passages inferring the deep time of experience and knowledge. The door handles at the entrance were sculpted in the forms of Adam and Eve to mark the 'beginning' of time; one entered a tall, blackened hall from which two staircases disappeared to the right and the left of the bulging form of a cylindrical inner temple, whose portal—an image of the portal to the building one entered from the city—was filled by stairs that rose to enter a rotunda whose dimensions were difficult to ascertain. This was the central reading room, lined with books on several levels. The walk from the street to the reading room could be taken to be and archaic ritual passage to knowledge.[29] There would seem to be some explanation for this character, shared in the work of other Nordic architects of the early twentieth century—among them Asplund's colleague Sigurd Lewerentz—which stemmed from a connection with the Mediterranean,[30] the Ancients, and ruins, that they cultivated on their own Grand Tours.[31] The spirit

(III) 35

of this was captured in Lewerentz's photographs of ruins and fragments of architectural elements and pavements, which reappeared in his architecture:[32] his Resurrection Chapel at Stockholm's Woodland Cemetery (1926), whose main volume resembled a funerary catafalque, was an image of the building's content, and decorated with a series of figures—a free-standing portico and a monumental window—drawn directly from his experience of those ruins.

The ruin as a reference point for architecture was proposed by surprising figures. Le Corbusier also took his own Grand Tour,[33] and his observations and declamations regarding the authority, vitality and currency of the Acropolis were arrived at after careful observation and attentive drawing. His polemic *Vers une architecture* (1923)[34] associated the precision of the Parthenon's design with that of a motorcar; his remarks about architecture as "the play of the magnificent forms revealed in light" were drawn from his peregrinations and encounter with ruins, which were intrinsic to his architecture. The Villa Savoye, in Poissy, outside Paris (1925) proposed a dwelling reduced to a *promenade architecturale*, a ramp rising through a framework of structure and skin, desiccated, hollow and nearly a ruin itself. The route, which wound through the house from the road to the garage and the vestibule to the rooftop, culminated in a view, through an aperture in the façade—continuing the pattern of the *fenêtre-en-longueur* but without glass—to the landscape, which was imagined in a drawing by as a fragment from a Nicolas Poussin painting, complete with a ruined temple. Le Corbusier was later drawn to the elemental character of Abbé le Thoronet, near Nîmes (1176–1200), which, in its apparent absence of being beholden to any function, presented itself as a perfect ruin: an assembly of forms and masses revealed in light, and so directly tied to his younger sentiments, and his invocation of elemental or Platonic forms drawn from ancient Rome. The existence of Le Thoronet seemed to give Le Corbusier licence to make the monastery—or *couvent*—he designed for Dominican friars at La Tourette (1960)[35] near Lyon an occupied shell. The material of the building, an extremely crudely rough-shuttered reinforced concrete, (what Le Corbusier called *béton brut*) emphasised this: the main chapel resembled a rectilinear cave, reinforced by the penumbral side chapel illuminated by coloured oculi or *canons à lumière* above each concrete altar; while the thin uprights of the windows of the *ambulatoire*, the library and the refectory—the *fenétre ondulatoire* conceived by Iannis Xenakis (the composer who worked in Le Corbusier's *atelier* at the time)—evoked withered saplings, casting shadows across the routes and rooms used by the monks when together, who, like the building itself, were removed from the world. They moved through the halls and voids of what presented itself as a complex shell left behind by others, a ruin.

Nearly in his 50s, at a moment that would be characterised as 'late-career', Louis I Kahn (1901–1974) also travelled to the ruins of the ancient world on his own Grand Tour in 1950, and drew the monuments as architect-in-residence of the American Academy in Rome. His encounter with the ancient remains transformed his thought, and he began to evoke ruins in his work thereafter: those of concrete and 'hollow stones'.[36] The façades of the Philips Exeter Library (1971) in Exeter, New Hampshire were conceived as discrete screens: on the outside, the four façades appeared to be detached from the body of the building, as though its contents occupied a ruin formed by those same façades; while on the interior,

(iii) 36–37

(iii) 38–39

Ⅲ 36

Ⅲ 37

Ⅲ 38-39

ⅲ 40

ⅲ 41

⬡ 42

a central room was bound by four screens of concrete, each punctured by great circular apertures, that seemed to have predated the construction behind it. The interior was reminiscent of a scene from a fantasy of Piranesi, perhaps the *Carceri*, occupied by young scholars.

⬡ 40

In Sher-e-Bangla, the National Assembly Buildings in Dhaka, Bangladesh (1962–1974), Kahn laid out a territory of stone plains, lawns and reflective pools for buildings that appeared on its horizon like monumental shells. Their interiors were spaces for the witnessing the play of overlapping structures and voids, and these were even more suggestive of the fantasies of Piranesi: they were ruins for the present and for a future age, in which a young nation might find its way. Many of his unbuilt projects, such as his plan for the centre of Philadelphia (1957), figured with titanic figures—such as cylindrical parking buildings, and a skyscraper using tetrahedral forms, angled columns and facetted nodes, made in collaboration with Anne Tyng, proposed themselves as beyond function—were also constructions to be appreciated over a vast historical span. The atmosphere suggested by this project was pursued in his plans for a convent or 'motherhouse' for Dominican sisters (1965–1968), and the Hurva synagogue in Jerusalem (1967–1974). The latter in particular was a great structure contrived as a ruin of itself.

⬡ 41–42

THE WAR, NEW RUINS AND THE PROBLEM OF RECONSTRUCTION

Europe and European architects were obliged to deal with very new ruins in the aftermath of two great wars. The Second World War created ruins throughout the continent, and the project of reconstruction affected everyone, all cultural protagonists, and all architects. In Germany, those ruins took on additional significance, as they were reminders of what totalitarian ideology had wrought. Therefore, in the West, reconstruction and building with and among ruins assumed a moral and political dimension. In Munich, Leo von Klenze's (1784–1864) Alte Pinakothek (1826–1836) was partly destroyed by Allied bombing. Its rebuilding was undertaken by Hans Döllgast (1891–1974), who set the work upon a path that approached the repair of the building in meaningful and deliberate phases, making the 'healing' of the scene of destruction (and thus the story of both the historical moment and the ruin) explicit.[37] Döllgast's incremental re-constructions, in which each stage of repair was evident, were part of the process of recuperation of the building in a form different from its pre-war form, and of the spirit of the society and culture it represented. This was a profoundly melancholic process of recovery, in which the ruin was always present, imparting its lessons incrementally and continuously, like a slowly healing wound whose scar always remains.

A different approach was developed in Italy at the same time, by the architectural schools and architect-protagonists of Rome, Milan and Venice, notably Luigi Moretti, Franco Albini and Franca Helg, Banfi Belgiojoso Peressutti e Rogers (BBPR), and Carlo Scarpa, respectively. In an evolving series of works, a working dialogue was established between the artefact of the past (or the ruin) and the creations of the manifestly present, which, though ceding to the character of the former, asserted their own distinct character, tied to their time. So germane to the post-war condition, and so ingrained became the conversation between the two, that completely new constructions, such as the apartment block *Il Girasole* designed by Luigi Moretti (1949–50), embodied both an imagined ruin—incorporating fragments of previous buildings and invoking the rough masonry of the past—and the new, which was, under the terms of the dialogue, episodic. The base of *Il Girasole* seemed to consist of a fragmented, rusticated body (with fragments of figurative sculpture)—a notion of *rustica*—from which a modern construction sprang, much in the spirit of the dialogue offered by Deane and Woodward in their design for the Natural History Museum in Oxford. In the lobby, one encountered architectural elements as fragments, and one's movement through its spaces was akin to picking one's way through a landscape of relics or ruins. One recalls here those walks traced through Soane's Bank of England, evoking the walks of the Grand Tour, though ruins of ancient Rome.

In the early 1950s, Franco Albini and Franca Helg[38] developed a language specific to permanent and temporary exhibitions, setting special constructions of steel and glass in contrast and contradistinction with the imposing historical structures in which they were staged, rendering their 'past-ness' visible and distinct, as 'ruins', regardless of their condition of repair. In the design for the re-constitution of the Palazzo Bianco (1951) and Palazzo Rosso (1952–1962) in Genoa as museums, the refined yet assertive nature of the contemporary elements designed for engaging viewers directly with works of art, were in sustained dialogue and partnership with the architecture of the rooms and these art works, which might be regarded as 'ruins' in their own right. Fragments of a sculptural group by Giovanni Pisano were set upon the arm of a hydraulically operated display that rose, fell and turned so that they could be studied from all perspectives; paintings were mounted on steel leaves that could be gripped by a viewer; iron easels supported others.[39] All of these were set against the architecture of the palazzi. Albini and Helg established both a paradigm and an orthodoxy that suffused the work of their contemporaries, who, faced with making displays in buildings whose war damage could not be repaired for lack of funds, made scaffolds for art out of material that was available, making the subject of display visible through frameworks of the present set amidst the ruins of the recent and distant past. The strategy of these architects persists in contemporary practices, albeit significantly diminished, in the 'old–new' opposition. The aesthetic associated with this Italian work is evident in the films of Michelangelo Antonioni (1912–2007), who was fascinated with architecture, and the scenes attendant on the post-war Italian city, which were poised between the ruination of the Second World War, the rapid industrialisation of its cities and countrysides, and the immanent prospect of annihilation in nuclear conflict. In films such as *L'Eclisse* (1962) and *Il Deserto Rosso* (1964), the theme of the ruin appeared as a metaphor for the end of civilisation, blown to oblivion in the twentieth century, imminent as our collective destiny, immanent in the structures all around.

The most elaborate dialogues were pursued in the work of the Venetian architect Carlo Scarpa (1906–1978), who imagined his work as added, in the manner of *bricolage*, to the deeply ingrained 'orientalist' traditions of construction and appearances of the city's architecture. The Castelvecchio in Verona[40] was configured internally so that one was always aware of the distinction between new constructions and existing fabric, which had been radically re-configured. The new was in some instances treated as thought it had emerged from a deep past, and in others, as though it was aggressively new. The building as a possible ruin containing this play of time was articulated at one end of the main body of the building, whose walls and roof appeared to be rent asunder, rendering them a blasted aedicule for the equestrian sculpture of Cangrande I della Scala (c1330), which, like the Pisano sculptural group isolated by Albini and Helg in Genoa, appeared to be suspended in air.

Similar to Scarpa's approach, although without his mannerisms, the Norwegian architect Sverre Fehn (1924–2009) developed a similar strategy, evident in the Hamar Bispegaard Museum at Hamar, Norway (1969–1973), in which board-marked concrete ramps glided through the spaces of partly ruined stone buildings, repaired by discrete constructions of walls and roofs in timber and tile, and sheets of glass fixed over rough openings left in the masonry walls. In his design for a new building for the Nordic pavilion in the *Giardini*, Venice (1962), an elemental structure of concrete walls, a folded column, two deep concrete beams and a phalanx of extremely fine concrete battens were built over, around and through a number of existing trees, preserving and making them the central figures of the composition of the interior. The new construction, ideally empty and an exhibit of itself, presented the identity of a ruin to its visitors, one grown through by the long-standing natural protagonists of the Giardini.

Ⅲ 43

Ⅲ 44

ⅲ 45–46

(iii) 47

RUIN AS STRATEGY FOR THE PRESENT

The discourse implied between buildings of the past, cast in the role of 'being of the past', and those constructions representing the condition of the present has continued to be potent, and poignant. The Grand Louvre in Paris, designed by Ieoh Ming Pei (1917–) of Pei Cobb Freed (1989; 1994), was proposed so that visitors would confront a structure, manifestly of the present, yet evocative of the forms of the ancient past—a glass pyramid—embraced by the arms of the pavilions of the Palais du Louvre. The contrast between Pei's structure and the palace seemed irreconcilable until one entered the pyramid, and found that it served as the lens through which the great pavilions were to be viewed. Immediately upon entering, one descended into a sepulchral space: a new crypt suggesting 'deep time' because it lay beneath the Palace and the city itself, even accommodating the foundations of the first fortified Palace on the site, exhibited in a vast and beautifully illuminated cellar. The ruin was constantly invoked. It was, of course, a play, in which the visitor imagined being an explorer or an archaeologist, wandering through vast, enigmatic halls erected by past builders, past citizens, past civilisations.

(iii) 45–46

This play, reminiscent of the Romantic period's assumption of the ruin as an object of reflection, has followed and determined many popular public interiors today. The latter days of the Palast der Republik in Berlin saw the building stripped of its representative materials and symbols after the collapse of the German Democratic Republic; it became a shell, a gargantuan construction of concrete cores and steel spans, a megastructure. The euphoria that greeted the fall of the Berlin Wall and the DDR affected the reception of the stripped out building, whose ruins were literally played on, and elaborated through an extensive programme of cultural events, from exhibitions and radical installations to concerts. The building was flooded for an exhibition on one occasion; on another, it was filled with an imaginary landscape.

(iii) 47

⑪ 48

⑪ 49

The ruin of the Palast enabled ludic abandon, and demonstrated that precisely this character of freedom from prescribed values and order affected a potent image for contemporary cultural space. In wandering over the ruins of the past, one was absolved of responsibility for them and for the present alike; and one could experience, at least fleetingly, the vertigo of freedom.

This sensation has prevailed in many spaces associated with culture and the pretence of connections to culture. The 'loft', emergent in New York and Berlin in particular in the 1960s and 1970s, drew upon artists' re-use of redundant inner-city light-industrial spaces for studios in which they could work and live cheaply. Inevitably, the character of their interiors became a stylistic trope for residential spaces and even for cultural spaces. Loft imagery cited that 'off-grid' history to bolster its own legitimacy, borrowing the sense of play associated with artists' practices and lifestyles (neglecting its crushing, attendant poverty). Spaces for contemporary art also used the artist's loft as a signifier, a motif that spoke of artistic production, conceptualisation, and again, freedom. Such spaces as the Haus für Neue Kunst in Schaffhausen, created by Urs Rausmüller (1982), used a former textile factory as space to display contemporary art in conditions offered as similar to those in which that art was produced. From those foundations, the conceit was executed in a more refined way in Max Gordon's transformation of a bus depot in west London into the cavernous spaces of the original Saatchi Gallery (1985). Such 'ruined' or 'as found' spaces were imitated in many artist-organised 'maverick' exhibitions, that occupied the 'ruins' of former industrial spaces which were fitted with white-painted gallery walls.[41] Herzog & de Meuron transformed a decommissioned power station designed by George Gilbert Scott for the Tate Gallery's outpost for modern art, Tate Modern (2000), proposing it in their 1994 competition project as an environment that would resemble the classic sites of artistic production and display: ruined industrial premises re-cast as contemporary art spaces. The inference was that the public could revel in the atmosphere of the artist's loft, and share the artist's rogue use of abandoned spaces that had fallen out of currency and usefulness: the ruins of industrialised urban culture.

The ruin, therefore, has given licence to a certain liberation of activity in the present. One might recognise the transformation by Lina Bo Bardi (1914–1992) of the factory complex in São Paulo into the cultural centre Fabrica SESC Pompeia (1986) similarly as a programme for emancipation, transforming obligations of work into opportunities for play, and transforming workers through engagement into citizens consciously and unconsciously living and making culture and enjoying leisure. Bo Bardi effected, designed and curated 'mis-uses' of the former drum factory, whose shell was made to accommodate quite different actions and atmospheres —leisure, study, creation—from those it was originally designed for, and in the design of new buildings that (quite intentionally, as posters showed the new 'chimney' belching out flowers)[42] assumed factory-like forms of raw and 'damaged' expression, particularly evident in the gouged shapes of the windows of the sport tower.

The industrial infrastructure of the nineteenth and early twentieth centuries has left an abundance of material for reinterpretation and transformation. In Paris, the former Gare d'Orsay—a train station parallel to the banks of the Rive Gauche of the Seine—was transformed into a museum dedicated to the nineteenth century

(iii) 50

(1980–1986) by Gae Aulenti (1927–2012). The Musée d'Orsay's main space was the glass-vaulted main hall, more *jardin d'hiver* than train shed. The conversion of this space in particular drew close to one's mental image of ruins, in that artefacts were displayed on walls that resembled the remains of an ancient complex, such as those around the pyramids at Cheops. The effect was that of a rather sober ruin, through which the past—evident in the entire fabric of Haussmannian Paris—was monumentalised. In that way, it was consistent with the programme of consolidating the Haussmann legacy that typified the various *grands projets* undertaken during the Presidency of François Mitterrand, including Pei's Grand Louvre.

(iii) 49

MODERN-DAY PALIMPSEST

The Palais de Tokyo, a building contained within the ensemble built for the *Exposition Internationale des arts et techniques de la vie modernes* in a stripped classical or late-Art Deco style 1937, had accommodated the Musée d'art moderne de la Ville de Paris and the Musée nationale d'art moderne in its two wings. This latter institution vacated the eastern wing for the Centre Georges Pompidou, and the conversion of the space into a centre for contemporary 'creation' in 2002 by Lacaton and Vassal saw the creation of a new ruin, the existing arrangements within the building torn out to reveal the structure's essential fabric. The building was treated as a resource in order to maximise the possibilities and opportunities for its use and interpretation. The interior thus stripped down no longer resembled a museum; rather, it resembled the remains of some centre of production; a monumental loft. This suited the architects' aim to create spaces that, like the loft model, were characterised by generosity, looseness and ambivalence. In this guise, it neatly aligned itself with the prevailing atmosphere of sites for contemporary art, as suggested earlier, and the fantasy that ran through them: namely, that in evoking the putative sites of art's production, the viewer was drawn into being an actor in

(iii) 50–52

(III) 51–52

that production, and was so transformed into a cultural maker. This position was consistent with the aims of contemporary art practices, in which the condition of art's visibility is not just a contingent factor, but part of the art's very substance. The artist Michael Asher (1943–2012), for example, stripped out a commercial gallery, the Clare Copley Gallery (1974), showing all its spaces, from showroom to office, as the site in which the public image or idea of art was ratified.[43] The transparency offered was a form of institutional critique, which has since been completely absorbed in the art world's modes of presentation and display. It was also the view propounded by the Palais's first (co-)director (with Jérôme Sans), Nicolas Bourriaud, who had coined the term 'relational aesthetics'[44] to describe practices that broke down boundaries between the artist and the audience of the work of art, and promoted more obvious forms of exchange between the two. The programme echoed that set by the Swedish curator Pontus Hultén, director of Stockholm's Moderna Museet, Kulturhuset and Centre Georges Pompidou, who had built these institutions around notions of interaction between people, and their empowerment. The impression for the visitor, despite the representative character that contemporary cultural production has assumed, has become one of freedom: freedom to see, to act, to intervene, and all within the wreckage or ruin of that which has gone before, acting out a ludic fantasy that cast the visitor was a working artist. It is of interest in considering the effects or affordances of the public interior that such a ruin might stimulate the public imagination and heighten the sense of agency of both the group and the individual.

The Palais de Tokyo cultivated an atmosphere of informality through the treatment or mistreatment of the building fabric, and was among those projects that in their manner of re-use of existing structures have been reliant upon the 'ruin value' of the structures that have accommodated them. The opposition has been central, as has been the aura of legitimacy provided to both the projects and the publics that use them. This might be regarded as a craving for authenticity, particularly in the face of new constructions that frequently offer only abstractions, whether in the clothing of minimalism, functionalism, deconstructivism or parametricism. These ruins have served the 'ego' of the public and its need for legitimacy.

The Neues Museum in Berlin (2013), as revived by David Chipperfield (1953–), presented another, graver atmosphere, also expressed through its attitude toward the existing structure—heavily damaged in fighting in the last days of the Second World War—treating it as a ruin. The ruin in this case assumed a character consistent with Romantic tastes: an artefact, or environment, of contemplation. The building was largely left 'as found', repaired or modified as needed. Remnants of the original *décor*, scarred and faded, were left as *momenti mori*; additions were executed in a manner sympathetic with that of the building—classical, symmetrical—yet were distinct. Rather than a sense of play, the visitor was led to assume an attitude of attention to the interiors' traces of narrative and their intimations of mortality. Of course, like Döllgast's Alte Pinakothek, it has proven impossible to detach the building from the historical circumstances that wrought its destruction, and the building has served as a witness to this, involving its visitors in the constantly unfolding of history and responsibility for that which has been and the here and now.

⑶ 53-54

Ⅲ 55

Ⅲ 56

57

NEW RUINS

When contemplating the public interior made anew, the ruin has remained an important theme: it has seemed to create distance and a correspondingly vertiginous feeling of freedom, in the manner of tourism (the notion of a Grand Tour has been rarely far from the surface of experience). It also seems to have heightened a sense of agency in the public's imagination. Recalling Piranesi's *Carceri*, whose terrible projections suggested a past that was impenetrable and cruel, hinting at the eternal suffering of its subjects, OMA used 'Piranesian space'[45] in its infrastructural interiors for Euralille in Lille (1994) and the Souterrain in The Hague (2004), in the first case as a spatial metaphor adequate to the task of conveying the dizzying multiplicity and simultaneity of layers of transport; and in the second case as a provocation, a heroic image in the midst—or under the streets—of a courtly provincial city. In this 'Souterrain' (literally, underground), the *dramatis personae* of the space—foot bridges, struts, coarse retaining walls, dramatic lighting, access ramps, moving cars, trams, and a vestige of nature bound by a roundabout—created an epic scene that suggested a world above, in whose cavernous cellars—as though left behind by another society—commuters carried on their daily cycle of transit, work and consumption. Like the city below the Earth in Fritz Lang's *Metropolis* (1927), the sprung wooden floors at the bottom of it all, where commuters embarked and disembarked from trams, provided the platform from which the elaborate staged scene could be viewed: a scene for a play in which, quite unlike Lang's fictional city, those involved felt ennobled.

I conclude with Herzog & de Meuron's design for 1111 Lincoln Road in Miami (2012), a multi-storey, multi-functional building with the appearance of an open-air multi-storey car park. It was indeed an open-air multi-storey car park, albeit one whose floor-to-floor heights had been stretched and compressed to different measures, seemingly randomly, to make the building at once emptier and more capable of accommodating different uses. Again, this is what it did, providing shelter for some stable uses, enclosed and controlled; and unpredictable events, which were by nature open and provisional. The building and its continuously unfolding space, whose interior was always an exterior, was at once also reminiscent of Le Corbusier's Dom-Ino House system (1914) and that prototype's anticipation of and thousand-fold reiteration in half-constructed Mediterranean villas, whose scarcely half-made-up-ness also suggested states of half-ruin, frameworks on which myriad futures could be projected, or upon which could be imagined myriad pasts.

(iii) 01
Braun, Clément &
Co. (French, active
1877–1928)
The Roman Forum

(iii) 02
Bosra, Syria. Photo
© and source: Mark
Pimlott

(iii) 03
Palmyra, Syria.
Photo © and source:
Mark Pimlott

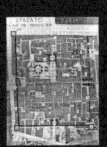

(iii) 04
Restitution of
the Porta Ferrea
of Diocletian's
Palace, Split, 1912.
© Public domain.
Source: *https://
commons.wikimedia.
org/wiki/File:SPLIT-
Palace_remains_
1912.jpg*

(iii) 05–06
San Sebastiano,
Mantova. Leon
Battista Alberti,
1458. Photo © and
source: Marius
Grootveld

(iii) 07
Andrea Palladio.
Villa Capra, near
Vicenza. Photo
courtesy © Marius
Grootveld

(iii) 08
Andrea Palladio,
Il Redentore, Venice.
Photo courtesy
© Marius Grootveld

(iii) 09
Andrea Palladio,
Vincenzo Scamozzi.
Teatro Olimpico,
Vicenza. Photo
courtesy © Marius
Grootveld

(iii) 10
Pantheon, Rome
(1990), Photo
Thomas Struth.
© and source:
Thomas Struth

(iii) 11
The Forum, Rome.
Photo Carla Tavares
© CC BY-SA 3.0.
Source: *https://
commons.wikimedia.
org/wiki/File:
Ct-fororomano1.jpg*

(iii) 12
Plate representing
a celestial hall with
figures, c 17th
century. Giuseppe
Galli Bibiena.
Victoria and Albert
Museum, London
S.329-2009
© and source:
Victoria and Albert
Museum, London

(iii) 13
*Ruins of a sculpture
gallery at Hadrian's
Villa at Tivoli*,
18th century. Yale
University Art Gallery
2012.159.11.93
© Yale University Art
Gallery

(iii) 14
Campus Martius.
Robert Adam,
Giovanni Battista
Piranesi, 1762.
© Public domain.
Source: *https://
commons.wikimedia.
org/wiki/File:
Piranesi-10013.jpg*

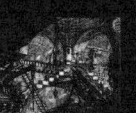

(iii) 15
The arch with a shell
ornament. Giovanni
Battista Piranesi,
1761. British
Museum, London
1910.1214.26
© and source:
Trustees of the
British Museum

(iii) 16
View of the Tower
of the Winds in the
eighteenth cen-
tury, 1762. James
Stuart, Nicholas
Revett. © Public
domain. Source:
*The Antiqvities of
Athens. https://
archive.org/details/
antiqvitiesAthe1Stua*

(iii) 17
Illustration to
Stuart and Revett,
The Antiqvities of
Athens; elevation
of the Tower of the
Winds, 1762. British
Museum, London
Hh,13.1.28
© and source:
Trustees of the
British Museum

(iii) 18
Plan of the Bank
of England with
an elevation of the
South Front, 1831.
Sir John Soane's
Museum P350
© and source:
Sir John Soane's
Museum, London

(iii) 19
Bird's eye view
of the Bank of
England: 'The Bank
in Ruins'. John
Gandy. Sir John
Soane's Museum
P267 © and source:
Sir John Soane's
Museum, London

(iii) 20
Rotunda of the
Bank of England,
drawn in the year
of its completion
1798, but showing
the structure as
it were a Roman
ruin. Joseph Gandy.
Sir John Soane's
Museum P127
© and source:
Sir John Soane's
Museum, London

(iii) 21
Number 13, Lincoln
Inn's Fields, Sir John
Soane's House and
Museum. Sir John
Soane. Photo © and
source: Marius
Grootveld

(iii) 22–23
Number 13, Lincoln
Inn's Fields, Sir
John Soane's
House and
Museum. Sir John
Soane. Photo © and
source: Marius
Grootveld

(iii) 24
Project for a Royal
Library, Paris.
Etienne-Louis
Boullée, c 1780.
Morgan Library,
New York 247385
© and source: The
Morgan Library and
Museum, New York

(iii) 25
Cénotaphe à
Newton, interior.
Etienne-Louis
Boullée, 1784.
Bibliothèque
nationale de France
ark:/12148/
btv1b7701015b
© and source:
Bibliothèque natio-
nale de France

(iii) 26
Altes Museum,
Berlin. Karl Friedrich
Schinkel, 1824.
Photographer
unknown, c 1900.
Library of Congress
LOT13411, no.
0338. © Public
domain. Source:
Library of
Congress Prints
and Photographs
Division,
Washington DC

(iii) 27
Charlottenhof,
Potsdam. Karl
Friedrich Schinkel,
1826. Photo © and
source: Marius
Grootveld

(iii) 28
Charlottenhof,
Potsdam. Karl
Friedrich Schinkel,
1826. Photo ©
and source: Julia
Hegenwald

⊞ 29
Charlottenhof, Potsdam. Karl Friedrich Schinkel, 1826. Photo © and source: Marius Grootveld

⊞ 30
Tintern Abbey: The Crossing and Chancel, Looking towards the East Window. Joseph Mallord William Turner, 1794. Tate D00374–Turner Bequest XXIII A. © and source: Tate, London

⊞ 31
Musée nationale de l'Histoire naturelle, Paris. Galéries de la paléontologie et de l'anatomie comparée. Ferdinand Dutert. Photo Flickr user: Ewan Munro © CC BY-SA2.0. Souce: https://www.flickr.com/photos/55935853@N00/3188065950

⊞ 32
Pennsylvania Station, New York. Main waiting room. McKim, Mead and White, 1910. Photographer unknown. © Detroit Publishing Company. Source: Library of Congress Prints and Photographs Division, Washington DC

⊞ 33
Pennsylvania Station, New York. McKim, Mead and White, 1910 (demolished 1963). Photo Berenice Abbott. Getty Images PH1979:0441:034A © and source: Berenice Abbott/Getty Images

⊞ 34
Kärtner Bar, or American Bar, Vienna, Adolf Loos, 1910. Photographer unknown. Source: Mark Pimlott

⊞ 35
Stockholm City Library. Gunnar Asplund, 1927. Stairs towards the north. Photo Ingrid Johansson. Stockholms stadarkiv 52003 75 12 © CC BY-NC-SA 2.5 SE. Source: Stockholmskällan, Stockholms stadsarkiv

⊞ 36
Villa Savoye, Poissy. Le Corbusier, 1928. Photo Paul Koslowski © FLC/ADAGP c/o Pictoright Amsterdam 2015. Source: Fondation Le Corbusier

⊞ 37
Villa Meyer, Neuilly-sur-Seine. Le Corbusier, 1927. Plan FLC 31514 © FLC/ADAGP c/o Pictoright Amsterdam. Source: Fondation Le Corbusier

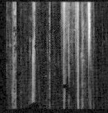
⊞ 38
Couvent Sainte-Marie de la Tourette, Eveux. Fenêtre ondulatoire. Le Corbusier 1960. Photo © and source: Hélène Binet

⊞ 39
Couvent Sainte-Marie de la Tourette, Eveux. L'ambulatoire. Le Corbusier 1960. Photo © and source: Hélène Binet

⊞ 40
Philip Exeter Academy Library, Exeter NH. Louis I Kahn, 1971. Photo David Schnabel © David Schnabel. Source: https://www.flickr.com/photos/dschnabel/10278339946/in/photostream

⊞ 41
Sher-e-Bangla, National Assembly Building, Jatiyo Sangsad Bhaban, Dhaka. Louis I Kahn, 1962–1974. Photo Wikimedia user Lykantrop © CC BY-SA 3.0. Source: https://commons.wikimedia.org/wiki/File:National_Assembly_of_Bangladesh,_Jatiyo_Sangsad_Bhaban,_2008,_3.jpg

⊞ 42
Sher-e-Bangla, National Assembly Building, Dhaka. Louis I Kahn, 1962–1974. Photo Raymond Meier © Raymond Meier

⊞ 43
Castelvecchio, Verona. Interior. Carlo Scarpa, 1958. Photographer unknown. Source: Mark Pimlott

⊞ 44
Hamar Bispegaard Museum, Hamar. Sverre Fehn, 1969–1973. Photo © and source: Hélène Binet

⊞ 45
Grand Louvre, Paris. Entrance hall. I M Pei of Pei Cobb Freed, 1989. Photo © and source: Mark Pimlott

⊞ 46
Grand Louvre, Paris. Foundations of the original, fortified Louvre. I M Pei of Pei Cobb Freed, 1989. Photo © and source: Mark Pimlott

⊞ 47
Palast der Republik, Berlin, in 2006. Wikimedia user: Agadez © Public domain. Source: https://commons.wikimedia.org/wiki/File:Palast_der_Republik.jpg

⊞ 48
De Meerpaal, Dronten. Frank van Klingeren, 1967. Photo Jan Versnel. © Jan Versnel/MAI. Source: Maria Austria Instituut | MAI

⊞ 49
Musée d'Orsay, Paris. Gae Aulenti, 1980–1986. Photo Flickr user: DaveKav © DaveKav. Source: https://www.flickr.com/photos/d-kav/8289427658/sizes/l

⊞ 50–53
Palais de Tokyo, Paris. Lacaton et Vassal, 2001; 2012. Photo © Phillipe Ruault. Source: Lacaton et Vassal architectes

⊞ 53–54
Neues Museum, Berlin. David Chipperfield architects, 2013. Photo © and source: Mark Pimlott

⊞ 55
Souterrain Den Haag The Hague. OMA, 2004. Photo © and source: Mark Pimlott

⊞ 56
The Gothic Arch, Giovanni Battista Piranesi, 1761. Princeton University x1938-13n © and source: The Trustees of Princeton University

⊞ 57
1111 Lincoln Road, Miami. Herzog + De Meuron, 2010. Photograph © and source: Nelson Garrido

IV
THE SHED

ⓘ 01

Consider the modest shed. The shed is something we are very familiar with; it suggests nothing more than a kind of shelter where things are kept to prevent them from getting wet. If one thinks of a shed at a larger scale, used by many people, one is led to a motif that at first makes its appearance as a nomadic tent thrown up in the settlement, an exceptional figure in the gathering of more permanent structures, a shelter for exceptional events in the clearings of the settlement. The shed appears as a more permanent figure, and a public interior, as it accommodates those exceptional, quotidian and unruly aspects of the city, the metropolis and its territories. Such sheds, from the tent, to the covered markets and halls[1] of the medieval period, have held long-established relationships with settlements, yet they came into their own as major figures within the nineteenth- and twentieth-century metropolis. In these contexts, in which their scale acquired monumental proportions, sheds demonstrated their capacity to provide—in our view—the most modern public interiors of the city, in which all contents and people within were visible and conceptually unified. The shed of the nineteenth century was an artefact yielded by the circumstances and technologies of the industrial revolution and the requirements of the metropolis for halls with ever-greater spans for machines such as trains, engines and turbines; for functions such as stations, urban markets, great exhibitions and museums.[2] Perhaps with the exception of the skyscraper, these structures could be taken to be both the most impressive and the most representative of modernity; and their interiors perhaps the most impressive and compelling.

One will note that the shed was a figure that came with modest associations, those approaching invisibility. It suggested little, it alluded to nothing; its world of evocations was rather small. The shed functioned, covered, sheltered, and contained. And yet, it came to provide the modern city with representative figures and interiors. It did so at a historical moment of profound change in Western cities, when major centres had grown to sizes that forced the issue of their management, the direction of their populations, and the coordinated control of their functions: the shed found its importance at the time when the greatest cities assumed the condition of the metropolis, and when modern states assumed the condition of elaborate bureaucracies. The shed, for all that was generic about its character, became a useful tool for the management or containment of complex situations raised by the metropolis. The shed could contain anything that required containment, and by its nature, it could make itself and that which it sheltered available for apprehension at a glance, thus presenting a very simple image and character, regardless of the complexity of its accommodation. Furthermore, it tended to set itself apart from its contexts, so that only their interiors appeared, and contexts either ceased to exist or were 'idealised'. This characteristic, one of whose consequences is interiority, has been central to the shed's effectiveness as a model for public interiors.

With everything visible within one shelter—or under one roof—a number of possibilities for the experience of the space within the shed emerged: first, that the contents it sheltered became its central and most visible protagonists, rendering both the shelter and its figure invisible; second, that the container itself became a dominant figure, rendering the shed that contained everything the primary figure in the composition and the expression of the space and its experience; or third, that contents and shelter were fused into a complete experience, rendering its interior an 'environment'. The greater the shed, the more extensive and complete the environment within became, and correspondingly, the greater the effect of interiorisation it produced. In its 'gift' of allowing anything to occur under its shelter, the shed came to offer the condition—as Ludwig Mies van der Rohe would describe it—of 'universal space'. Architects went on to propose such a condition as 'democratic' space. Depending on the uses to which such interiors were put, contradictory outcomes resulted.[3]

A collage of Mies's Project for a Theatre (1938) presented the most emblematic image of a paradigm within the Modernist canon, one that has retained its relevance to the present. Under the structure of a pre-existing aircraft hangar (designed by Albert Kahn for the production of military aircraft), a few paper shapes indicated specialised uses of space within a general space. These were complemented by sculptural figures: two different versions of this collage by Charles Danforth showed a sculpture of a reclining figure, probably by Kolbe; the other an ancient Egyptian sitting figure. The pictured space represented Mies's emerging idea of a universal space in which a structural architecture could provide large, clear spans and the possibility of multiple interior spatial configurations. Mies, in his teaching, often directed his students' attention to the Gothic cathedral—and that of his place of birth, Aachen (Aix-la-Chapelle, the seat of Charlemagne) for the clarity of its construction. The cathedrals' interiors were the most significant in any town: voluminous, monumental spaces that, beyond their dedication to worship and directionality toward the altar, pulpit and choir, offered extensive interior terrains for wandering about; interiors in which the idea of a meeting between God and Man could be contemplated. Mies was concerned with establishing a structural architecture that was representative of its epoch:[4] the cathedral—specifically, the Gothic cathedral—was an expressive and ethereal structure that sheltered a vast space limited only by the capacity of its vaults and its membrane-like walls of stone and glass.

ⓘⓥ 01

Consider these great cathedral and church interiors as 'sheds'. As painted by Pieter Saenredam (1597–1665) in the mid-seventeenth century, the interiors of great Dutch churches, such as St. Bavo in Haarlem or the Buurkerk in Utrecht, possessed an expansiveness that one might have been able to appreciate in the contexts of the towns in which they appeared. This character was undoubtedly exaggerated by the effects of iconoclasm in sixteenth-century northern Europe, when the iconographic, stained glass windows were stripped out and replaced with clear glass, the altars removed, the seats repositioned and the walls whitewashed, rendering the interiors even more, abstract, 'empty' and shed-like. These churches could be understood as great shelters of space, quite unlike any other construction. They were not halls embedded in other buildings; rather, they stood freely in the midst of settlements, dominating them, their interiors utterly separate and different. In the northern European countryside, pilgrimage churches stood free, like giant barns, with capacious and otherworldly interiors: vast sheltered clearings, reaching up to open air, with the vaults of heaven above. The gothic cathedrals' spaces suggested Paradise, the enclosed garden of everything. Columns and vaults were the structural components of these buildings and were formed as one; their thin walls were, conceptually, absent, allowing them to be substituted by large areas of glass, simply defining or separating their interior spaces from the rest of the environment around them. They were the noblest forms of shelter, with their structure

ⓘⓥ 02–03

Ⅳ 02

Ⅳ 03

ⅳ 04

ⅳ 05

(iv) 06

and spaces bearing the aura of significance. This characteristic was grasped by Mies: the cathedral space, as he idealised it in his teaching,[5] was a charged shelter, which, through its precise proportions, measure and materials, could ennoble its contents and its occupants. It is the shed's capacity for wonder, for the charging of experience to which the architect of the public interior has turned to so frequently.

EARLY HALLS AND MARKET HALLS

Developing at the same time as these churches, there were also interior halls for trade and exchange that became representative of common purpose. The first town exchanges could be thought of as grand civic barns, with interiors set aside for trade or commerce, and their central motif, the civic room, carried over into other building types, such as town halls. The two were often combined, the hall of exchange on the ground floor, with the town offices directly above.[6] In the south of the Netherlands and Belgium, the *halle* was a very significant public building, that rivalled the scale of the church. This motif was persistent, and evident in the interior of the Beurs in Amsterdam (1896–1903), designed by Hendrik Petrus Berlage (1856–1934), whose rationalist medievalism, can be seen as the re-construction of an ideal gothic architecture and the *halle*. In this case, the ribs of gothic vaults, suggesting the branches of trees, are re-interpreted as iron structures supporting a glass roof, attaching the interior to heaven while separating it from the city. In Italy, the Palazzo dalla Ragione in Padua (1219) was particularly notable as such an interior: its vast, voluminous (81.5 by 27 by 24m high) hall or *salone* (1420) was sheltered under a vaulted timber roof for civic meeting. Resting over an arcaded ground floor, the great form enclosing it dominated the city's central *piazza*.

(iv) 04

IV 07

Existing alongside the spaces of cathedrals, often adjacent to each other in the representative centres of villages and towns, medieval market halls became foci of public interaction and communication. These halls arose in already established market towns, whose trading activities required increased regulation and segregation from other activities of the town. Their monumental sheds, open timber and stone structures set upon clearings within the town's fabric, sheltered market trade and represented, in their mixing of local buyers and regional traders, the idea of town and country coming together. During those hours of trade, their interiors became centres of the world, as meeting places of others. It is worth noting that in being distinct from the fabric of the rest of the town, the market hall was effectively isolated: its worldliness and its accommodation of others, was set apart. Market halls, emptied out on many days of the week and at night, became empty monuments within the fabric of towns, occupying important places in their midst. Structures of columns or sections of wall in stone supported their roofs, which often featured elaborate internal structures due to their large spans. Emblematic of these constructions were the seventeenth-century Bastide markets in the South of France; the Market Hall of Richelieu (1630); or their equivalents in English village markets, such as Chipping Camden in the Cotswolds (1627). In Italy, *loggie* in the midst of the fabric of cities were analogous to these kinds of market halls. The Mercato Nuovo in Firenze (1547–1548) featured an elegant open colonnade that stood amidst the compact gridded streets of the centre.[7] Such structures were more formally refined than those in France and England, and more obviously monumental. Refined versions of market halls appeared in the Netherlands, too, apparently inspired by Italian *loggie*: one, the Graanbeurs, in Middelburg, (reconstructed from a much earlier original, re-cast as *Podio del Mondo per l'Arte* or 'World Plinth for Art' by the artist Marinus Boezem in 1976), typified such representative structures, appearing as a small, open civic 'room' on a raised dais, with classical columns supporting a ceiling and a slate roof. These shelters

IV 05–06

IV 07

Ⅳ 08–10

(IV) 11

or sheds that lacked the pretence of being 'complete' buildings provide a model for the theme of the shed as proposed here: a charged shelter in the midst of the world.

In the case of the markets of the Rialto district in Venezia, stalls for vegetables and fruits occupied open clearings, while the market halls at their ends were sheltered spaces with offices above—'empty' buildings—nestled among shops and houses in the small streets and squares (*calle* and *campi*) of the area.[8] The carefully wrought stone columns and carved timber ceiling beams of the buildings of the *Mercato del Pesce al Minuto* offered an ennobled realm for trade. The openness of the sheltered spaces to the streets and spaces around them, amidst the fullness of their setting and their interior bounty, rendered them significant. With offices and useful rooms directly above them, no other functions compromised the simplicity of the market halls themselves. It was and continues to be bound to the life and movement of the city around them, and along with the interiors of churches, the most significant shared interior spaces of the city.

(IV) 08–10

METROPOLITAN MARKET HALLS

The market shed, without any narrative other than its transient use and its untiring accommodation of diverse contents, citizens and strangers—yet with a form, a structure and an image of its own—provided a compelling model for the public interior. The lightly representational structural architecture of the shed, with its own story of structure and span bridging several types of use, rendered it central to accounts of the trajectory of Modern architecture, notably that of Sigfried Giedion.[9] The widespread industrialisation of Western European economies and its chain of interrelated consequences, the rapid increase of populations of cities, and concomitant growth of railways in the second half of the nineteenth century caused the problem of size (and subsequently, scale) to enter all building problems, giving rise to the re-evaluation of all building types, and in some cases, the invention of new types. As rural populations dwindled and agricultural production and distribution changed, the figure of the shed in the guise of the Market Hall took its place in the burgeoning metropolitan centres, at a large scale, serving ever-growing populations,

(IV) 11

IV 12–13

167. PARIS — Les Halles Centrales

(IV) 17

responding to pressures of centralisation. Markets of very similar characteristics appeared throughout major European cities in the second half of the nineteenth century. Paris was of course central to this phenomenon, but their appearance was tied to all cities undergoing fundamental change. The format for these halls was consistent: large-span shelters with structures of iron and glass, well ventilated, with natural clerestory lighting and market stalls in street-like arrangements below. As the needs of such markets were relatively universal, so too seemed the solutions that were evolved in order to address them.

The market of central importance was the extensive Halles Centrales, designed by Victor Balthard and Félix Collet, and constructed in a series of phases between 1853 and 1857 in Paris, which occupied an enormous area of Châtelet, with the church of St-Eustache to the north, and to the west, the Bourse de Blé or Wheat Exchange. Its market sheds were demolished in 1971.[10] Balthard was architect of the city of Paris from 1845 and known for his experimental developments in structures of iron, the slaughterhouses of La Villette, and steel churches (St Augustin 1860–1871). His initial proposal for a predominantly masonry structure (1843) was abandoned in 1851 under pressure from both the Emperor Louis Napoléon III and Baron Georges-Eugène Haussmann. The Emperor was moved by the construction of the Crystal Palace (1851), seeing it as a structure befitting a metropolis, which, in his mind, London was, and Paris was not. The train shed at Gare de l'Est fitted his idea of the metropolis's necessary clarity and efficiency, which should serve as a model for Paris. Haussmann, as responsible for the construction of the city as Prefect of the Seine, declared in sympathy with Louis Napoléon III that the new structures of the market should be 'only iron' and 'iron umbrellas'. Balthard's new project therefore offered a series of pavilions in iron, glass and brick, linked by *galéries* covering internal streets, that were parallel in character with the sheds of those new urban infrastructural projects—the train stations—that served the city.

(IV) 12–16

(IV) 18

Les Halles featured the repeated deployment of two sizes of model pavilion—ten of them, augmented by four special pavilions framing the circular Bourse de Blé—with the 'standard' characteristics previously described, creating an urban market zone arrayed in a gridded network of one central glazed avenue and five lateral streets, four of which were covered with glass, facing and integrated with the streets of the district, in which informal market activities gathered. The market complex or zone suggested a social hierarchy nevertheless. Inside, order reigned, and the bourgeoisie could be found within; in the streets around, the chaos associated with the less advantaged of the city was much in evidence, disparities that were described by Emile Zola in his novel *Le Ventre de Paris* (1873).[11]

This arrangement afforded a standard type, built of pre-fabricated elements, a high degree of specificity: the building fit in its context, communicated its idea, and 'charged' its urban setting in a manner much like the *loggia* and *halle* markets of the sixteenth and seventeenth centuries. The cast-iron and glass sheds seemed suited to the pressing demand for utility that the metropolis imposed. In Barcelona, the Mercat St Josip (1840; 1910), and Mercat Sant' Antoni, designed by Antoni Rovira i Trias (1882), were representative of the new order of interior under iron roofs, integrated with the street systems of their locale, while the biggest single space of all was that of the Great Market Hall in Budapest, designed by Samu Pecz (1897), which offered itself as a complete interior urban district.

(IV) 17–18

The spaces of Les Halles Centrales were not completely foreign to Paris; they relied to some extent on potent motifs or types that were germane to the Pre-Haussmannian city,[12] namely the *passages*, the interior pedestrian streets of the first and second *arrondissements*. Among the working sheds of Paris were the slaughterhouses (La Villette in Paris designed by Balthard), but our concern is with those sheds that represented the metropolis's new public interiors, and so it is important here to introduce the train stations: not the stone blocks that faced the various squares cleared for their consumption and expulsion of travellers, but their train sheds behind, which generated among the most representative scenes of the city in modernity. Their huge spans would shelter many trains, platforms and people all at once,

IV 19–20

ⓘⓋ 21

vast shelters or 'rooms'. These were not the evocative spaces of the Crystal Palace; rather, they were sheds, or hangars (whose etymology suggests origins in both 'hamlet' and 'enclosure')[13] for everything and everyone, accommodating the chaos of metropolitan transit, its new locomotive machines, and the machinery of the movement of crowds in a most organised way. The Gare de l'Est (admired by Louis Napoléon III), Gare de Lyon (trains for the South), Gare Saint-Lazare (trains for the South-east, painted by Édouard Manet), and Gare du Nord (trains for the North, painted by Claude Monet) were (and remain) important public interiors, in which an entire populace could be imagined and the city's population could be seen on the move. These sheds came to be characteristic of Paris, London, Berlin and New York among other cities, and representative of the condition of the city as manifested in the metropolis. We have to remind ourselves that such models as they emerged from the metropolis were widely, almost universally applied in cities across Europe and the West. These sheds' design was usually dominated by their engineered structures, and the application of technology to issues of purpose: the public interiors that emerged were products of necessity and efficiency. However, such interiors affected an order of consciousness in users that one would associate with more self-conscious modes of design and their representations. Two stations developed slightly later than their Parisian counterparts showed that this character, fused with more narrative programmes, created interiors of great invention and visual power, invoking, respectively, the Gothic tradition, in the case of Liverpool Street Station, London (Edward Wilson and W. N. Ashbee, shed by Messrs. Lucas Brothers 1874); and the antique world, in the case of Pennsylvania Station, New York, designed by McKim, Mead and White (1901). The utilitarian therein assumed a civic, representational dimension.

ⓘⓋ 19–20

ⓘⓋ 21–22

IV 22

⓵ 23

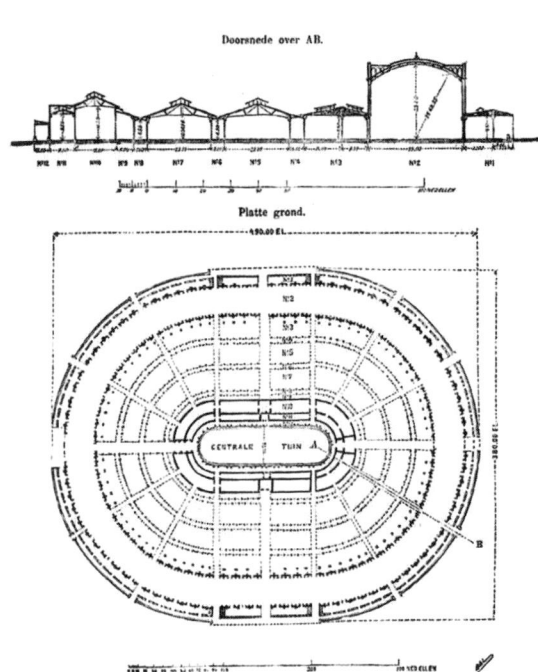

⓵ 24

(IV) 25

INTERNATIONAL EXPOSITIONS AND UNIVERSAL SPACE

The Crystal Palace (Joseph Paxton, 1851), as we have seen, was regarded more an achievement of technology and engineering than a work of architecture, yet its status as a unique and powerful interior was unquestioned. A vast shelter that contained everything, it established a position that would allow the figure of a capacious shelter to be suitable for similar uses in the future. The Crystal Palace was, as we have seen, erected for an international exposition, a type of event that took place many times over the remainder of the nineteenth century and slightly less frequently through the twentieth century. Such events were outward expressions of the desire for an international metropolitanism. The Expositions featured pavilions from nations who promoted themselves through their industry or resources on a great stage in collective displays of production, which was in constant and rapid development. This development mirrored the enormous changes affecting major urban centres such as Paris, London, New York, Chicago and St. Louis, which all hosted such expositions before the First World War. Paris alone hosted nine of them[14] before the Great Exhibition in London, any many more after, typically featuring groupings of small structures for individual nations or industries, and large, collective structures. There was always an aspect of artificiality to the former; they amounted to little more than fantastic *décor*. The collective 'utilitarian' structures, however, provided spaces that were extensive, and stretched the limits of construction technology and the perceptions of space. Buildings such as the *Galérie des machines* designed by

Ⓘᵥ 26

Ⓘᵥ 23–25

Fréderic Le Play for the Exposition of 1867 was a structure of concentric oval sheds that could be navigated by walking around each of their circuits, in which industrial products were organised by type; or by cutting across these rings, each of which were dedicated to single nations or groups of them. The route through the exhibition yielded concrete experiences of comparative analysis and universality. The *Galérie des machines* designed by Ferdinand Dutert and Victor Contamin and produced for the later Exposition of 1889 was a single clear-span structure over 110m wide and 420m in length: a pure engineering structure with a glass roof that contained everything, and which could be appreciated at a single glance. The structures of the great exhibitions were frequently memorable and influential. At times they were obliged to cede to tradition: the Grand Palais, designed by J.-A. Bouvard for the Paris exhibition of 1900, still in use as a space for large art and fashion exhibitions, was a great glass shed encased in a confection of stone and stucco in the neo-Baroque style of the *Belle époque*.

Ⓘᵥ 26

As the Crystal Palace was adopted, adapted and re-interpreted in such types as the department store and the *jardins d'hiver*, train sheds and industrial hangars were adopted for the representative structures of the great expositions of Paris, affecting perceptions of what a public interior could be. In such structures, the characters of the Crystal Palace, market hall and train shed were fused into a single, useful expression. The expansiveness of those spaces of display for the masses was matched by the scale of their ambition—to show everything, to everyone. The ever more ambitious

(IV) 27

treatments of structure and span required to do so led to the clear span becoming representative in its own right. In the service of 'universal' exhibitions, clear span spaces could become universal spaces in which there was only structure and space, with all audiences and functions contained within a single representative interior, clear to all: the world under one roof. Such structures had no need for the rest of the city with the exception of their infrastructure: the axis connecting the Champs de Mars and the Tour Eiffel was indeed in Paris, yet otherwise disconnected from the life of the city. The interior worlds they sheltered were—for all the metropolitanism of their effects and spectacle and their intrinsic utopianism—anti-urban. They were capable of appearing in parks, or out of town: their structures were indifferent to their contexts, regardless of their representative nature.

THE SHED AND THE AMBITIONS OF INTERNATIONAL MODERNISM

The large-span structures of markets, stations and exhibitions directed to very large public gatherings causes us to think of them as models for the public interior. Because of the clear and overwhelming imagery provided by these structures, they have communicated their messages at great scales. The great sheds, in accommodating and communicating to masses of visitors and users, have inevitably represented the shared or collective experience of those masses, and became—perhaps by default—a motif for space designed for the broad public. This potential was as true for the nineteenth century as it was for the twentieth: the exposition buildings of Montréal in 1967 and Osaka in 1970 were regarded as experimental, and in terms of technology and media they were; but they adhered to a formula that had been set over one hundred years earlier. The emblematic structures of Expo67 were the American pavilion, a geodesic dome designed by R. Buckminster Fuller; and the German pavilion, a tent structure designed by Frei Otto and the Institute of Structures of Stuttgart. Fuller's dome represented a fragment of a larger, utopian project to re-build the world in lightweight self-sustaining environment-structures,[15] for which he proselytised and had conducted considerable research. His project for a dome over a portion of Manhattan (1960) imagined an interior that was in fact a perfect environment, an 'eco-sphere' whose

(IV) 27–28

(IV) 29

(IV) 30

THE SHED

(IV) 31–32

(IV) 33

inhabitants would occupy the streets and, in the thickness of the light-transmitting dome, the sky itself. At Expo 67, his geodesic structure was the setting for imagery and artefacts of American culture: a fusion of memorabilia, Hollywood iconography, Pop Art and paraphernalia of space exploration.[16] People moved across platforms and through the exhibition scenes that occupied the dome via very long escalators, suspended in the volume of the dome as though traversing the space across both the 'ruins' and the future of American culture that were contained within the pavilion's environmental bubble. In contrast, Otto's tent provided a free terrain on the ground and on raised decks for technological and cultural artefacts which people could explore, as though on an archaeological dig of contemporary material. Fundamentally, these pavilions operated as those in nineteenth-century expositions in Paris, but with different forms. The most significant pavilions at Expo 70 in Osaka, Japan—at which the Welcome pavilion designed by Arata Isozaki featured a plaza covered by a giant space frame, and the American pavilion, an inflated shallow dome designed by Davis Brody Associates—followed the conventions once more, in an exhibition that was full of clear-span space frames, and suspended and inflatable structures, all proposed as universal spaces, prototypes for future public interiors and future formations of society.

(IV) 29

(IV) 30

MIES VAN DER ROHE AND UNIVERSAL SPACE

Ludwig Mies van der Rohe, in his many clear span projects dating from 1942, spoke of making representative, 'universal' spaces of complete adaptability. Among these projects were those for theatres, including the collage that we encountered earlier, that proposed the idea in the setting of a hangar (1938); a competition project for a Theatre in Mannheim (1953) that featured a clear span shed raised on a plinth sheltering two auditoria under its span; projects and realisations for museums, such as the 'project for a Museum for 194X' designed for *The Architectural Forum* magazine (1943);[17] the realised Neue Nationalgalerie in Berlin (1968) with its clear span steel shelter poised on four columns set on a monumental plinth; his vast Project for a Congress Hall for Chicago (1956); and

(IV) 31–33

(iv) 34

in its smallest iteration, a single family dwelling called the 'Fifty by Fifty House', with a clear span of over fifty feet (approximately fifteen metres) on each side (1950–1952). Mies's objective was to create an architecture that was representative of its 'epoch', which he described as 'structural architecture'.[18] What was notable about all of Mies's clear-span projects was their interior visual organisation, wherein the user's view was led ineluctably toward the horizon through the pairing of ceiling and floor about a horizontal axis of symmetry[19]; and how, regardless of their appearances, this organisation provided these interiors' most persistent visual tendency and most communicative aspect, even when the expression of the main constituent elements—ceiling and floor—tended toward abstraction and bore no overt material or visual qualities. When, for example, ceiling and floor were white, horizontal planes, the contents of the interiors appeared to be especially significant. The aura of the contents in all cases was entirely dependent upon their visual frame, and the 'image' of the shed that enabled their existence. This was evident in designs spanning from the Barcelona Pavilion (1927); through the courtyard houses of the 1930s; the Resor House (1940); project for 'A Museum for 194X' (1942), and the Neue Nationalgalerie.

Mies's colleagues and collaborators extended this idea in projects both realisable and hypothetical. Konrad Wachsmann, who taught at the neighbouring Institute of Design in Chicago, designed a project for a civic centre in California City (1966–1971), whose interior was represented by an image of a structure whose span appeared to be stretched taught across a landscape, framing the view and the horizon. The clear span's supports—great anchors holding the cable structure in tension—were not visible: the span replaced the sky, charging the ground below and all actions and contents resting upon it. The project offered itself as a 'last project', without image, placed at the centre of the world.[20] Reginald Malcolmson, a colleague of Mies at the Illinois Institute of Technology, designed a project for a museum of Natural Sciences in much the same spirit. A huge external steel arch truss supported a suspended ceiling of great span, an interior within which only the significant permanent elements within appeared: two people, a skeleton of a Tyrannosaurus Rex, a polygonal silhouette suggesting an auditorium with a stair, and surprisingly, the Moon, which hovered over a grid on the floor that stretched to an apparently infinite distance. Malcolmson seemed to infer that all time and space were collapsed and replaced by this singular interior. The project was improbable, yet it demonstrated the shed's capacity to serve the idea—epitomised by Paxton's Crystal Palace—that a whole world could be under one roof. The architect and engineer Myron Goldsmith—who trained and worked with Mies (and later Pier Luigi Nervi), and ran a studio at IIT with Fazlur Khan—set projects for students on the theme of large span and clear span structures as public interiors.[21] The object of their studios concerning clear-span structures was to research the feasibility of interiors made for public life in a dispersed or territorial city through representative structural architecture; the structures' tasks were to create spaces that could accommodate myriad activities all at once. In all cases, those activities were framed by orthogonal and largely clear-span structures whose features never imposed themselves upon the scenes they framed. They removed themselves from view, yet were inescapable: great sheds in the tradition of the early market halls, and the metropolitan sheds that followed them.

These academic projects were effectively realised in Italy by the engineer Pier Luigi Nervi, to whom Myron Goldsmith turned in order to learn more about structure, interrupting his studies with Mies at IIT. The interior of Nervi's design for the Palazzo del Lavoro, for the international expostion in Torino (1961) was immense, a great space sheltered by the meeting of a set of muscular steel columns that cantilevered outwards at the top to form 'umbrella' roofs that did not quite touch. The project was representative of Nervi's hangars and clear-span spaces for market and event halls, stations, stadia, and auditoria: single-space shelters that could accommodate any event or circumstance, regardless of their nature or scale; structures that were exercises in monumental architecture and universal space.

FUN

Universal space, as interpreted by Cedric Price and his sponsor, the theatre director Joan Littlewood in the provisions of the Fun Palace (1958–61), was framed by the playful and even feral possibilities of the pleasure garden, and specifically Vauxhall Gardens (c 1650–1840; 1841–1859). The Fun Palace, which we have described before, was proposed as a very large shed, or perhaps more accurately a hangar, with its giant structure a scaffold for capsules, stages, tribunes, media-oriented events and entertainment. It offered a model of partnership between structure-as-infrastructure and structure-as-architecture that was emulated by architects thereafter, in the service of either culture or commerce. The Centre Georges Pompidou, Paris (1977), designed by Renzo Piano and Richard Rogers, offered its spectacular long-span structure of elaborately articulated and clear spaces at the service of whatever cultural manifestation was desired: its structure-as-infrastructure-as-architecture accommodated open public lobbies, event spaces, a public library, a research institute, the national museum of Modern art, restaurants, cafés and public terraces. Everything about the building's expression—again, like an open-air *Meccano* toy—suggested the servicing of these programmes and the people that used them. Despite its spectacle, and the destruction of the local *milieu* wrought by its construction, it was a rather gentle building. This was most apparent at the ground floor, which had a character of

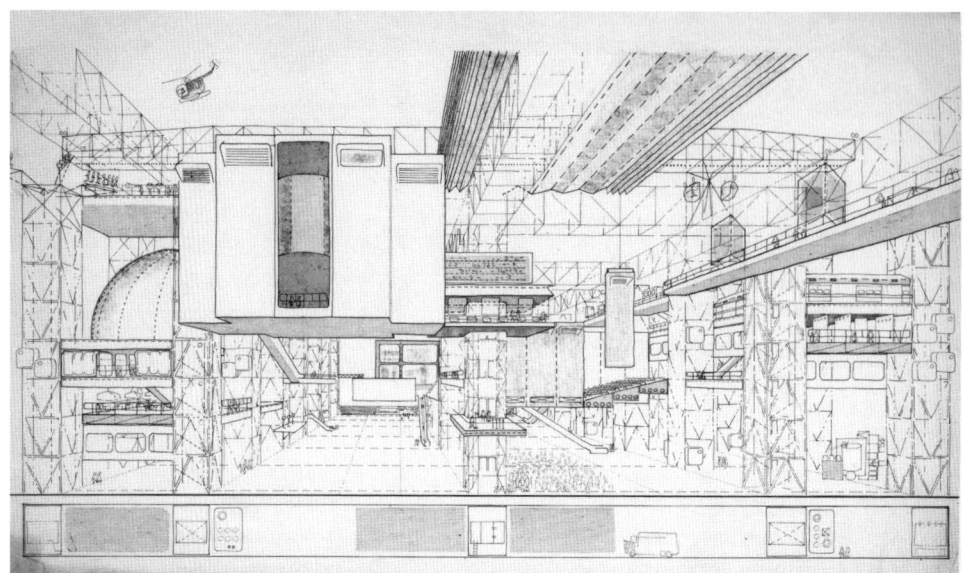

Ⅳ 35

Ⅳ 36

a vast industrial living room directly connected to the sunken, sloping, public square in front of the building. The building 'withdrew'—a paradox given the exaggerations of its structure—in order to serve its public, who gathered there to look at art, or study, meet or simply indulge in *flânerie*. The building visibly dominated its site and its interiors, communicating its matter and substance more than any of its contents; yet it did so in an accessible and even liberating way. This was consistent with the attitude conveyed by its founding director Pontus Hultén, who wished to open the site of cultural creation to the broad public, who in fact created culture. The feeling of the Centre Pompidou in its early years—rambled over by thousands of users each and every day—was something approaching 'democratic', of being free for all, its structure providing a multi-level shelter for intellectual and social pleasures. That quality was sadly eroded over a series of restorations and renovations, which instituted many 'permanent' structures within—such as Gae Aulenti's re-design of the spaces for the *Musée nationale d'art moderne* (1986)—and removed facilities from their previously easy accessibility, both in fact and in atmosphere.

DEMOCRATIC SPACE: FRANK VAN KLINGEREN AND LINA BO BARDI

In making democratic space in the spirit of experimentation that was characteristic of the 1960s, the shed was deployed to accommodate everything and everyone, encouraging random and unpredictable activity. In two projects by Frank van Klingeren—an engineer by training—all manner of activities took place under one roof: in the first case, the multi-functional centre De Meerpaal in Dronten (1967), a glass box in a new low-density urban setting, whose interior was articulated by an extremely simple, black-painted steel structure carrying lights, projection screens (for television) and murals, in the manner of a well-equipped warehouse.[22] The structure—the architecture—withdrew from the scene. Yet the scene was virtually impossible to imagine without the structure's determinations of space and geometry. The shed's structure was a constant presence, a sign for the building and all that happened there, whether it was a play, a market, lessons for adults or children, or games. The building promoted an atmosphere of freedom, aligned with the contemporary revision of social norms, particularly those that permitted existing social desires and activities to become visible and public. In the second building, 't Karregat in Eindhoven (1970–73), a complete experiment for social interaction was conducted under one articulated shelter, that, again, was very present as the visible background and protagonist to very real activities: two schools, a nursery, a scout club, doctors' offices, a library, restaurant, bar and even a supermarket. There were clearings for events, which featured fragments of a playful, imaginary landscape, represented by painted rocks. The interiors of De Meerpaal and 't Karregat were both conceived as *agora*: gathering places for people that might encourage social and naturally political activity. Within such shelters, Van Klingeren hoped, people could make their way, their lives, their communities, or, by extension, their idea of the State. The important aspects of his projects were connected to his insistence—manifested in his structures—that a space for free social interaction must be sheltered and accommodated, sympathetically. The modesty of his architectural expression

IV 37

was suitable for the communities and activities his buildings served. One can only speculate on the manner he may have used for larger, more generalised metropolitan conditions and their cosmopolitan publics.

Returning briefly to Mies van der Rohe's 1938 'Project for a theatre' and its central motif of adaptation of an existing hangar, the status of the existing structure was subject to an extreme reinterpretation in its re-use: in this case, the original purpose of the structure was subverted. Its structure was reinterpreted so it might serve a purpose opposite to that which it was built for: it was 'mis-used'. In its new guise as a theatre, its space would be dedicated to the construction rather than the destruction of culture in its role as a factory for bomber aircraft. Mies's proposition was emblematic of the possibilities offered by the shed, which would make something new work, regardless of or even in direct opposition to the original uses of the spaces sheltered and defined by the structure. The obverse adaptation of a shed was both possible and productive: the shed would be both changed and *charged* by its re-use as mis-use. This was from where much of the strength of Mies's proposal was drawn from, as was Lina Bo Bardi's project for a cultural centre—or a centre for the unfolding of culture through leisure—in a former industrial area of São Paulo—SESC-Fábrica da Pompéia (1977–86), which we have already encountered. The factory buildings, formerly used for the making of steel drums, were transformed—and subverted—through simple operations of opening walls and bridging structures: the walled site as a whole was invoked as a *cidadella*,[23] which was made plainly accessible and that had been claimed already by the people in the neighbourhoods around it: children and adults had breached the site through its one gate, and 'played' there. The *cidadella* was an interior by virtue of its enclosure, a safe haven for rest and

IV 38–40

Ⅳ 38–40

(IV) 41

creation in the midst of the city. Existing structures were cleared of their tools and other signs of work, while new structures were built and connected over terrains that could not be built on. The emptying or internal clearing out enabled the complex of buildings and access routes to be claimed, reinterpreted and put to new uses. Simple structures of concrete and block-work for study and work areas gave the impression that anyone could build them; a steel fireplace was suspended from the rafters, suggesting domesticity; a shallow, serpentine pond was cut into the floor. These episodic gestures were superimposed on users' memories of the complex's original use, creating a new condition that derived its aura from the residue or legacy of those uses, and from interventions that were openly in playful opposition to them. The shallow pond was perhaps the most disruptive of all the interventions, preventing the floor being used as an industrial work-floor ever again. Similarly, the internal lanes crossing the site, formerly used for transporting material, were transformed into streets for people and their interaction. Two new buildings, which assumed the image of production buildings in rough-shuttered concrete, were also dedicated to leisure and play, accommodating bars, gymnasia, swimming pool and changing rooms, connected by an array of aerial bridges. Their window openings were amorphous holes that appeared to be selective works of demolition. The sport facilities were intentionally designed not to meet the conditions for competitive events, rather encouraging 'amateur' play. The atmospheres of both the former factory interior and the new towers built alongside were charged by their curated subversion, which in turn affected their users. The factory was transformed from a place of work and oppression into one of social interaction, liberation and play; while the user was transformed from a worker, and an agent of others, into a cultural maker; independent, and in the best spirit of the word, a player. The factory shed that sheltered the spaces of this transformation became the central figure of the representation of that transformation, and its emancipatory idea.

VARIATIONS ON THE THEME, FROM THE BANAL TO THE SUBLIME

The Shed was a format or theme that seemed bound to succeed due to its capacity to be open to re-interpretation or mis-use; this same capacity has rendered it open to abuse. The distinct and separate nature of the shed, in which it could work without obvious relations to those contexts upon which it depended, or be apparently indifferent to them, allowed it to accommodate entire interior worlds, and in its outward aspect, to seem anti-urban. This characteristic allowed the shed to thrive in suburban conditions. In the context of the so-called Free Market, the shed became the space that granted licence to a sort of free-for-all, whose spaces were used to hold their users captive, and to oblige them, for example, to consume in predictable patterns. The markets we have seen typically controlled their expression through sets of standard rules that placed all traders on a level ground of competition for business. This came to be overthrown in the 'big boxes' of suburbia by the principles of a 'free market', wherein the impulses of 'self-expression' and its ideological bedfellow 'self-realisation', have become dominant, rendering the Shed a space of 'free expression', supplanting hard-won agreements with the ideology of *laissez-faire*; elective exchange with unbridled competition; human nature with 'survival of the fittest'; and enfranchisement of the public with the incentive of the boundless capacity to consume. This was not new; something similar drove the assumption of the *grand magasin* as a public interior in the nineteenth century.

(iv) 41

These tendencies manifested themselves in the buildings designed for 'Big Box' retailing, inevitably realised in industrial sheds, filled with material ripe for high-volume consumption. The 'Big Box' achieved its aim in a straightforward way, offering consumers what appeared to be a direct link to the imagery of the space of manufacture or storage (a reminder of the warehouse origins of the American department store), apparently eliding the spaces of production with those of consumption, such as in the case of hardware stores, do-it-yourself stores, sporting goods stores, furniture and lifestyle stores and the like. Conversely, the Big Box proposed itself with interiors of more complex imagery: sheds full of distractions and diversions, achieving something close to monumentality, such as the Mall of America in Bloomington, Minnesota, designed by Jon Jerde Associates (1992).[24] In this case, the shed was not a mere warehouse, but a receptacle for spectacle; for entertainments that were parallel in spirit to those offered in the American department store as it was transformed from being a mere warehouse in the latter part of the nineteenth century. Jerde, who understood the performance of commercially oriented environments very well and tried to translate this understanding into architectural *mise-en-scènes*, filled the space of the Mall of America to its capacious limits with imagery of fantasies attendant upon consumption. The interior clearly displayed its construction: open-lattice columns and beams suggested that the whole interior was a space-frame—not unlike the Fun Palace—ready to be filled with fun. However, unlike the Fun Palace, the users were given neither the opportunity nor the responsibility to generate the interior's 'special effects'. Rather, these effects were imported, courtesy of the architect and developer (the Ghermezian brothers being modern-day versions of Aristide Boucicault, the creator of 'Au Bon Marché) and designed to give the impression of itineracy and ephemerality, like a visiting circus.

(iv) 42

Ⅳ 42

Ⅳ 43

ⓘⱽ 44

This imagery was borrowed, of course, from that of Archigram's 'Instant City' project (1968),[25] which was fantasised as a device for the transformation of sleepy English provincial towns through the overnight deployment of dirigible-transported tents, robot-installed rigs, and stages. The functional and provisional structure of Jerde's Big Box was the rectangular 'tent' or shed that made the spectacle in the logistical centre of a suburban region of Minnesota possible.

Positioned somewhere between Jon Jerde's shed for the consumer experience and Mies van der Rohe's projection for a Theatre, which made a space for high culture under the shelter of steel steel trusses, was Norman Foster and Associates design for the Sainsbury Centre for Visual Arts at the University of East Anglia, Norwich (1974–1978).[26] The institution, placed on a green sward of the campus, preserved its contents of rare cultural artefacts in a technological hangar. Its enclosure, which could be very easily understood at a glance from without and within, was conceived as a life-support unit, a 2,4m thick 'skin' that contained all building services and modulated light from above and its sides, sustaining the interior. The objects and visitors all shared a space that seemed to offer a gentle, comforting shelter, open to the landscape at its ends, with natural light filtered through its enclosure. Its displays of vitrines and stands were intimate, yet highly managed elements of technological design, consistent with the architectural legacy of the universal expositions. (iv) 43

Another shed with the ambition of charging its programme and its occupants—and aspiring to the condition of instant divine communication—was The Crystal Cathedral in Garden Grove, California (1981), designed by Philip Johnson of Johnson and Burgee, a glass-clad polygonal space frame whose interior was designed to impress its congregation through its capaciousness and a corresponding evocation of the sublime. The space-frame was painted white, achieving a kind of diaphanous ethereality, under whose structural filigree were ranged thousands of worshippers' seats, a stage, and a monumental organ. A profane equivalent to this spiritually charged shed was the Jacob K. Javits Convention Center in New York, designed by Ingo Freed of Pei Cobb Freed (1986), a very large glass-clad space frame shed whose external form was composed of an uneven cluster of beveled cubes, rendering the interior complex, but still legible as one space. Both this and the Crystal Cathedral were huge versions of the shed as a generic structure whose idiosyncratic articulations were intended to lend them architectural qualities, and were vaguely reminiscent of those glass houses and *jardins d'hiver* of the nineteenth century that seemed capable of accommodating any variety of functions and events.[27] The communication of purpose within these buildings—whether for worship or congress—was supposed to be affected through the forms they assumed. However, it was their status as sheds that communicated their simple messages: that anything and everything could occur under their shelter. (iv) 44

SHED AS COMMUNICATIVE MOTIF NOW

In Lacaton and Vassal's transformation of a disused boat warehouse—a precast concrete structure several storeys high—on the harbour of Dunkerque into a regional centre for contemporary art, or FRAC (2013), the original building was kept in its entirety and a double in precast concrete, galvanised steel and translucent polycarbonate cladding was fixed directly it to its side.[28] The first structure, a shed, (iv) 45–46

Ⅳ 45–46

THE SHED

(IV) 47–48

was left as it was—empty—and adapted to its new use through connections to the new structure. The second structure was an interpretation of the first, a shell clad in transparent and translucent plastic harbouring a stacked precast concrete construction of galleries. The original shed served as a lobby or great single room for the new shed of galleries, the latter 'plugging into' the former, in a configuration identical to that of the Turbine Hall and galleries of the converted Bankside Power Station into Tate Modern in London designed by Herzog & de Meuron (2000). From a distance, the building conveyed the image of a double shed that could be read at a glance: partly old, and partly renewed. Both the shell of the existing shed at FRAC Dunkerque and the modest, almost provisional quality of the construction of the new shed promised a kind of freedom of access and use that characterised the affordance of its public interior.

In the centre of Ghent, Paul Robbrecht, Hilde Daem and Marie-José Van Hee built new municipal facilities for the city's Town Hall under a new public square, between the churches of St Nicholas and the Belfry. The terrain had been used as a car park since the 1960s, when a series of buildings were demolished in anticipation of an extension to the Town Hall that never came to be realised.[29] Between the spaces of three squares of the original fabric, and extending to the local Korenmarkt, the architects built a large underground space for the town hall and bicycle storage, but of most importance was the monumental shelter at street level, that signified the Stadshal (2012). The structure—a great shed—evokes memories of both the covered markets and the *hallen* of Dutch towns we have described earlier. Its roof is supported on four colossal legs, one of which accommodates a great open-fire hearth, as if to exaggerate the almost archaic character of the structure, presenting an image that both serves and represents communal gathering. Sitting on the formerly abused terrain, the structure shelters a recovered clearing in the centre of the city, confers upon it the quality of a room, and bestows upon its occupants— citizens—the pleasure of looking at the city from within, and at each other. In so doing, the building revives a special characteristic of the historic sheltering hall, and fashions a profoundly public space, a place shared between citizens, one in which all are gathered together, in which all are equal, and all are other.

In many of these 'sheds', we have seen the assumption and transformation of a structure of necessity into one that has represented freedom of use, movement, and association. The ambiguity of the open market and its relation to the plan of the city around it created the situation of a free clearing in the midst of a settlement, and myriad possibilities for use and engagement. In the cases of Les Halles Centrales, Mies's Project for a Theatre, the Fun Palace, De Meerpal, SESC-Fábrica Pompéia and the Town Hall in Ghent, the affordance of the Shed—a sheltering structure—has been liberating, giving licence to uses and behaviour aligned with the feeling of clearings, in which public life could be made anew.

01
Project for a Concert Hall. Ludwig Mies van der Rohe, 1938–1942. Charles Danforth, collage. Museum of Modern Art 0123664 © Scala Archives. Source: Museum of Modern Art, New York

02
Sint-Bavo, Haarlem. Photo © and source: Mark Pimlott

03
Interior of the Buurkerk, Utrecht. Pieter Jansz. Saenredam, 1645. Kimbell Art Museum AP 1986.09 © and source: Kimbell Art Museum, Fort Worth

04
Palazzo dalla Ragione, Padova. Photo courtesy © Marius Grootveld

05
The Market Hall, Richelieu. Photo Flickr user Malcolm Webb © Malcolm Webb. Source: https://www.flickr.com/photos/48308261@N04/19297600555/

06
Bastide Market, Cadouin. Photo Richard Kalvar. Magnum 55007742 © Hollandse Hoogte. Source: Magnum Photos

07
Graanbeurs, Middelburg. Photo Flickr user: Ben Willemsen © Ben Willemsen. Source: https://www.flickr.com/photos/mojekieke/7682791342/

08
Rialto, Mercato del Pesce, Venice, 1910. Photo © and source: Mark Pimlott

09–10
Rialto, Mercato, Venice. Photo © and source: Mark Pimlott

11
Halle aux Poissons et aux Huiles, Bruxelles. Photo © and source: Marius Grootveld

12
Les Halles centrales, Paris. Victor Balthard, 1875. Photo Roger Henrard 1952. 51936-6 © Hollandse Hoogte. Source: Roger Viollet

13
Halles centrales de Paris. Interior of central pavilion. Victor Balthard, 1875. Bibliothèque nationale de France RC-A-23881 © and source: Bibliothèque nationale de France, Paris

14
Les Halles centrales, Paris. Victor Balthard, 1875. Photo Charles Marville. 70249-15 © Hollandse Hoogte. Source: Roger Viollet

15
Halles centrales de Paris. Interior. Victor Balthard, 1875. Photo Charles Marville. 72147-17 © Hollandse Hoogte. Source: Roger Viollet

16
Les Halles centrales, Paris. Victor Balthard, 1874. Post card c.1900, photographer unknown. 25379-1 © Hollandse Hoogte. Source: Roger Viollet

17
Mercat Sant' Antoni, Barcelona. Antoni Rovira I Trias,1882. Photo © and source: Mark Pimlott

18
Mercat de la Boqueria (De Sant Josep), Barcelona. 1918. Photo Ritma C_025_157. © and source: Arxiu Fotogràfic de Barcelona

19
Gare du Nord, Paris. Photo © and source: Mark Pimlott

20
Gare du Nord, Paris. Photo © and source: Mark Pimlott

21
Liverpool Street Station, London. Photo © and source: Mark Pimlott

22
Pennsylvania Station, New York. Photo Berenice Abbott. New York Public Library 482562 © and source: The New York Public Library, 2016

23
Exposition universelle, Paris 1867. View on le Champs-de-Mars. Photographer unknown. © Public domain. Source: https://commons.wikimedia.org/wiki/File: Exposition_universelle_de_1867.png

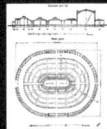
24
Galeries des machines. Exposition universelle, Paris, 1867. © Public domain. Source: Scan from: "De Opmerker Jaargang 2–1867"

25
Side view of the Galerie des machines, Paris. Ferdinand Dutert, 1889. H.-C. Godefroy. © and source: Brown University Library

26
The glass roof of the Grand Palais, Paris. Girault, Deglane, Louvet and Thomas, 1897–1900. Photographer unknown. 4380-3 © Hollandse Hoogte. Source: Roger Viollet

27
United States Pavilion, expo67, Montreal. R Buckminster Fuller, 1967. Photo Sam Tata. ARCH261911 © and source: CCA Collection Centre Canadien d'Architecture/Canadian Centre for Architecture, Montréal. Gift of May Cutler

28
United States Pavilion, expo67, Montreal. Interior. R Buckminster Fuller and Cambridge Seven Associates. Photo Sam Tata. ARCH261911 © and source: CCA Collection Centre Canadien d'Architecture/Canadian Centre for Architecture, Montréal. Gift of May Cutler

29
West Germany pavilion, expo67, Montreal. Frei Otto, 1967. Photo Sam Tata. ARCH266306 © and source: CCA Collection Centre Canadien d'Architecture/Canadian Centre for Architecture, Montréal. Gift of May Cutler

(iv) 30
United States Pavilion, EXPO70, Osaka. Davis Brody Associates, 1970. Photographer Unknown. © and source: Davis Brody Bond

(iv) 31–32
Neue Nationalgalerie, Berlin. Ludwig Mies van der Rohe, 1968. Photo © and source: Mark Pimlott

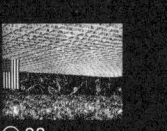

(iv) 33
Project for a Congress Hall, Chicago. Interior perspective, preliminary version. Ludwig Mies van der Rohe, 1954. Museum of Modern Art 572.1963 © Scala Archives. Source: Museum of Modern Art, New York

(iv) 34
Project for a train station. Students of Myron Goldsmith and Fazlur Khan, IIT. Source: Mark Pimlott

(iv) 35
Fun Palace. Interior perspective, Cedric Price c 1960. Centre Canadien d'Architecture/ Canadian Centre for Architecture DR1995:0188:123: 001 © Cedric Price fonds. Source: CCA

(iv) 36
Centre Georges Pompidou, Paris. Piano and Rogers, 1977. Photo © and source: Mark Pimlott

(iv) 37
De Meerpaal, Dronten. Frank van Klingeren, 1967. Photo Jan Versnel. © Jan Versnel/ MAI. Source: Maria Austria Instituut | MAI

(iv) 38–40
SESC-Fábrica Pompéia Sao Paulo, Brasil 1977–1986. Photographer unknown. © and source: Instituto Bardi, Sao Paulo

(iv) 41
Big Box store, Montréal. Photo © and source: Mark Pimlott

(iv) 42
Mall of America, Bloomington MN. Jon Jerde Associates, 1992. Photo © and source: Fenella Clemens

(iv) 43
Sainsbury Centre for Visual Arts, Norwich. Foster Associates, 1978. Photo Ken Kirkwood © Ken Kirkwood. Source: Norman Foster and Partners

(iv) 44
'Crystal Cathedral', Garden Grove Community Church, Garden Grove, CA, by night. Johnson Burgree architects, 1981. Photo Gordon H. Schenk. © and source: by permission of PJAR Architects

(iv) 45–46
FRAC Nord-Pas de Calais, Dunkerque. Lacaton et Vassal, 2013. Photo Philippe Ruault. © Philippe Ruault. Source: Lacaton et Vassal architectes

(iv) 47–48
Markthal/Stadshal, Ghent. Robbrecht en Daem, Marie Jose Van Hee, 2012. Photo © and source: Marius Grootveld

V
THE MACHINE

The machine has served as a metaphor for both the modern state and the metropolis throughout modernity. Nineteenth-century metropolitan Paris, in its transformation by Baron Georges-Eugène Haussmann, was regulated and organised like a machine. Its construction followed norms that aligned with those characteristics of repetition, efficacy and efficiency that were germane to machines. As the setting for the daily lives of millions, its aesthetic—its full expression—was impressed upon them through its forms. The appearances of Paris did not conform outwardly to those of many-wheeled metal behemoths—the machines of the infernal factory—yet were consistent with their nature. With the advent of electric light, the underground train (*le Métropolitain* or *Métro*) and the emergence of the motorcar, the aesthetic of the machine in the city, delivered by advances in technology, came to both represent the city's image and its traumas.[1]

In emerging modern states, procedures, regulations, organisations and formats were developed so that they might function with some degree of predictability; their many aspects were regulated so to be in balance, with their effects transferred to those working to execute them as well as those subject to them. The Western metropolis—a phenomenon of the mid-nineteenth century—came to rely upon more rigorous organisation and rationalisation of its processes, governance, bureaucracy, and ultimately, its forms. As each of these aspects grew in order of complexity, ever-more rigorous solutions were sought to relieve them, pursuing efficiencies and arriving at the design of systems—of organisations and 'structures'—to achieve them. The development of the modern state and that of the metropolis were in parallel; the metropolis was the most evident manifestation of both the problems of management of populations and physical solutions to them. The metropolis was subject to rapid growth and specific and myriad social and physical problems that were a consequence of that growth. The metropolitan condition was a phenomenon of great complexity that was difficult to control without extensive regulation. Populations grew in relation to the development of industry, which often found its place expediently, and the problems of housing, sanitation, health, public order and poverty soon emerged, their proliferation following the pressured conditions of the environment.

The assertion of control in the metropolis and the state was realised through attention to the issue of improvement, so that all aspects of their operations and functions would perform to expectations. This attention was not necessarily consistent in focus or motivation: it was taken up by various protagonists, some within government, some within the burgeoning civic society, and some independently, businessmen, philanthropists and philosophers among them. Yet by and large, common to these efforts of improvement were—because of their scale—approaches that reflected the efficiencies delivered by systems that tended to render organisations, processes, performance and structures (phenomenal and literal) within each subject of concern as effective and predictable as possible, repeated so to achieve clear and regularly occurring outcomes, whose workings might be comparable to those of a machine: one that could work without human interference. The scale of the system might be attuned to a specific task, or to the operation of much more complex organisations and their correlate objectives. The modern state constructed systems to address its formidable burdens of society, economy, bureaucracy, institutions, and their management. The term 'state apparatus' indicated the vast complexity and *machine-like* character of the means of the bureaucratic—and often authoritarian—state that arose in modernity. This machine-like character was reflected in the shaping of institutions; in the forming of professions; in professional education; in the realisation of policy; in buildings and the organisation of activity within them; and in the city—the metropolis in particular—and its spaces, all of which were used and experienced by citizens, who were furthermore shaped by them. The state's systemic address of the problems germane to it were reflected in the programmes and methodologies of scientific and engineering academies and their approaches to problems of the equipment of the state and the city: its institutions and infrastructures and the approaches to their construction, as well as the forms of institutions for improvement, repair and even reform of the body and the mind. The governance of the state was reorganised, and the city was recast as a complete infrastructural system, including its form and its representations, at all scales. A regulated and formulaic approach was applied to the places and interiors of the city, and the metropolis in particular.

Mechanisation in factories increasingly met with ideas geared to increase the productivity of their workers. The principles of scientific management founded by Frederick Taylor (1856–1915) scrutinised processes of work in the factory and the office in order to improve their efficiency, and this too led to machine-like conditions in the places of work. Interpretations of Taylorism would see workers acting in complete symbiosis with their machines; their bodies fitted and groomed to the machines they operated. The machine as representative of the repression of the worker and the metropolitan citizen, and the corresponding overthrow of the machine as a motif for the emancipation of the worker has been an abiding theme since the advent of industrialisation, from the Luddite movement (1811–1816) to the fictive revolution of subterranean workers in Fritz Lang's *Metropolis* (1927). In contrast, the machine-metropolis was embraced by Futurists such as the architect Antonio Sant'Elia, the poet Filippo Tomasso Marinetti and the painters Umberto Boccione and Carlo Carrà, who saw the mechanisation of the city and its citizens positively, realising the modern epoch's potential. Le Corbusier's ode to the machine's purity and corresponding beauty, in his *Vers une architecture* (1927); his declaration that a house was a 'machine for living' and his enthusiasm for aerial machines and their capacities for ennoblement of the human spirit and surveillance of the urban condition was representative of an aesthetic of the machine. Modernism's 'machine aesthetic,' which was more than a matter of appearance, but a matter of its total performance and its relation to its users and subjects, was innate to Modernism in architecture, and the 'International Style'[2] in particular, and incorporated and fused into the scientific management systems that characterised corporate modernism and the architecture of the office from the 1950s onward.

THE MACHINE

The emergence of the modern nation state and the metropolis was met by the development of building types whose object was to process their users, and whose organisation and spaces were instrumental in achieving certain patterns of behaviour in them, handling them and shaping activities to achieve predictable effects. There were those that transformed their users from one way of being to another: from unwell to well; from criminal to reformed citizen; or from citizen to consumer or citizen to passenger. All of these transformations were effected within their interiors, whose spaces engaged or handled significant numbers of people who were treated as a mass. Individuals entered, things happened to them, and they were passed through staged processes, events and experiences. There were core conditions, such as convalescing in a ward, or shopping in a mall, or watching a spectacle, or even dancing, but therein there were always processes that sent people, with great efficiency, to the exit and/or into the world, with something having been done to them; with some change effected. These interiors were conceived as machines, in operation if not in appearance. In our view of the public interior so far, we have repeatedly encountered the phenomenon of the metropolis and the distended city, which, because of its size and complexity, has been a testing bed for solutions regarding the very problems it has generated. The metropolis as a designed phenomenon—in opposition to the intensity of its chaos—has demonstrated its makers' consciousness of its ambitions in legislation, regulation, its spaces and its appearances and a corresponding desire for identity in architecture. These ambitions have been proposed to its citizens, asking them to involve themselves in the metropolis's abiding fictions; while the shared and public interiors of the metropolis—wherever its ideas have been manifested—have been the spaces in which they have been tested, and where the city's idea of itself has been displayed and played back to its citizens, reinforcing their identification with it, with each other and their ways of behaviour. The public interior has at once accommodated its users (its subjects), played to them, charmed them and manipulated them.

The modern era does not have an exclusive hold on the machine aesthetic, its full range of attributes and ensuing relations that it implies: the collective complexes of ancient Rome dealt with the issues of use specific to large numbers of citizens, for leisure and spectacle. The Colosseum is renowned for its workings and its managements of audiences, prisoners and animals, all in the service of mass spectacle. The great Baths of Diocletian and Caracalla were giant working machines, not only in the sense that they kept water for ablutions at various temperatures (*Caldarium*, *Tepidarium*, *Frigidarium*), but managed the movement, processing and pleasures of a great many people—perhaps some 3,000 at a time in the case of the Baths of Diocletian, 1,600 in the Baths of Caracalla—through the prescribed processes inscribed in their chambers. The spaces of the Baths of Caracalla and their management of people directly inspired McKim, Mead and White's design for Pennsylvania Station in New York (1910, demolished 1968), which we have encountered on several occasions, concerning the quotation of the 'ruin' of the Baths of Caracalla as imagery, and the relation of the iron structures of the shed in relation to these 'ruins'. The main hall's appearance was derived from historical reconstructions of the Baths in their pomp, and effectively reconstructed and re-presented in a manner consistent with approach to the construction of American institutions at that time. Beaux-Arts Classicism legitimated the American project, insofar as it replayed European themes, and McKim, Mead and White were its representative architects. The hall's orchestration of the complex movement and interaction of many travellers, paths, connections and trains echoed the Baths of Caracalla's organisation, conduct and distribution of crowds. The Baths and the station both operated to achieve predictable and highly controlled performances, despite the diverse and individualised experience within them. The machine-like organisation of each—spatial, functional and technological—was given a representational form that communicated the character of its ideas to their users. In the case of the Baths, they assumed the imagery of Roman basilicas and their aura of higher purpose, while the station assumed the imagery of the Baths to borrow the ancient city's aura of ultimate centrality. This 'dressing' of the machine was closely bound to its aesthetic and its workings. We shall see machines that, in the service of control, left their workings brazenly visible; and those that clothed, decorated or disguised their workings in order to make their prescriptions more palatable, and even pleasant, to their users.

From the onset of modernity in the mid-eighteenth century, demands particular to scale and number—essential dimensions of both the nation state and the large city—were accompanied by the need for an increasing variety of building types that could accommodate increasing specialisation within the operations of society. These new types would come to represent the authority of the nation state through institutions that demonstrated mastery of the complexity of the tasks they faced. There were problems that were exacerbated by increasingly larger numbers of people that threatened the state's operation: issues of health and behaviour; problems of governance, of order; of storage. New institutions, serving the workings of the state and those serving the state of society, could address them. Their creation, and that of other fiscal and regulatory devices required extensive work on methodology, and the ordering, regulation management of an entire state and society, which would be both realised and represented through buildings.

TYPE

Formal and organisational problems of buildings and infrastructures particular to a new order of scale required solutions that could be applied and repeated broadly. Notable schools in France pursued this: the École Polytechnique, and highly specialised institutions concerned with training those who would enact operations of the state at strategic, bureaucratic and instrumental levels, such as the École Nationale des Ponts et Chaussées (1747). Their efforts—representative of Enlightenment thought—were put to the purpose of reforming the institutions of state and society on the basis of reason and scientific method. So it followed that the devices and equipment provided for society—its institutions and infrastructure—would follow rational bases and improve society. In buildings, this was reflected in the design of institutions that were centred on the achievement for desired forms for a vast society, as well as its reform: the reform of the body through the hospital, the reform of the individual through the prison. This was paralleled by efforts of individuals and movements concerning the inequitable consequences of industrialisation, and the desire for the reform of the conditions of working people, represented by projects for ideal communities and/or communal dwellings.

Jean-Nicolas-Louis Durand (1760–1834), Professor from 1795 at the École Polytechnique (founded as the *École Centrale des Travaux Publics* in 1794), taught architecture through the exposition of types. The idea of the *type*—through which essential and abstract characteristics form indelible bases for architectural models to follow—was developed by Antoine-Chrysostome Quatremère de Quincy (1755–1849),

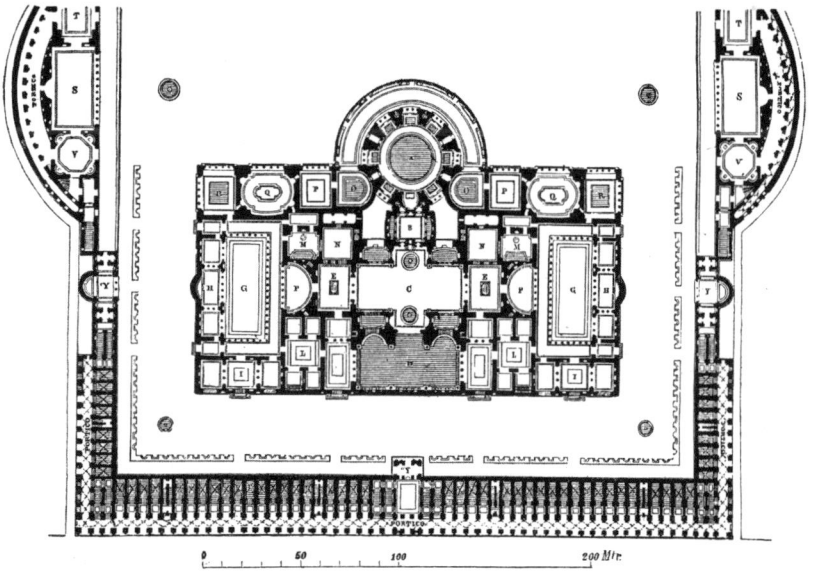

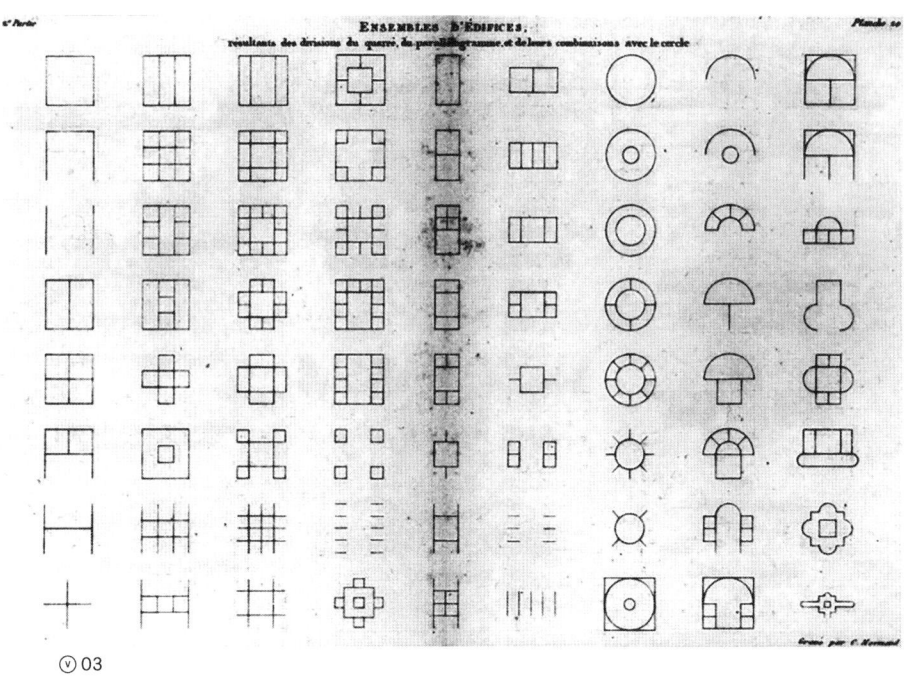
ⓥ 03

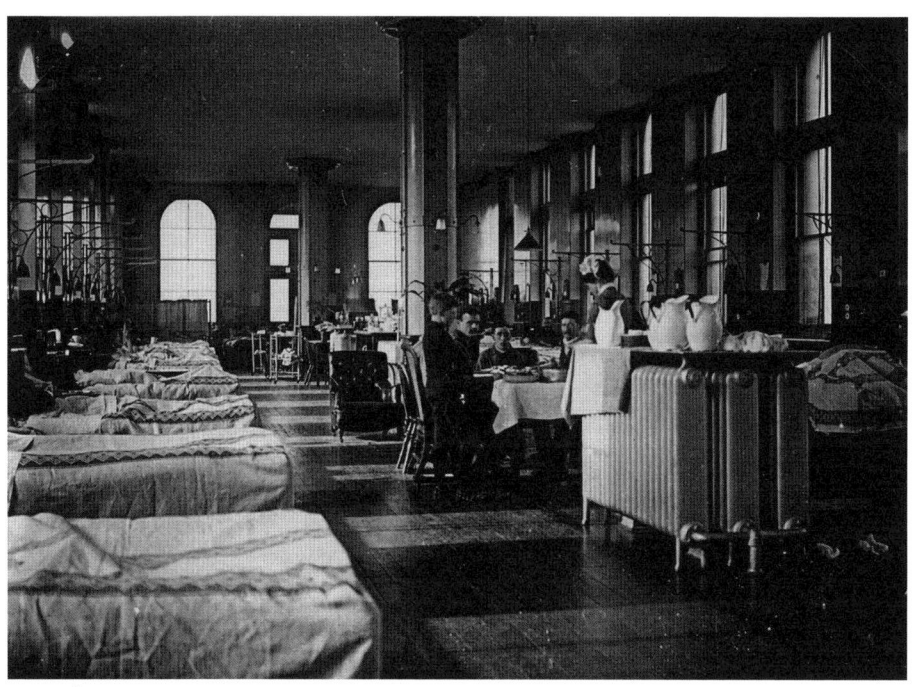
ⓥ 04

and articulated in his *Dictionnaire d'architecture* (1788). The type as described by Quatremère de Quincy emerged from his assessment that the origins of architecture were the outcome of specific environmental and cultural conditions that forged characteristic figures, whose essences repeated themselves within locally specific architecture: a deep and culturally specific structure at the origins of subsequent constructions and their styles.[3] In a sense, type persisted as a deep pattern, and its implementation acted as a guarantor for a designed structure's workings, the engine within an architectural vehicle. Durand's architectural education system, based within classicism rather than any locally specific language, seemed to use this idea, as the pattern diagrams that accompanied his course suggest. Durand's two great contributions were a study, *Recueil et parallèle des edifices de tout genre, anciens et modernes* (1799), and a summary of his lectures, *Nouveau précis des leçons d'architecture données à l'École polytechnique* (1809). Durand prescribed the classification and ordering of buildings according to deep patterns visible within the plan (in particular), and offered a rational basis for architectural organisation that constituted a set of guidelines or rules of engagement for architects. If followed correctly, the architect would arrive at an appropriate solution, within which the logic of the type was deeply inscribed, bound to the composition of the plan and its volumes, and the determination of its structural and representational order. The idiom in which these patterns were articulated was inevitably classical, though one might imagine these patterns served by any manner appropriate to the conditions in which they would be applied. Durand considered these published works 'encyclopædia' or 'architectural museums'.[4] The patterns set out by Durand were employed to build structures that represented the large and far-reaching apparatus of the State. The elemental structures offered to illustrate his *Leçons* can be seen inscribed in the proposals of the visionary architect Etienne-Louis Boullée, and generations of École des Beaux-Arts-trained architects that followed. These patterns were the foundation of the architectural language of the nineteenth-century institution in France, and were influential internationally thereafter. International students from the École des Beaux-Arts brought its principles back home with them, and early twentieth-century architecture in the United States vividly illustrates their influence.

Ⓥ 03

THE SICK, THE INFIRM, THE INSANE, THE DEVIANT

Among the earliest issues that demanded rational and consequent attention was that of the sick and infirm, and their care and treatment in hospitals. The task of the earliest of these was palliative care. The first hospitals emerged from religious foundations, in halls and cloisters. Religious communities of monks and nuns provided care, shelter and food for the poor and the sick, in institutions before the age of dedicated institutions, such as in the Hôtel-Dieu, Paris (651). Their work was reinforced by Charlemagne's declaration, consistent with his plan for the restoration of hospitals in the late eighth and early ninth centuries, that all cathedrals and monasteries in the Holy Roman Empire should have hospitals attached: the Benedictine Abbey hospital at Cluny (910) was exemplary. In England in the sixteenth century, the dissolution of monasteries by Henry VIII (1540) set hospitals in the hands of citizens. There and elsewhere, the Enlightenment saw the emergence of what we

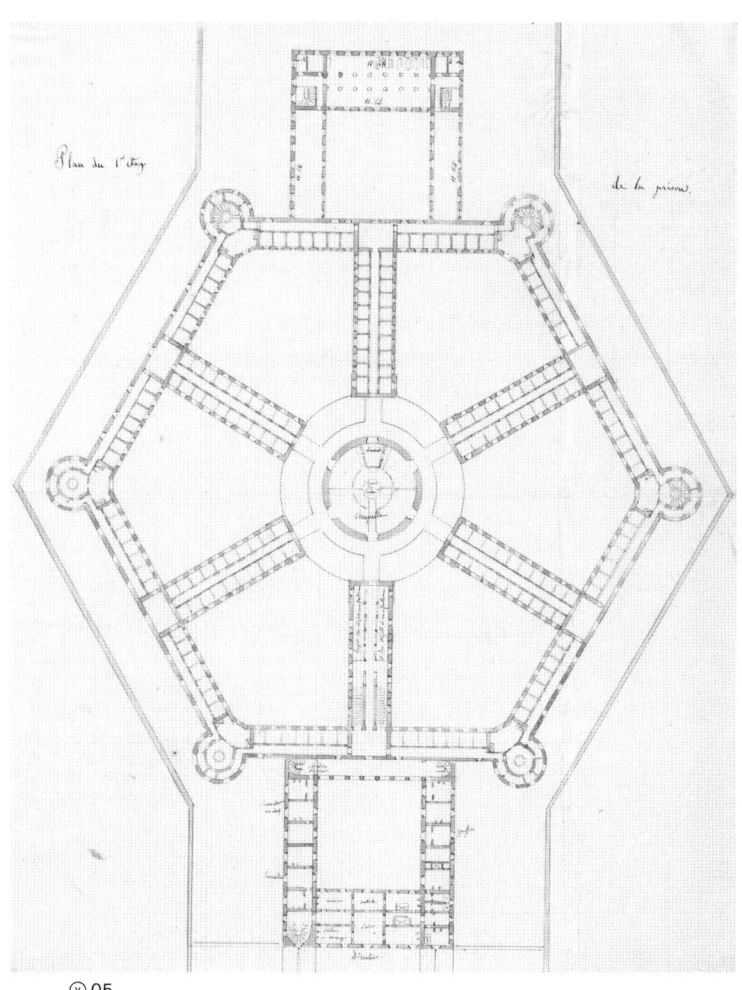

ⓥ 05

ⓥ 04

consider the modern hospital or the hospital as a machine: organised on the bases of observation of patients, and the isolation and treatment of specific types of ailments in different departments. In Britain, following the Apothecaries Act of 1815, professional medical practice was mandatory: hospitals[5] became places in which physicians practiced medicine on professional basis, and where medical education and training occurred. Florence Nightingale (1820–1910), witnessing the appalling suffering of soldiers in field hospitals during the Crimean War, campaigned for the modernisation of patient care, nursing, hospital administration and sanitary conditions, which had a profound influence on the architecture of patient wards that can be recognised still. These wards were rational, and, despite their bases in human care and contact, relentlessly regular in character and form.

The organisation of hospital plans echoed the processes of treatment contained within them, and represented machine-like approaches to the solution of problems. This was particularly apparent in plans for hospitals for the mentally ill or the insane, as they were generally categorised, such as St Mary of Bethlehem (known as Bethlem, or Bedlam) in South London, designed by James Lewis (1815) and Robert Smirke (the architect of the British Museum (1835 and after)), and those institutions—largely in the United States—that derived from it, which shared many

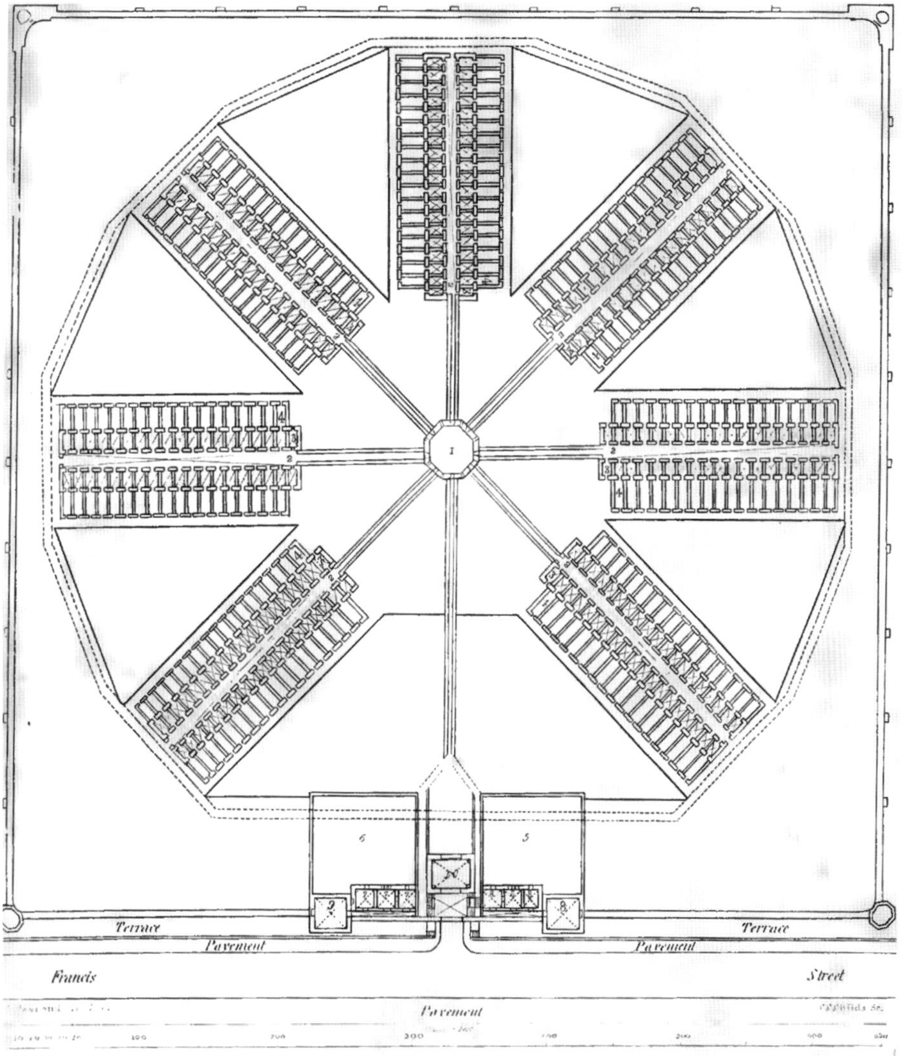

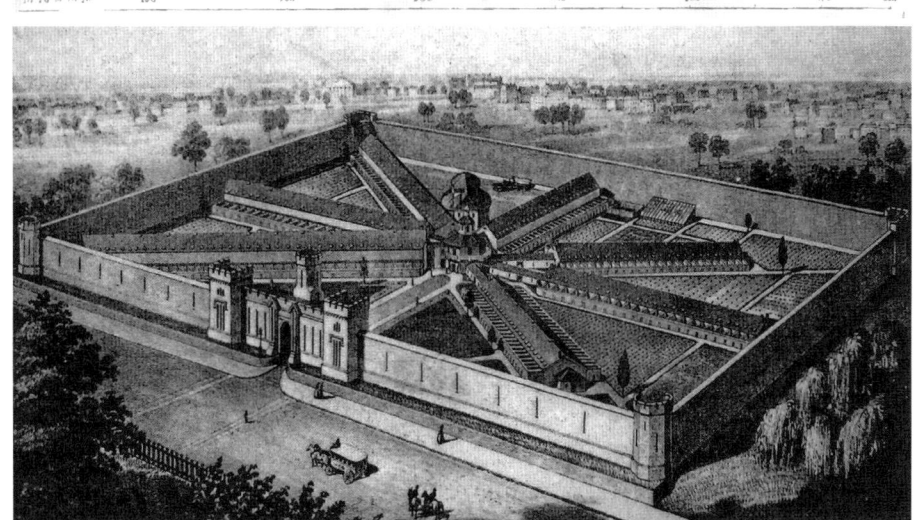

ⓥ 06–07

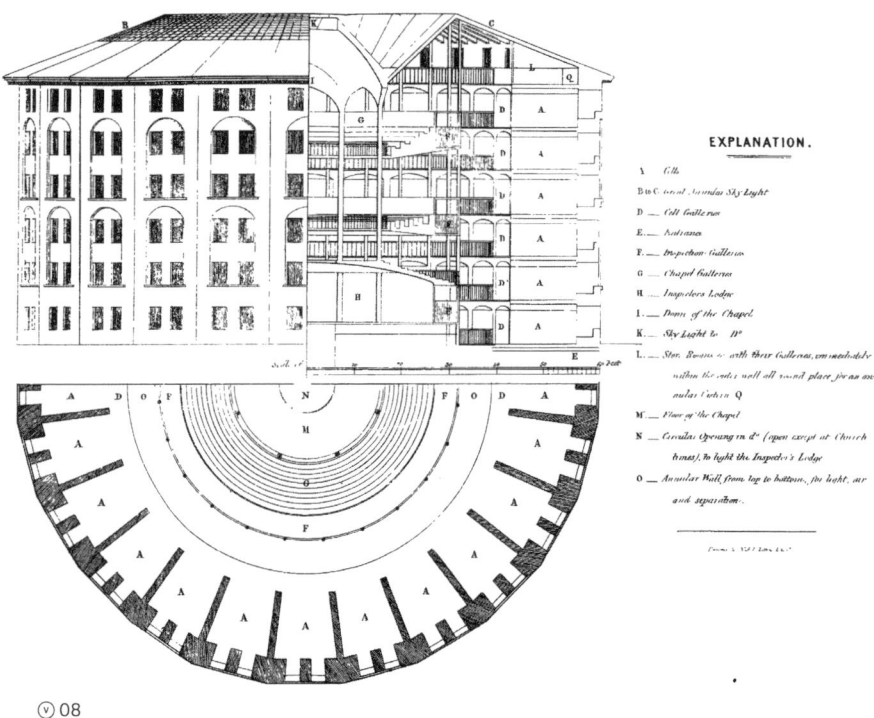

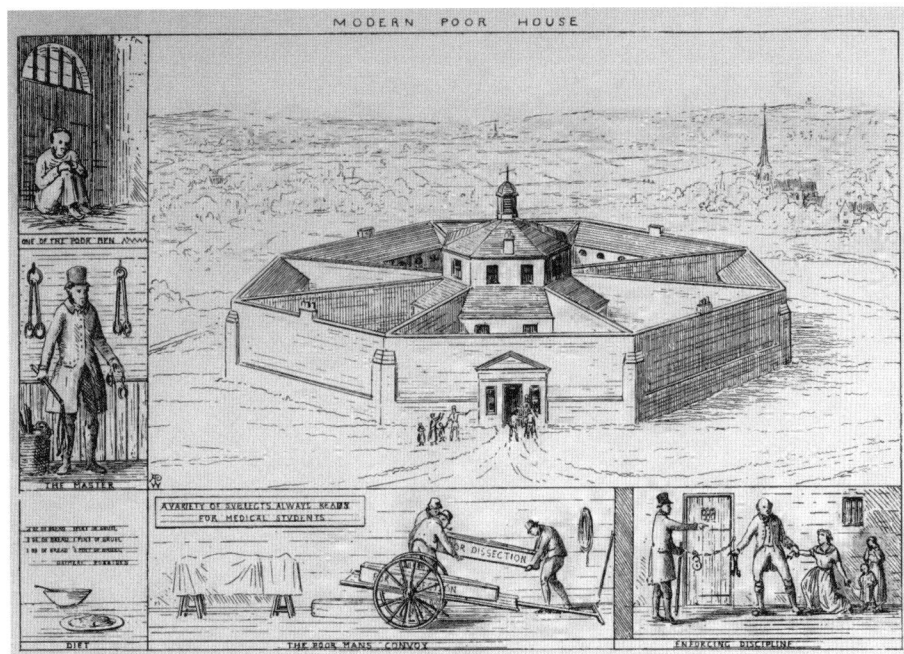

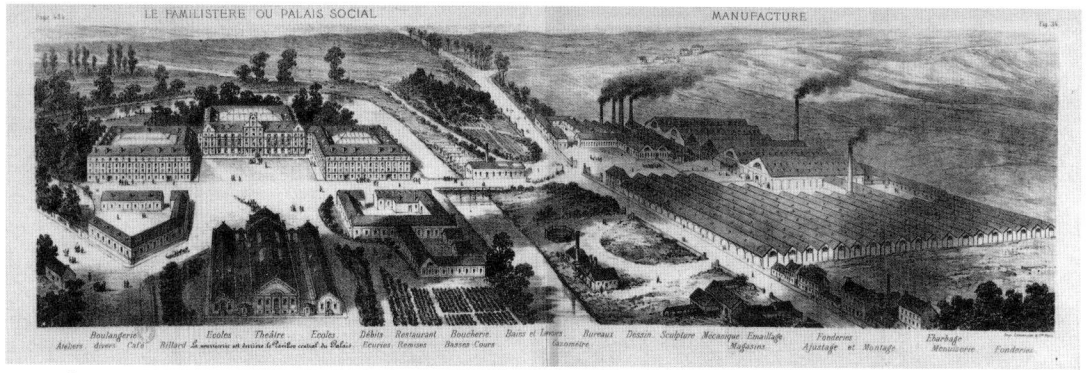

of the characteristics of the design of prisons. In these, convicts were placed under supervision, isolated from one another and controlled, as in rationalised hospital design, where patients suffering from contagious conditions were isolated from each other. In prisons, criminals and deviants were to be punished and *transformed*; a transformation that would be achieved through restrictions of the body and association with others, segregated and surveyed. The design of prisons approached that of machines for 'breaking' offenders. The philanthropist, philosopher and reformer Jeremy Benthem (1748–1832) devised a prison design—the Panopticon (1797)—in which all movements of prisoners could be effectively surveyed through an invention that made prisoners believe they were being watched at all times. The design was centred on a central interior watchtower. All prison cells would be closed to each other but open, through barred doors, to the view of the tower and the gaze (or not) of a monitor who occupied it, who could watch all the cells at once. The prisoner could not see the occupant of the tower due to its design, and could not determine whether he was being watched or not. The only conclusion the prisoner could arrive at was that he was under constant surveillance, and therefore induced into behaving in accordance with the tightly proscribed regime of the prison. The gaze or its idea from within tower was palpable in all cells and to all prisoners and, in its representation of the complete authority of the State itself, inescapable. Michel Foucault wrote that the Panopticon was 'the diagram of a mechanism of power reduced to its ideal form.'[6]

COLLECTIVE HEALING

Through much of the nineteenth century, the treatment of the poor shared characteristics with that of criminals: their freedoms were sacrificed so that their debts might be redeemed through work. Their behaviour was controlled and reduced as a consequence; accommodation for the poor—debtors and their families—often resembled that of prisons. There was a desire to reform this situation, and to find other, more humane means to relieve the poor. It was thought that new building types might help create a better society, and provide models for social utopias that would transcend the venality that was so often characterised as the lot of the impoverished, and the scourge of society.

In his book *Contrasts* (1836), Augustus Welby Northmore Pugin (1812–1852) presented the decency of certain kinds of care for the poor, in the medieval cloister as an alternative model contrasted with the prison-based workhouse.[7] The cloister model offered by Pugin, in which people were meant to be inspired to live 'correctly'

Ⓥ 12

Ⓥ 13

within a complex that balanced worshipful practice, family life and work, was also an ideological model that could be repeated and deployed *in toto*: a machine for better living.

The reform movements were at once a legacy of the Enlightenment and critiques of the prevalent inequalities within society, including those embodied by the metropolis. Models were offered—arrangements, plans, buildings, interiors and urban propositions—as agents for an improved society. Some radical reformers proposed overturning the existing order, and imagined new societies and new devices to deliver them, often in the form of new settlements isolated from the harmful effects of the world. Charles Fourier (1772–1837) and his colleague and disciple Victor Considerant (1808–1893) proposed utopian communities, given form— *phalanstères*—which they characterised as 'grand hotels' but we might regard as palaces put to the service of workers rather than rulers, whose occupants would be liberated through their free choice of work, their own education and their freedom to pursue individual passions and capacities. Their object, according to Fourier—a visionary with many progressive views (and several that were lamentable)—was to completely transform civilisation, which he saw as constrictive and punitive. His view was that labour should be transformed into pleasure, and to achieve this, labour had to be attractive, and so the passions of individuals needed to be recognised and cultivated so that they might develop completely fulfilling existences. His theories about people and their passions generated the *phalanstère*'s characteristics: twelve common passions were thought to yield 810 types of character, and taking into account male and female—who Fourier regarded as equals—he determined each 'phalanx' or 'colony' should accommodate 1620 adults, who would pursue their work and their interests with joy. The radicality of Fourier's proposal was reflected in the composition of collective dwellings proposed by the Russian Constructivists (such as Moisei Ginzburg's Narkomfin building in Moscow, 1929). The ideal buildings of the *phalanstère* were presented with the outward form of palaces or workers' Versailles: they were hierarchical, with those of greatest individual motivation at the top. The American Fourierist colonies—Utopia in Ohio or La Réunion, founded by Considerant in Texas 1855 with the help of Jean-Baptiste-André Godin—were short-lived. However, another with a rather less radical yet generous social programme—a *familistère*—was established in Guise, in northern France, and devised and sponsored by Godin, in 1865. It was a phalanx-like community tied to a stove and cooking equipment factory, and accommodated in a grouping of buildings for living that included a *palais social*. In its interior, apartments on several levels were arranged around a central, top-lit space 20×40m, and connected by galleries. The day-lit courtyard—the representative interior of the *familistère*, and partner to its palatial exterior—was designed to relieve the workers of inclement weather conditions, and to allow children to play indoors throughout the year. Day nurseries were also provided so that children's parents might be free for some time to carry on their own interests. The courtyard also served a social space for communal events under the light of the sky. In this collective interior, all residents and the hierarchies that defined their place in that closed society of 1,200 people living in 350 apartments were visible to each other.

ⓥ 14

COMPANY TOWNS

Reform movements dedicated to the improvement of the lot of the worker frequently prescribed machine-oriented remedies for the conditions of repression and dehumanisation wrought by the machine, and idealised life that would be played out in new settlements or institutions of a 'mechanical' character that shaped behaviour. The *familistère* at Guise bound Godin's company and its workers together into one 'society', which could be claimed to be a voluntary agreement between the company and its workers. However, arrangements 'tying' workers to companies in set architectural arrangements abounded in the nineteenth century in Europe and North America: larger communities in which a whole town would be dedicated to the production of one company, in which working and living would be incorporated in one design, were called company towns. These towns, their shared spaces and interiors, embodied the idea of how their citizens were to relate to their employers (patrons) and each other. The configuration and expression of those spaces were controlled in order to effect predictable behaviour in its citizen-workers, which were reinforced by informal legislation and contractual obligations.[8]

ⓥ 14

The town of Chaux-Arc et Senans (1804), designed by Claude Nicolas Ledoux (1736–1806) was a precursor to the company town. The town was in fact a salt works, in which all of its buildings spoke of their labour through their *architecture parlante*. All parts of its radial layout led the eye to its representative administrative centre. Company towns dedicated to the production of single commodities sprang up across Europe: Alfred Krupp effectively transformed Essen into a company town for his steel works in the 1860s; in the United States, the most well known company town was Pullman, outside Chicago, established in 1880. Chicago hosted a series of such towns in its expansive territories, connected to the city by rail, keeping workers under control and apart from each other, so they could not gather or protest about their working conditions. George Pullman's objective was to create an environment in which workers and production could be completely controlled through a complex of 'soft' measures. The workers, isolated from agitators in the city, could consider the satisfaction of their improved living conditions in a quasi-urban setting, at whose heart was a factory that produced luxury railway carriages. In town, the behaviour of workers and their families was monitored and moral pressure was asserted through internal legislation and conditions—on rent, for example—and through its normative architecture and plan.[9] The plan's repetitive layout rendered the hierarchy of the company town visible, with the company and its benefactor central to the town's representative imagery, with its theatre, hotel arcade and view of the factory premises contrasted with the fabric of dwellings rented by its workers, and its regular

15–16

distribution of places of worship. All were entirely dependent on George Pullman. The designs of the houses were carefully controlled, their distinctions calibrated, and residents under the conditions of their leases were obliged to maintain their appearance. The entire town—its houses, churches, streets, park and arcade—was subject to a condition of interiority whose total design impelled norms of behaviour determined by its sponsor, owner and operator. The buildings around the town's most public space were arranged to demonstrate the hierarchy of power and the limits of 'citizenship' therein; shopping was ordered within an arcade that was contained, rather than leading anywhere. One might regard the Company Town, and Pullman in particular, as a model of how the relation between corporations (and the states that advocate on their behalf) and workers were idealised: as interiorising machines in which workers' working, domestic and public lives could be controlled and instrumentalised within carefully calibrated representative environments.

THE CITY AS MACHINE

Some urbanists of the nineteenth and twentieth centuries asked if a working model could be devised at the scale of a self-contained colony or company town, why couldn't a system be arrived at for a larger urban structure, taking care of the distribution of dwellings and places of work, integrating necessary connective infrastructure and integrating the urban construction with landscape and its structures? The solutions for so-called linear cities all attempted to solve problems of urban distribution, growth, transport and hierarchy within single gestures, in which the infrastructure of transport and services would be central. All other urban functions would be connected to this infrastructure, which would become the central representative figure of the shared urban interior. All of these linear cities, from Alberto Soria y Mata's Ciudad Lineal for Madrid (1882), through Edgar Chambliss's Road Town (1910), Ivan Leonidov's and the OSA group's projects for Magnitogorsk (1930), Paul Rudolph's Manhattan Expressway (1967–1972) and Michael Graves and Peter Eisenman's project for a Linear City (1969) were effectively megastructures, whose outward forms and correlate interiors primarily represented their organisation and hierarchy, which were inevitably in the hands of administrative or political authority, and dependent upon their vitality.

ⓥ 15–16

There was something in these projects of the spirit of Eugène Hénard's work in Paris at the end of the nineteenth century: indeed, Hénard, to whom we will return, was re-evaluated in the 1960s by architects[10] who recognised that new architectural projections increasingly tended toward the condition of infrastructure: pursuing this tendency would yield a new kind of public interior that reflected the structure of the city as a whole. The megastructure, that monumental framework that contained and determined all subsidiary components—a complete infrastructure of exaggerated structural expression—was characteristic of the urban projections of the 1960s.[11] The Manhattan Transit Authority terminal, New York (1962) designed by Pier Luigi Nervi was one such realised project, which extended the George Washington Bridge, incorporated the terminal, and served as the core for a chain of office blocks above with interiors that bore the character of its grounding in traffic management. Paul Rudolph's later project for the Lower Manhattan Expressway,[12] commissioned by the Ford Foundation imagined—like Hénard's projections—

ⓥ 17

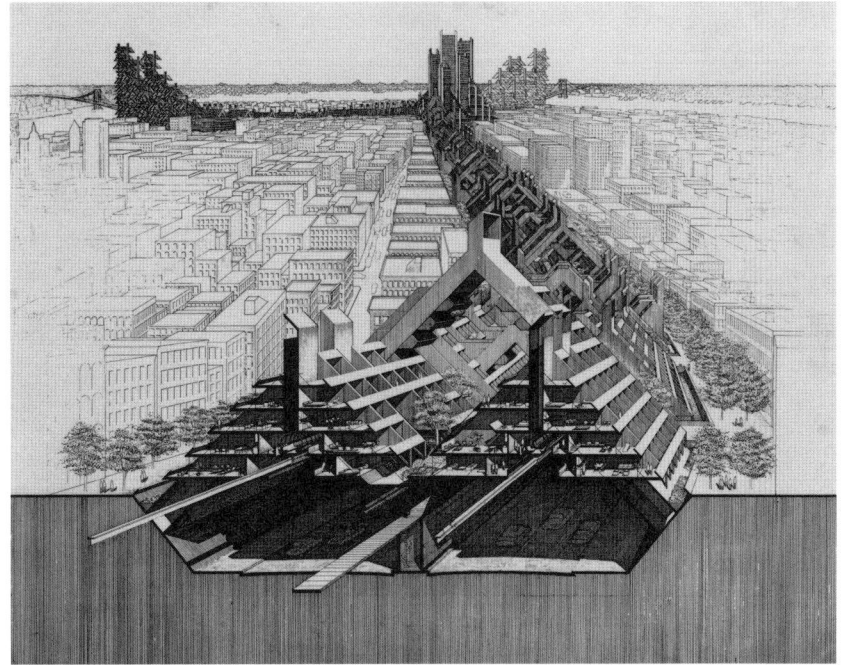
ⓥ 18

the whole city as an interconnected structure: a network, and a great piece of processing machinery. The megastructure embodied the idea of the processing and distribution of services, vehicles and people (in that order of priority). Every part of the megastructure's large-scale construction was subservient to a central structural motif, which ultimately depended on a central administrative or directional authority. This dependence was a structural weakness, so the megastructure came to a formal dead end despite its international currency among architects.[13]

ⓥ 18–20

HAUSSMANNIAN PARIS AS MACHINE

In the guise of reform, one could observe the development of an instrumental architecture, and appreciate its spatial consequences, particularly in the public interior. In the construction of the metropolis, many devices were created that managed the movement and behaviour of crowds, from the railway station through the department store. We have considered Paris repeatedly in these chapters, primarily because of its pre-eminence as the Western metropolis of the nineteenth century. The treatment of the masses in Paris after 1850 was an integral aspect of its design; from its regulation to its infrastructural systems and architectural expression, it bore the character of a carefully adjusted and well-appointed machine.

The radical modernisation of Paris as devised by Baron Georges-Eugène Haussmann, Prefect of the Seine Department under the Emperor Louis Napoléon III, entailed the complete re-organisation of the city fabric and its administration (1853–1870). The city was partitioned (and bound) by a new system of avenues and boulevards cut through the existing street pattern, involving extensive compulsory purchases and demolitions, work that can be described as the destruction of medieval Paris.[14] The city's new thoroughfares divided the city into different administrative zones or *arrondissements*, each with their own responsibilities and authority for collecting taxes. The new roads also provided the opportunity to revise the city's

ⓥ 21–26

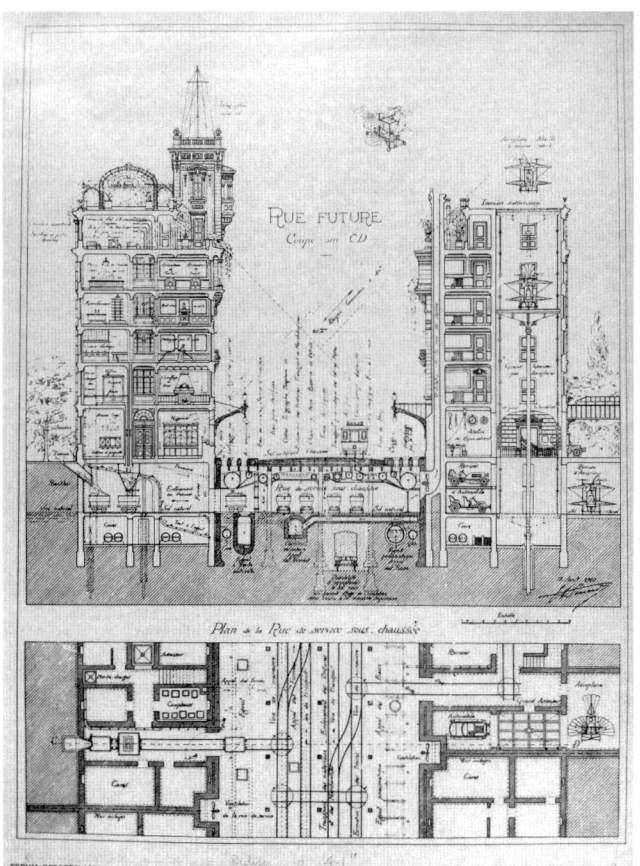 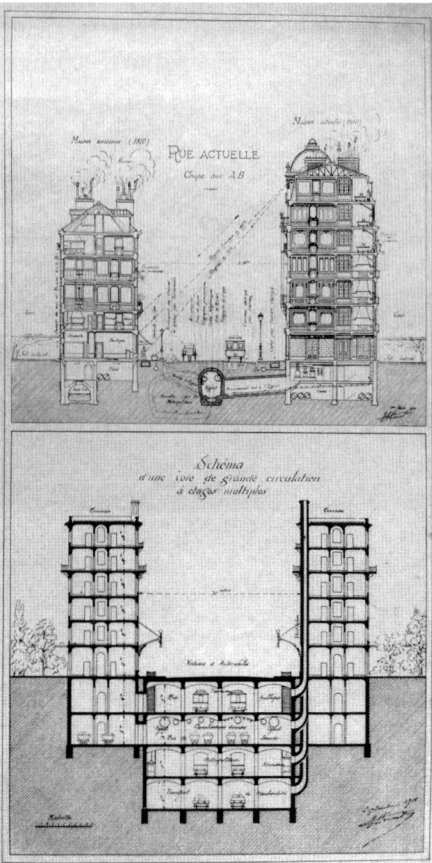

ⓥ 19–20

infrastructure (water, sewage, métropolitain railway, pneumatic post), and became express routes for the rapid deployment of emergency services (and armed forces). They furthermore provided building developers with many kilometres of 'new' real estate to exploit, producing many kilometres of new building façades. These gave the city a completely new appearance—derived from its previous character, but altered—and set out an orthodoxy regarding Paris's self-image that would be projected into the future. New façades were obliged to conform to strict codes of appearance, composition, expression and materialisation. The buildings—or *immeubles*—were organised in compliance with legislation, visible both in their elevations and their sections, which suggested how the various levels of the social hierarchy might be distributed within their interiors. Outside in the street, and from rooms within buildings, one knew one's place in the city and within the social order. The new streets of Paris built under the Haussmann directives were widely decried as alienating, yet they produced a recognisable and ordered metropolitan environment that would condition the populace's behaviour therein. The new city-wide public interior thus created—full of effects—was animated by an array of standardised street furniture including lamps, bins, urinoires, kiosks, advertising columns and benches; while its myriad cafés, and their own standard equipment and fare constituted an infrastructure in their own right.

The streets' regularity—a network of broad, straight routes—allowed them to be easily monitored, thereby deterring insubordination in the citizenry: military

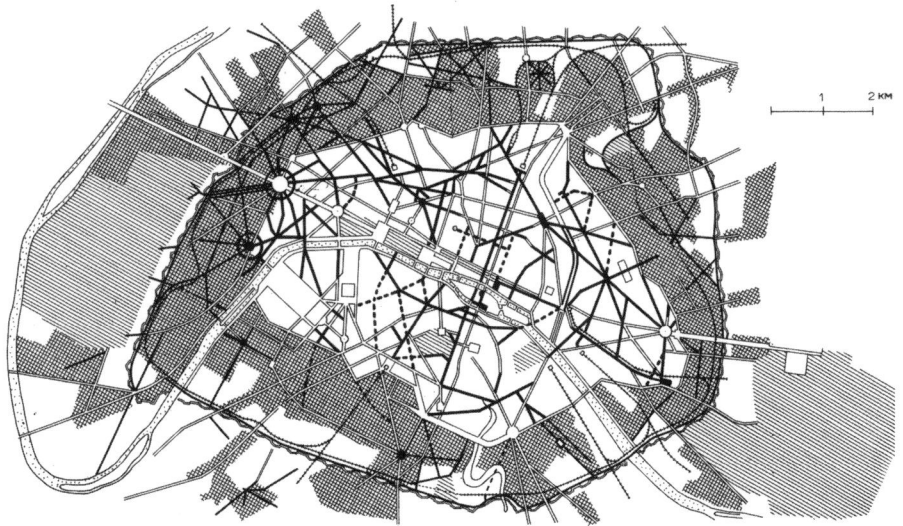

79 - Esquema de los *percements* efectuados por Haussmann; en blanco las calles ya existentes, en negro las abiertas durante el Segundo Imperio; en cuadrícula los nuevos barrios; en rayado las zonas verdes.

ⓥ 21–22

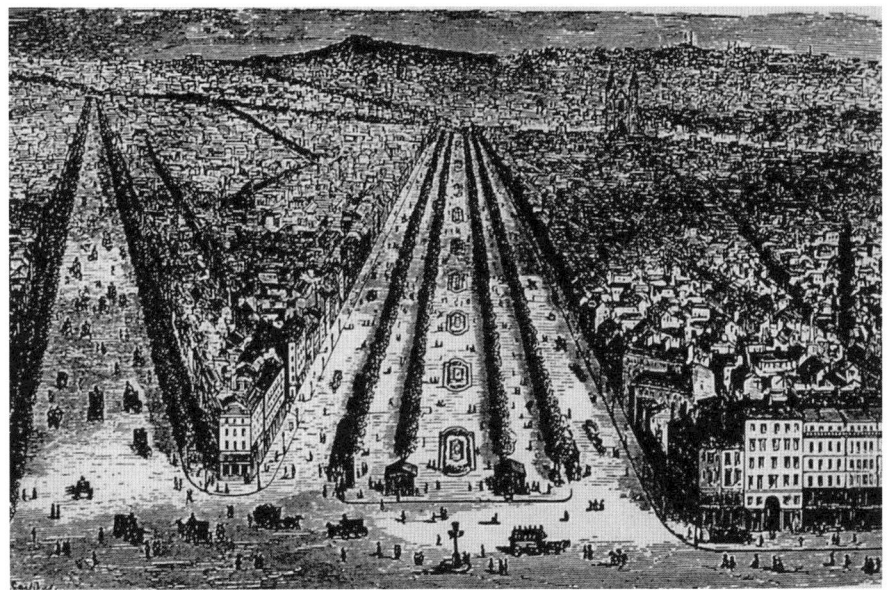
(v) 23

(v) 24

ⓥ 25

forces could be deployed quickly across the city to dispel disorder and suppress insurrections. Within this framework—a vast device for both control and performance—there were fragments, interiors in particular, that extended or elaborated its workings, and presented these as spectacle. The department stores or *grands magasin* that we have seen on several occasions in this series were machines for consumption, designed to effect expenditure at a maximum level.[15] The circulation within and the relations of displayed items to its movements were devised to effect maximum visibility according to the principles of the correct placement of goods in relation to the consumer and his/her itinerary through the space of the store. These principles have come to be developed to a very high degree—as a kind of science based in psychology—in both the contemporary department store and the shopping mall.

In this context, Les Halles Centrales (1853–1857) could also be regarded as a machine, one that worked efficiently within the network of neighbouring streets, and in its totality, its arrangement of sheds and streets operating as a system that

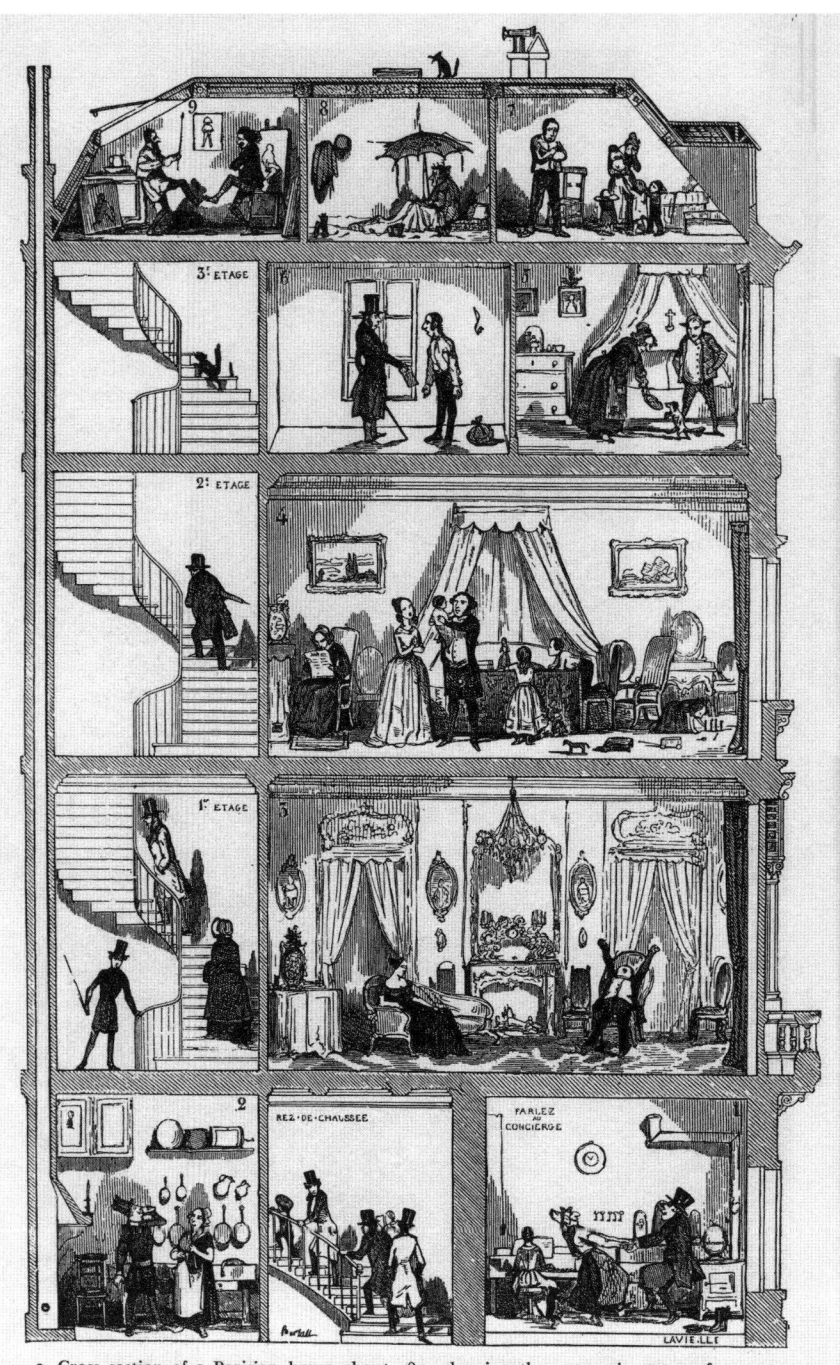

3. Cross section of a Parisian house about 1850 showing the economic status of tenants varying by floors. (Edmund Texier, *Tableau de Paris*, Paris, 1852, I, 65.)

processed and distributed the various products under its roofs. The planning of Les Halles was consistent with that of Haussmannian Paris, and was continuous with its principles. The structures of Les Halles worked like one coordinated machine, and they shared this characteristic, evident in their representative spaces, with the more monumental new figures of the metropolis.

SPECTACLE

The Opéra (1860–1875) designed by Charles Garnier (1825–1898) was a spectacular building, or rather, a building offered as a spectacle. It was placed at the end of the new diagonally oriented Avenue de l'Opéra that had been carved into the city by Haussmann, and was the most conspicuous ornament of the entire plan. The interiors were very elaborate both in their decoration and their interrelation, and together, they choreographed the movement of audiences as they arrived, lingered and departed. This movement began from a great distance away from the building, and the view of its main façade from the *Comédie française*. The new Avenue acted as a conveyor belt for the movement that was designed within the theatre itself. For the majority, stairs from the Place de l'Opéra led into the interior, and the visitor was swept into the sequence of spaces that ultimately led to the auditorium. All were decorated in the manner of a palace, and indeed the features of the interior suggested the sequences of movement associated with the palace that we have encountered earlier, and the object of transformation of audiences that was germane to the palace as both a phenomenon and a type. A grand salon situated on the *belle étage* looked back down the Avenue and, with a curiously artificial atmosphere, played the part of being the great ballroom for the city's *élite* for the evening. However, what was most remarkable about the Opéra was its management of discrete sequences of movement within its interior, for distinct social groups and hierarchies from not only the Avenue, but three additional points of access that signalled their exclusivity. Entries for the Emperor, special subscribers and artists all had special lobbies, stairs and *salons* dedicated to them, placing them, ultimately, in their correct places in the auditorium, without having to meet those outside their circle of contacts, not dissimilar to how residents, visitors, staff and trades were separated in large villas and palaces. The interior marked out the privileges particular to each of those groups, discreetly, and so reinforced the social order of the metropolis even within its *élite* classes, demonstrating that the public interior was capable of subtle calibration, just like the city's *immeubles*, in which social order was inscribed. The *bourgeoisie* followed the central route from the main front, entering the auditorium through the elaborate central staircase. The movement around the stair replicated the excitement that could be anticipated within the auditorium itself. The stair embraced the gathering throng in a wide opening movement, which was then split into two streams, each of which would arrive at the first floor to either side of the auditorium, and ultimately moved into a ring of space around the staircase itself and the perimeter of the auditorium. Small balconies, like theatrical box seats, were suspended from this ring of space around the stair, and a few steps down from the level of the rest of the first floor. The audience already arrived was able to look at the audience arriving, and *vice versa*, replicating the effects of the auditorium. One could see over the whole plan a similar streaming

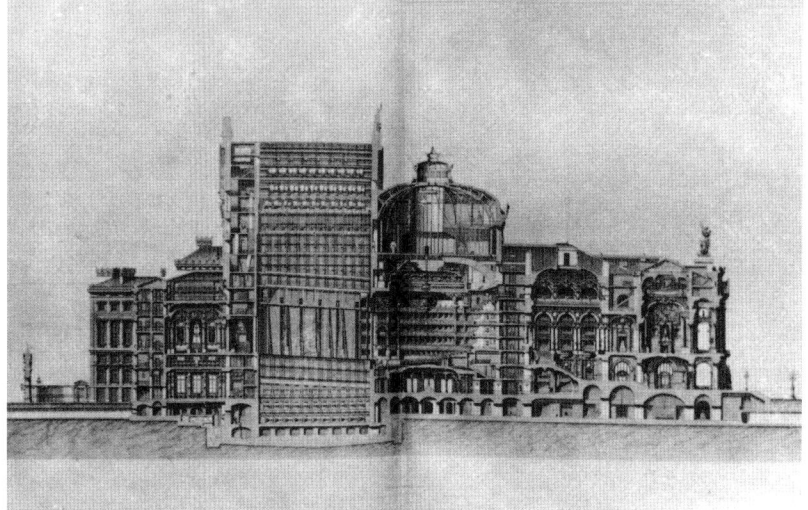

27–29

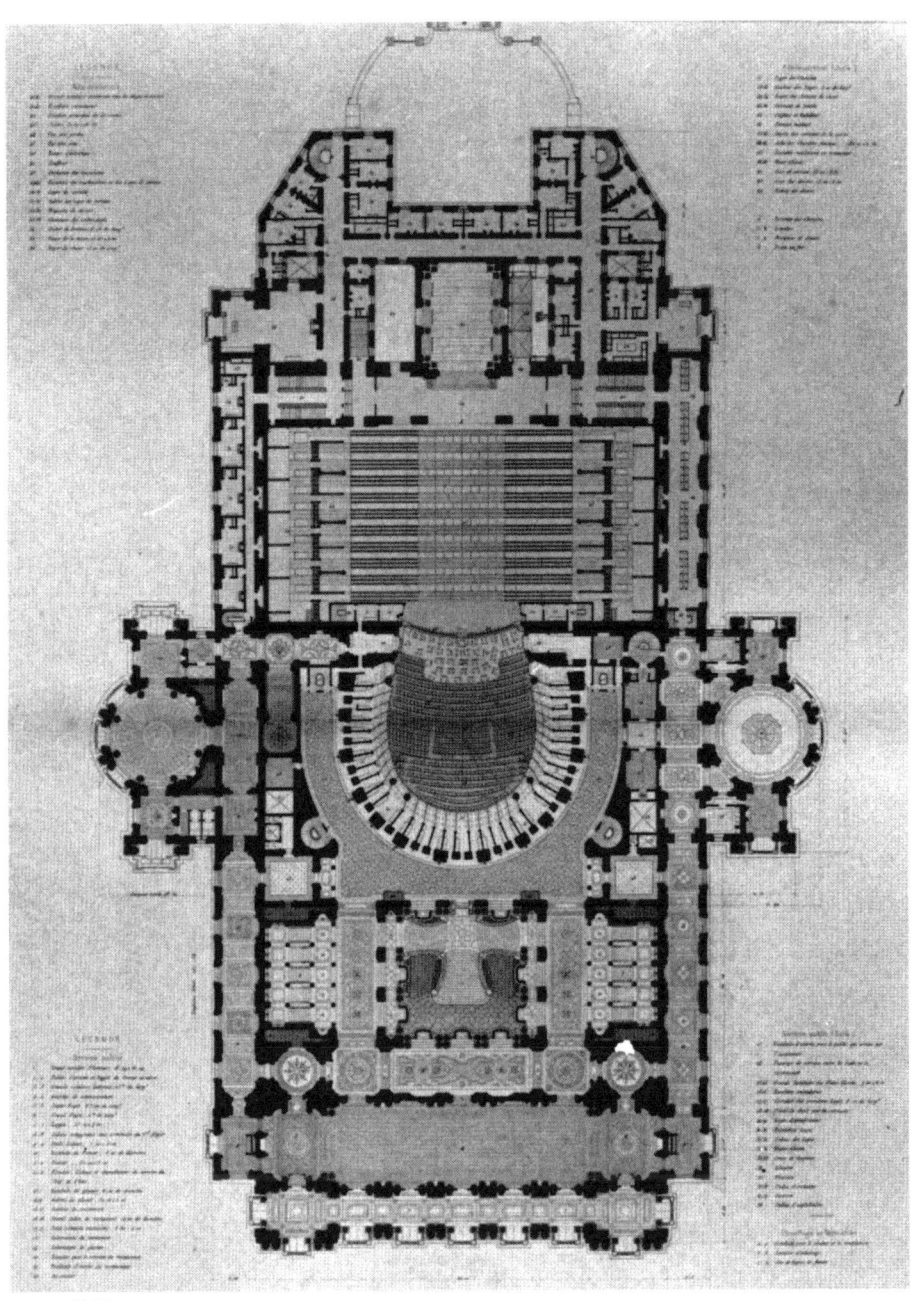

ⓥ 31–32

of movement, for the audience, the performers, the stage sets and equipment. The longitudinal section through the building demonstrated that the whole was devised as an elaborate machine for spectacle, involving both the effects of the theatre and those provided by the metropolitan audience itself, whose adornment about their persons was mingled with the *décor* of the public rooms. The Opéra was a machine that effected transformation through its allusions, illusions and artificiality. This was all described in great detail by Garnier in *Le Théâtre* (1871):[16] he completely unpackaged the aspect of theatricality within the design and the artifice that was required to sustain it, as well as the urban and social task that his machine both resolved and represented. The auditorium itself did what every opera theatre had done before it: its horseshoe-shaped plan provided a special focus on the events of the stage and deep space that receded behind the proscenium, and another upon the audience itself. As within the staircase, the audience looked at itself and a picture of the entire social hierarchy, including a dedicated section—a box within an aedicule—for Louis Napoléon III, who gave the impulse to the transformation of Paris and its new structures, and his wife, the Empress Eugénie. The boxes looked to other boxes, the boxes to the stalls, and the stalls to the boxes. The visit to the Opéra could be imagined as a kind of frenzy of metropolitanism, an almost automated event: the Futurist painters understood this characteristic and represented it years after Garnier had articulated it.

The plans of Eugène Hénard (1849–1923) for a thoroughly modern Paris seem to take the city as a mechanistic device to an extreme, but his proposals were merely extrapolations of conditions that were already in place. They included plans for ideal streets, including all their infrastructure, street crossings and roundabouts, and

⊙ 33

ⓥ 34

further projects to complete or upgrade the Haussmannian idea. Hénard proposed technologies that were meant to accompany these devices, such as moving pavements: 'futuristic' technologies we are familiar with from our use of underground public transport systems and airports. Hénard's propositions gave a central role to that aspect of modern Paris that made it work—its infrastructure—and recognised it as a functioning armature and the pre-eminent representative realm of the city, wherein an underground passage could be regarded as a public interior, worthy of attention just as much that of the Opéra.

AMERICAN METROPOLITAN MACHINES

In the United States, public buildings in the late nineteenth and early twentieth centuries were also being proposed as machinery: the Auditorium Building in Chicago (1889), by Dankmar Adler and Louis Sullivan, was a complex that combined a university, hotel and public theatre, in an interlocking puzzle or collage of programmes, each with its own circulation, and each scientifically considered, much like Garnier's project (such as the case of sight lines of the auditorium), so that it might work best. It operated and processed its users like a machine, with great efficiency, keeping its apparently contradictory contents apart while integrating them into a complete structure. This was best represented in the construction of Grand Central Terminal in New York, to which we will return in the final chapter, designed by Whitney Warren and Charles Wetmore (1910). In various cutaway sections, one saw that the complex was a distributive device, with the central concourse as its network's—and its machinery's—central theatre. Cutaway views that combined the attributes of the plan and the section were applied for all those 'machines' that were miracles of the new, from Leonardo da Vinci's sketches of a new, ideal city (c. 1485), through the famous section of the Haussmannian *immeuble*, Pierre Cuypers's Rijksmuseum, Louis Sullivan's Auditorium Building, Harvey Wiley Corbett's plans for a multi-level

ⓥ 34–37

Ⓥ 35–36

ⓥ 37

Manhattan, the Waldorf Astoria Hotel, ocean liners, and wherever the metropolitan project 'appeared'; in linear cities, in underground cities that echoed Fritz Lang's *Metropolis*, in the New York World's Fair's Futurama as a section of the future at work, in fighter jets and spacecraft, megastructures of the 1960s, and Norman Foster buildings of the 1970s: all machines that showed the possible condition of the metropolis as it was proposed. The drawings proposed a reading of the city that pertained to the metropolitan project, particularly as realised in New York, Paris, and London, one that celebrated the city as both a great, connected mechanism, and as a network, re-presenting the spectacle of what Rem Koolhaas, when discussing Manhattan, characterised as the 'delirium' of its 'culture of congestion'.[17] Again, the spectacle of mechanical processing germane to the numbers within the metropolis was part of its total expression—its aesthetic—regardless of its outward architectural style. Grand Central Terminal established a visual theme representative of the city and the public interior for the twentieth century. In the case of the hospitals, asylums and prisons of the nineteenth century, the machine-like distributions of and within buildings assumed control and exercised policy, authority (and power) invisibly and securely. But in the working monumental machines of the American metropolis, it was important that processes were seen. In its public interiors, the metropolis as a phenomenon was demonstrated through the form of spectacles of its own operations. The public interior was its principle theatre, whose *ballet méchanique* was and remains germane to the metropolis and its spectacle.

MACHINES FOR WORKERS

The character of the machine was adopted by other 'new' types that arose at the end of the nineteenth century, as a consequence of the emergence of the labour movement and a correlating space—both political and social—for workers and the working class in cities. This may be seen as a continuation of the idea that assuming

ⓥ 38–39

the controls of the machine might achieve emancipation for the working class. Buildings with this ambition were addressed to needs for assembly, education and health. A great many buildings and interiors could be discussed, but we are concerned with the imagery that some of the most well known of these assumed, their adoption of machine aesthetics and what they may have communicated through their appearances as products of an industrialised society, and as machines whose controls were in the possession of their users, the working man and woman.

The Maison du Peuple in Paris-Clichy designed by Eugène Beaudouin, Marcel Lods, and Jean Prouvé (1935–1938), which we have already encountered, contained local offices, conference rooms, a market, and a multi-functional space with machine-like characteristics that could be arranged in various configurations through folding and sliding partitions, and open to the sky by a sliding roof. The appearance of the building and the interior was redolent of both a machine and a hangar, one that had been put to civic use. Its multivalence evoked that of Walter Gropius's theatre for Erwin Piscator (1927), which proposed a radical re-appraisal of player-audience relationships by rendering both the stage and the audience's seating mobile, and capable of completely different configurations. Its idea was that the audience might be completely immersed in the experience of the performance, and this immersion, or the capacities imparted by its adaptability and enabled by its evident technology, would also seem to be at the heart of the project for the Maison du Peuple. The building as an operable machine enabled the agency of its users, who could shape their environment in accordance with their desires, reinforcing their capacities to affect their conditions, and their lives. The building furthermore embraced the industrial condition, echoed its expressions, and legitimated them as public forms, placing them in the hands of those who laboured in spaces of industry (the original users of the building), doubly reinforcing the idea that its users would, as they mastered its spaces and their representations, be masters of their own destinies.

ⓗ 27–28

This idea was extended in other community-oriented buildings: the apartment building at Rue des Amiraux, Paris designed by Henri Sauvage (1927), contained a public interior that also invoked the machine. The appearance of the exterior of the building, clad in white glazed bricks, advertised the prospect of light and hygiene. It was meant to be one of a series of identical ziggurat-form blocks, distributed over an urban district, whose arrangement of terraces would provide fresh air to every inhabitant. Its interior, a public facility containing a swimming pool, reflected the ziggurat form of the building without, a tapered hall surrounded by galleries of changing rooms. The clearly recognisable relationship between the unconventional yet communicative external form and the public interior allowed for a reading of the whole block, outside and in, as a single device: a machine for the good of residents of both the building and the whole neighbourhood.

ⓥ 38–39

The transformation of machines from agents of control of the state or industry into catalysts for the improvement of conditions for working people was established in these projects; the appearance of the machine as protagonist, inverting the standard order, communicated their agency. The Pioneer Health Centre designed by the architect-engineer Owen Williams (1936),[18] contemporary with the Maison du Peuple at Clichy, was another such benign and beneficial machine, specifically geared toward the betterment of life of the working class population of an impoverished area of

ⓥ 40–41

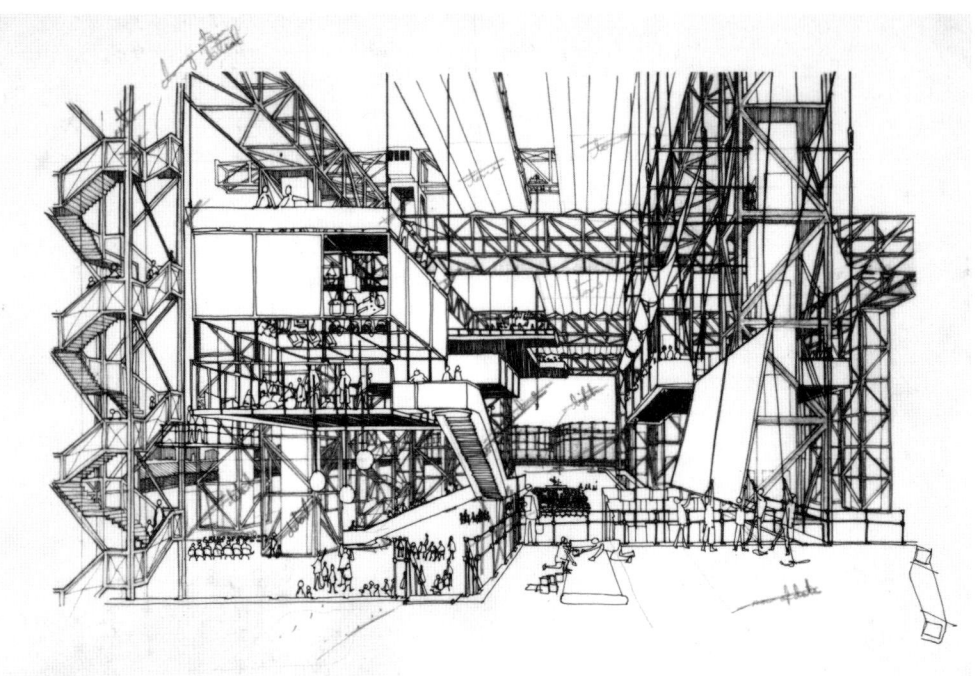

ⓥ 42

ⓥ 43

southeast London, which offered a variety of collective activities and access to family health care. An initiative of the Peckham Experiment by the doctors George Scott Williamson and Innes Hope Pearse to study general health as a medical condition,[19] it was intended that the whole package of facilities would improve local health and wellbeing, and that the effects of providing care in combination with those facilities such as a swimming pool, gymnasium, dance hall and nursery would be observable and their relations could be studied. Both the exterior and interiors of the building assumed the guise of a public factory for good living.

The aims of the Pioneer Health Centre anticipated those advanced twenty years later by theatre director Joan Littlewood and the architect Cedric Price in their project—which we have discussed several times—for a Fun Palace (1958–1962) for London's East End, which, like Peckham, was poor compared to the rest of the city and lacking any public facilities of a scale concomitant with its largely working class population. The building and its vast interior was presented and designed to operate as a giant machine, complete with moving parts, for the purpose of 'fun' in its broadest sense, intended to activate inter-subjectivity and myriad impromptu interactions, implicitly political in nature. The machine was to serve its public by inspiring and responding to individual and group desires, prompting sociability, and free and unpredictable behaviour. The input of the cyberneticist Gordon Pask, who with Price studied processes of decision making with regard to the programmable possibilities of the Fun Palace reinforced an emerging tendency toward the treatment of architecture as individually responsive machinery. This was proposed by many architects in the 1960s and 1970s in relation to individual environments, such as Joe Columbo's Total Furnishing Unit (1972); Ugo La Pietra's 'La Casa Telematica' (1972),[20] in which domestic technology at the command of user transformed both the home and the collective condition, or another kind of public interior; the Archigram projections of David Greene, 'Electronic Tomato' (1969), and Michael Webb, 'Cushicle' (1964) and 'Suitaloon' (1967), which responded to and provided sensory stimuli; and to public environments, in Archigram's 'Instant City' (Peter Cook, Ron Herron and Dennis Crompton, 1968–1970), in which a whole city was proposed to be dropped in on an unsuspecting town to demonstrate the possibilities of completely mutable quasi-urban experience. Critique came in the form of Archizoom's No-Stop City (1970) project, in which the entire environment was a machine, a dominant condition already in existence but without concrete form, in which the general working and consuming population played a role, agreeing to and engaging with those devices that ensured its enslavement.

It was Cedric Price's and Archigram's suggestions that could be felt in Richard Rogers and Renzo Piano's design of the Centre Georges Pompidou (1977), wherein the machine became the image of the building: its users were encouraged to expect it to respond to their demands for access to its facilities; the machine imagery sustained the idea that their access and its corresponding flexibility would be realised. As we have encountered previously in the Palast der Republik in Berlin (1976), a building could be seen as a huge device that represented the ideal view of the state: a machine, in this case, that delivered both the state's ideological message and its intended correlated social image. The building was clearly a mainframe—its components evident—into which disparate activities were inserted. The Palast deployed, rather obviously, imagery of the ideal workers' democracy, in a manner consistent with the ideology of the State. The building was the device upon which this imagery was suspended; and after it was stripped out and awaiting demolition, it became a device that was played on by its emancipated visitors.

AMERICAN SUBURBAN MACHINES

The imagery cultivated by the Palast der Republik, which suggested continuity between it and its society's ideal, could also be deployed within a much larger environment, whose size made it difficult to perceive as a single entity. The distended city of post-war America was typically organised as a regional network of residential areas, industry, retail and entertainment facilities and offices, whose unifying elements were the individual automobile and the motorway. The distended city was a grand device in the service of a regional and national economy, with a set of carefully elaborated (and predictable) working elements that tied the dwelling to suburban settings and the suburb to urban centres and sites of production, consumption and entertainment, all of them caught up in connective webs of motorways.[21] These were constituent elements of a network—the theme addressed in the final chapter—but its individual components were efficient, market-tested machines, connected by machines, and filled with machines that delivered, in the case of the dwellings, comforts the same as those of one's neighbours and those advertised openly and subliminally in media. The shopping mall, where such goods were purchased, delivered predictable outcomes to retailing strategies. The shopping mall was a direct outgrowth of the regional shopping centre, which was placed within the network of motorways to serve the vast suburban developments that emerged in the 1940s and 1950s as a consequence of federal policies intended to transform the war-time, weapon-producing economy of the United States into a peace-time consumer-goods oriented economy, one in which home ownership, individual mobility and the 'freedom to consume' were cornerstones. The individual dwelling was a mass-marketed and mass-produced consumer 'durable',[22] and intended to be the receptacle for consumer goods and the representative site and figure of standardised values and predictable social behaviour, begetting predictable patterns of consumption, production and performance.[23] The suburban dwelling had been rendered public by its absorption of predetermined characteristics and mediated imagery. The climate-controlled shopping mall, arrived at or invented by the Vienna-born architect Victor Gruen, was to be at once a social, quasi-public space, a commodity distinctly absent in suburbia, which Gruen bemoaned,[24] and at the same time, a high-performance retail machine, organising a 'society' of retail units of different goods and scales into a coherent 'experience', thus maximising the profits of individual stores and the shopping centre development as a whole.

The shopping centre was a privately owned building, with an interior that was considered to be public by its users. The first indoor mall, designed by Gruen, was the Southdale Center, in Edina, Minnesota, a suburban nexus outside Minneapolis, which we have discussed earlier. The extremes of weather—very cold in the winter, very hot in the summer—caused Gruen to think that the sales and profits of a shopping centre could be increased, the number of days amenable to and

ⓥ 44

ⓥ 44

pleasant for shopping could be maximised. It was necessary to design an interior that would give shoppers the impression that they were liberated from both the weather and their cars, and so free to mingle, associate and shop. (Gruen had observed that suburban dwellers actually walked around open-air malls on Sundays just to experience something like an urban social experience.)²⁵ The Southdale Center was placed on its site and manipulated in its section so that it could be serviced and stocked without obstructing consumers' vehicles. Internally, it was arranged so that the thresholds between consumers and goods were perceived to be as minimal as possible, leading to the blurring of boundaries between promenades and shop interiors. The environment that framed all of this was the mall itself, which Gruen designed to resemble a kind of village square, with stylised furniture, planting and sculpture creating scenery (the sculptor-designer Harry Bertoia designed a monumental decorative screen). The interior was not a village square; rather it was a stage set that consumers could identify with, particularly given its resemblances to scenes seen on television, and interestingly, to corporate office lobbies. Gruen's design eschewed obvious statements to become 'natural', and, as a medium for the relationship between the consumer and the consumer object of desire, 'transparent'. The mall was a machine, but one that appeared in completely benign attire. The machine aesthetic had been adjusted so that its appearances were consistent with the total representation of 'normality' that saturated American media. The Southdale Center was the working prototype for outdoor malls to follow, notably by Gruen himself, who saw their characteristics as solutions to inner-city blight. The model continued to develop in suburbs and city centres alike, in North America, Europe, Africa and Asia. The mall was the ubiquitous, unrecognised and maligned[26] public interior that had been sustained, until quite recently due to the dramatic transformations of consumer habits, by its dependence on the machinery of motorway and automobiles.

MONEY MACHINES

Those machines dedicated to relieving American consumers of excess income have been epitomised by Las Vegas casinos, which have used their interiors to dissociate their visitors from the outside world. Within, a completely different condition has prevailed that has preplaced the world without with one of endless interiority and acute artificiality. Robert Venturi, Denise Scott Brown and Steven Izenor wrote of the disorientation affected by the interiors of Las Vegas casinos,[27] largely through artificial lighting that confused visitors, disrupting diurnal cycles and offering illusions of boundlessness. At the time of their research in the late 1960s, casino spaces were mostly horizontally oriented, but in contemporary casinos, such as Caesar's Palace (a subject of their earlier studies), a fully three-dimensional confusion reigned. The casino has demonstrated itself to be an elaborate machine for collecting money, filled with machines, gaming tables, bars, restaurants, shops, malls, hotels and entertainment venues, whose various aspects and identities have been integrated through their continuity and efficiency, much of it learned from the science of the layout of shopping centres. Fittingly for Caesar's Palace, its abiding fantasy contrived to be the evocation of the luxuries of ancient Rome; and to this end, boundless extravagance and *kitsch* poured forth—golden statues, fountains, and gaudy wall-to-wall carpeting, entwined with spatial and polychromatic effects worthy of the Baths of Caracalla. In this instance, gamblers and tourists were encouraged to ascend the heavenly vaults of a contemporary plasterboard monument via spiralling arcs of helical escalators, in scenes of spectacular historical one-upmanship. The Las Vegas machine, having learned from the Romans, and from McKim, Mead and White's homage to the Baths of Caracalla at Pennsylvania Station, proclaimed itself as bigger and better than all of them. The public, immersed and mesmerised in this interior realm of the spectacle, was seduced and contented by the all-too-obviously artificial outward representation of the casinos' own machine aesthetics, and volunteered to assist in its workings. The casino, the ultimate machine of indulgence and corruption, represents a cautionary tale for the public interior.

WORKING MACHINES

The 'umbilical' was the word used by the architect Kevin Roche to describe the motorway that tied the place of dwelling and the place of work together, and in fact the entire dispersed American urban condition. He made the point that the boundaries between the dwelling and the office were increasingly illusory, yet the bond tying them together was strengthened by communication technology.[28] The office interior was to him therefore a part of urban experience, intimately tied to the experience of the dwelling, which was in many respects, as a product of external formation through media, a public space, its claim to be a private realm a fallacy. For the regionally situated Union Carbide World Headquarters in Danbury, Connecticut (1976–1982), Roche and John Dinkeloo plugged the building directly into the motorway system; workers drove directly into the building from a spur road, erasing the

v 45–46

ⓥ 47

ⓥ 47

distinction between the regional network and the building which was a part of it, or, in Roche's thoughts, the dwelling, the automobile, and the office, with motorway as the 'umbilical cord' maintaining their codependency. The office interiors were developed through questionnaires with individual (executive) employees, which frequently led to the quite literal extension of the décor of their homes into them. The building—a megastructure in the woods—was an articulation of the distended urban machine and its family of representations.

The interior of the office has been introduced as a public interior here not because of its accessibility to everyone, but because it has been a space that has shaped the experience of workers in the manner of a small society, one that has attempted to replace 'real' society. In 'corporate culture', sets of agreements have been imposed on employees, often embodied in architecture and in particular, in the design of the interior. In its history of development, the office could be regarded as a kind of machine that has produced obeisance to the hierarchies of its society's 'culture'. The office as machine was established as early as the Uffizi in Florence (1560–1581), and was much in evidence in iconic buildings such as Frank Lloyd Wright's Larkin Building in Buffalo (1901). Its object was to increase productivity and effect allegiance. The office building designed by Norman Foster and Associates for the insurance company Willis Faber Dumas in the market town of Ipswich (1975) was, similarly, such a machine, organised about a central bank of escalators rising

ⓥ 48–50

diagonally through its three-storey structure. The offices were contained within an undulating, dark glass curtain wall, each floor plate an open expanse oriented toward the horizon, defined by grass-green carpeting and reflective metal ceilings. The idea was that the building would avoid the cramped and manifestly hierarchical arrangements that characterised the company's offices in the City of London, replacing its effects with openness, transparency and a measure of environmental comfort. Leisure and health facilities were provided to complement the office spaces.

⊚ 48

49–50

A swimming pool on the ground floor and a canteen and lawn on the roof and the offices between were connected by escalators, redolent of both the department store and the airport interior. The section of the building and its interiors as a machine was legible as one passed between its floors on the escalators; one worked in the guts of the gadget. The curtain wall, open plan and reflective ceiling suggested an endless space of free movement, despite its confinement. The escalators provided places for casual meeting and informal surveillance, from which all workers could be seen at once. The facilities above and below encouraged workers to spend 'quality time' at the office before, during and after work, and reinforced the idea that the workplace was a self-sufficient society. The drawings for the building varied between two opposing paradigms: in arguing for its friendliness, Foster commissioned the newspaper cartoon artist Frank Dickens to have his protagonist, the long-suffering office worker Bristow, pad around the proposed spaces of the building contentedly, representing a happy employee-Everyman.[29] The architectural drawings for publication, in contrast, showed the building as an elaborate, serviced construction in cutaway perspectives and exploded axonometric projections, in the manner of *Popular Mechanics* or *Scientific American* magazine illustrations, or those from technical manuals, again, a trope typical of descriptions of architectural 'machines'. The truth of the building, like so many of Foster's in the 1970s, lay somewhere between two extremes: it was a machine, yet a soft machine impelling its users to savour its many technologically-sustained benefits. It gave the impression of being benign, but it was designed so that it might consolidate the corporate culture of its sponsor, and effect predictable outcomes of employee behaviour and performance in its interiors, its 'world'.

This idea of performance was, of course, well known to the history of office design. Frank Lloyd Wright's Larkin Building, innovative in many respects— particularly in environmental comfort—was also an exercise in Taylorist principles of scientific management, as may be seen in the design of the furniture (office chairs integrated with desks, ergonomically designed for typing, into which one swung). The office design communicated—often directly, through well-placed inscriptions equivalent to today's motivational posters—the ethos and hierarchies within the company, which to the outside world, appeared in the guise of a blank, masonry monolith. The elaborate and vivid interior regime was defended by its outwardly enigmatic public image, as was the case of innumerable Modernist corporate headquarters, and precisely so in the case of the inscrutable black glass façade of Foster's Willis Faber Dumas Building; its continuously undulating surface following the irregular contour of its site.

FLYING MACHINES

Airports, our transport hubs are often charged—like Grand Central Station—with reconciling competing infrastructural components; and furthermore, must divide departing and arriving passengers through complex and discrete interior realms in the pursuit of security. Along the way, they have been compelled to ensure that their users are coerced into consuming goods and services voraciously. The most transparent and unapologetic about the necessarily mechanistic character of this Herculean effort of management has been the Charles de Gaulle airport (1969–) in

ⓥ 51–52

ⓥ 53–54

ⓥ 51–52   Paris, designed in several phases over the last forty years by Paul Andreu. The first terminal in particular was a constructed diagram of the positioning and distribution of people and airplanes and the crossing of their myriad paths. The torus-shaped building received automobiles directly from the regional *autoroute* system, drawing them into its orbit, while airplanes docked at regularly spaced satellites to and from which passengers were conveyed by extremely long travelling walkways in snaking, cavernous tunnels. The torus accommodated, on several levels, all service roads, check-in desks, passenger facilities, security checks and baggage halls. Due to the processes involved, passengers were obliged to pass from one section of the torus to another, often opposite each other, at different levels. This was achieved by crossing the void at the centre of the torus, conveyed along moving walkways encased in tubes of curved glass. The many overlapping routes traversing the empty provided a spectacle suggesting a futuristic, mechanistic, Piranesian *carcero*.

Such extraordinary scenes have been difficult to achieve in airports, given that the increasing burdens of air passenger traffic and economic imperatives have obliged them to adapt and adopt new external and internal arrangements on a con-
ⓥ 53–55   stant basis. Schiphol, outside Amsterdam, has become such an airport. Originally a simple structure of great clarity and elegance designed by Marius Duintjer and Kho Liang Ie (1967),[30] from its architecture to information and graphic design, the airport has undergone constant modification by Benthem Crouwel Architects since 2000. This work has been made to accommodate far greater passenger numbers, the integration of the motorway system, train network and the burden of an expanded obligation to security measures and retail facilities. Airports have for the last decades had to generate income well beyond that provided by air carriers, and so have become retail centres. Benthem Crouwel Architects have tried to create public interiors as clearings within the nexus of passageways and processing halls. The first and greatest of these—and to our feeling the most evidently public—is Schiphol Plaza, which receives train passengers and those on foot arriving from coaches, taxis and car parks. A sprawling, vaulted industrial shed–filled with access pavilions for trains platforms below, ticket machines and various kiosks, surrounded by concessions—serves as a place in which people orient themselves, meet fellow travellers and descend to trains or ascend to departure gates. *Passages* are arranged around the Plaza's perimeter. Once past security gates, clearings within each terminal provide the lasting image of the airport's 'public interior'. These are offered in the manner of shopping mall atria, with all the paraphernalia and phantasmagoria that attends such environments. Pavilions appear (including a putative fragment of the Paleis van Volksvlijt); directional and advertising signs; lights, sparkling surfaces and materials throughout that support the illusions or fantasies associated with consumerist wish-fulfilment. The retail spaces, often extracting what they can, ultimately propel visitors toward the wings of departure gates. The clarity of the spaces seems to be compromised by their effulgent surfaces, but navigation through them is necessary and so ensured through signage and announcements through the public address system, with, which its regularity, suggests a disembodied mechanical process of shepherding. Schiphol, as a device, is not merely a conveyor belt leading passengers to airplanes, but a retail machine that is obliged to charm, and cajole, and entice its captive 'customers' in order to

ⓥ 55

function. As a public interior, it frames the public in publicity and conveys them through it and to their aircraft in machine-inflected processes and atmospheres visible in the technique of the building itself. The moments of departure and arrival are mere episodes in the interstices of its working chambers.

Schiphol represents the current state of public interiors, which convey, in every aspect of their appearances and experiences, the theme of the machine. It is notable that descriptions of interiors within this particular thematic framework have been less spoken of in terms of their qualities than in terms of their performance, or 'quantities'. In the case of Charles Garnier's Opéra, the mechanistic distributions of several publics were accompanied by specific representational supports, each speaking the 'language' of recognisable building tropes (in tis case, that of the palace). Yet Schiphol also speaks a language, and its industrial structures are elided with sparkling surfaces that signal the casino and the mall. These particular identities are so common that they slip under the perception of the enormous numbers of people who use or pass through the airport; yet they are visible, and sweeten the pill of movement through the extensive guts of the airport's machinery. It may be that we have arrived at a moment when we might think of machinery that gives pause as it is used, or invites, like the Maisons du Peuples or Fun Palaces we have seen, the humanising events of engagement.

(v) 01
Baths of Caracalla, Rome. Reconstruction, Abel Blouet 1899. © Public domain. Source: https://commons.wikimedia.org/wiki/File:Caracalla_innen.png

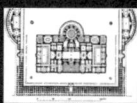

(v) 02
Baths of Caracalla, Rome. A reconstruction of the floor plan of the bath complex, 1908. © Public domain. Source: https://commons.wikimedia.org/wiki/File:Caracalla Grundriss.jpg

(v) 03
J.N.L. Durand, from Receuil et parallèle des edifices de tout genre, anciens et modernes, 1799

(v) 04
St Thomas's Hospital, A 'Nightingale ward', London 1910–17. © King's College, London. Source: King's College London Archives

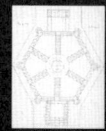

(v) 05
Prison de la Petite Roquette, Paris. First floor plan. Hubert Rohault de Fleury; Louis-Hippolyte Lebas c 1826. CCA DR1974:0002:015:036. © and source: CCA Collection Centre Canadien d'Architecture/ Canadian Centre for Architecture, Montréal

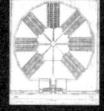

(v) 06
Eastern State Penitentiary, Philadelphia. Plan, 1830. Drawn by William Mason, engraved by C. G. Childs, printed by B. Rodgers. © Public domain. Source: University of Pittsburgh Library

(v) 07
Eastern State Penitentiary, Philadelphia. 1830. Source: Library Company of Philadelphia

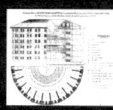

(v) 08
Plan of the Panopticon. Jeremy Bentham, 1843. © Public domain. Source: https://commons.wikimedia.org/wiki/File:Penetentiary_Panopticon_Plan.jpg

(v) 09
Interior View of Cell House, Illinois State Penitentiary, Stateville IL. Photographer unknown. © Lewis University. Source: Consortium of Academic and Research Libraries in Illinois (CARLI)

(v) 10
A comparison by Augustus Pugin of a new Workhouse plan, with his romanticised medieval ideal, Augustus Welby Northmore Pugin, 1834. © Public domain. Source: https://commons.wikimedia.org/wiki/File:Contrasted_Residences_for_the_Poor.jpg

(v) 11
Le Familistère ou Palais social. Jean-Baptiste André Godin, 1871. Bibliothèque nationale de France R-37424. © and source: Bibliothèque nationale de France, Paris (2014)

(v) 12
School children in the interior court of the Social Palace of the Familistère, Guise. (Ecoliers dans la cour intérieure du Palais social du Familistère),1896. Photographer unknown, 1976-01-078. © and source: Collection musée de Guise/Familistère de Guise

(v) 13
In the central courtyard of the Central Pavilion, the Birthday Ball. (Dans la cour du Pavillon central, le bal de la Fête de l'enfance),1909. Photographer unknown, (inv. 2006-33-1). © and source: Collection musée de Guise/Familistère de Guise

(v) 14
Pullman Company Town. The 1901 Sanborn Fire Insurance Map showing the overall area of Pullman, Illinois. © and source: The Pullman State Historic Site, 2016

(v) 15
A bird's-eye view of Edgar Chambless' Road town from The Independent. Milo Hastings, 1910. © Public domain. Source: https://en.wikipedia.org/wiki/File:Roadtown_Sketch.jpg

(v) 16
Edgar Chambless' Road Town, Railway below, public promenade above, 1920. Author unknown. © Public domain. Source: https://orchestratedcity.files.wordpress.com/2012/11/roadtown-edgar-chambless-1910.jpg

(v) 17
Aerial view of Manhattan Transit Terminal and I-95, New York, Pier Luigi Nervi, 1962. Photo Chester Higgins. © Public domain. Source: U.S. National Archives and Records Administration

(v) 18
Lower Manhattan Expressway, New York. Bird's-eye perspective section. Paul Rudolph, 1969. © Public domain. Source: Library of Congress Prints and Photographs Division Washington DC

(v) 19
Comparison of a New House 1910 with an Old House 1810, Paris. Eugène Hénard

(v) 20
Comparison of a New House 1910 with an Old House 1810, Paris. Eugène Hénard

(v) 21
Scheme for major incisions to the urban fabric of the centre of Paris. (Baron) Georges-Eugène Haussmann. Source: https://spargeland-fraise.files.wordpress.com/2011/05/haussmannparc3ads.jpeg

(v) 22
Demolitions between Rue de l'Échelle and Rue Saint Augustin, Paris, 1877. Photo Charles Marville © Public domain. Source: Brown University Library

(v) 23
Haussmann Paris. Aerial view of Avenue Richard-Lenoir. Source: http://ecosistemaurbano.org/urbanismo/desde-el-parque-de-gezi-hacia-rio-de-janeiro-el-urbanismo-al-frente/

(v) 24
Boulevard des Italiens, Gustave Caillebotte, 1880. © Public domain. Source: http://www.wikiart.org/en/gustave-caillebotte/boulevard-des-italiens

(v) 25
Man at the Window, Gustave Caillebotte, 1875. © Public domain. Source: http://www.wikiart.org/en/gustave-caillebotte/man-at-the-window-1875

(v) 26
Cross-section of a typical Parisian Apartment House, about 1850 showing the economic means of tenants varying by floors. Edmund Texier, *Tableaux de Paris*, 1852. I. 65. Source: https://architokyo.wordpress.com/exposition/

(v) 27
Opéra, Palais Garnier, Paris. Charles Garnier, 1875. Photographer unknown. 23429-20 © Hollandse Hoogte. Source: Roger Viollet

(v) 28
Opéra, Palais Garnier, Paris. Longitudinal section, c 1863. From Steinhauser, Monika (1969). *Die Architektur der Pariser Oper*, plate 7. Munich: Prestel. © Public domain. Source: https://commons.wikimedia.org/wiki/File:Palais_Garnier_long_section_-_Steinhauser_1969_plate7.jpg

(v) 29
Opéra, Palais Garnier, Paris. Longitudinal section. Karl Fichot and Henri Meyer. 1555-1 © Hollandse Hoogte. Source: Roger Viollet

(v) 30
Opéra, Palais Garnier, Paris. Plan, first *loge* level. 1880. From Garnier, *Le Nouvel Opéra* (1876–1880), folio I, plates 10–11. © Public domain. Source: https://commons.wikimedia.org/wiki/File:Palais_Garnier_plan_at_the_first_loge_level_-_Mead_1991_p101.jpg

(v) 31
The Opera House Grand Staircase Paris, France, ca.1890–1900. Author unknown. Source: https://nl.pinterest.com/pin/445715694348660138/

(v) 32
Inauguration of the Paris Opera, 5 January 1875. Edouard Detaille. © Public domain. Source: https://commons.wikimedia.org/wiki/File:Inauguration_of_the_Paris_Opera_in_1875_by_Detaille_-_Collections_of_the_Château_of_Versailles_cropped.jpg

(v) 33
Opéra, Palais Garnier, Paris. View and perspective of the central staircase. Charles Garnier, 1875. © Public domain. Source: *Monographie du Nouvel Opéra de Paris*: 12 of 44; La Bibliothèque de l'Institut National d'Histoire de l'Art

(v) 34–37
Grand Central Terminal, New York. Warren and Wetmore, 1910. Photo © and source: Mark Pimlott

(v) 38–39
Apartment building and public swimming pool, Rue des Amiraux, Paris. Henri Sauvage, 1927. Photo © and source: Marius Grootveld

(v) 40
Pioneer Health Centre, St Mary's Road, Peckham, London: the library and rest room. Owen Williams, 1935. Photo Dell & Wainwright © and source: Dell & Wainwright/RIBA Collections

(v) 41
Pioneer Health Centre, St Mary's Road, Peckham, London: view of the swimming pool from one of the recreation rooms. Owen Williams, 1935. Photo Dell & Wainwright © and source: Dell & Wainwright/RIBA Collections

(v) 42
Fun Palace: Interior perspective. Cedric Price, c 1960–1964. CCA DR1995:0188:525:003:001 © Cedric Price fonds. Source: CCA Collection Centre Canadien d'Architecture/Canadian Centre for Architecture, Montréal

(v) 43
Centre Georges Pompidou, Paris. Piano and Rogers, 1977. Photo © and source: Mark Pimlott

(v) 44
Southdale Center, Edina MN. Victor Gruen, 1956. Photo Minneapolis Star Tribune. Minnesota Historical Society © and source: Minnesota Historical Society

(v) 45
Caesar's Palace, Las Vegas. Advertising photo, 1960s. From Robert Venturi, Denise Scott Brown, Steven Izenor, *Learning from Las Vegas* (1968)

(v) 46
Caesar's Palace (2013). Photo Wikimedia user Tuxyso © CC-BY-SA-3.0. Source: https://commons.wikimedia.org/wiki/File:Caesars_Palace_shopping_center_Interior_2013.jpg

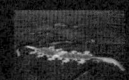

(v) 47
Union Carbide Corporation World Headquarters, Danbury, Connecticut. Roche and Dinkeloo, 1982. Photo Ronald Livieri and Chalmer Alexander. © and source: Kevin Roche John Dinkeloo and Associates LLC (KRJDA)

(v) 48
Willis Faber Dumas Building, Ipswich. Foster Associates, 1978. Photo Ken Kirkwood © Ken Kirkwood. Source: Foster and Partners

(v) 49–50
Willis Faber Dumas building, Ipswich. Foster Associates, 1978. Photo © Tim Street-Porter. Source: Norman Foster and Partners

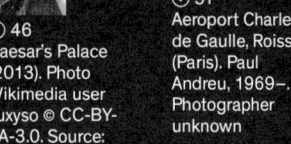

(v) 51
Aeroport Charles de Gaulle, Roissy, (Paris). Paul Andreu, 1969–. Photographer unknown

(v) 52
Aeroport Charles de Gaulle, Roissy, (Paris). Paul Andreu, 1969–. Photo © and source: Mark Pimlott

(v) 53–54
Schiphol Airport, Amsterdam. Marius Duintjer, Kho Liang Ie, 1967; Benthem Crouwel, 2000–. Photo © and source: Mark Pimlott

(v) 55
Schiphol Airport, outside Amsterdam. Photo © and source: Mark Pimlott

VI
THE NETWORK

VI 01

Networks lie at the very foundations of the human settlement as implicit and explicit lines drawn between disparate elements, places, and people. The very first connections between different settlements constituted networks, in the form of routes, such as the Silk Road, that tied many distant places and peoples together for the purpose of trade. The mingling of these routes and those already traced within settlements contributed to the reinforcement of their centres, and the creation of realms within them that witnessed the gathering of locals and others, and gave these realms lasting significance. Often, these nexus of routes were given form, in structures of particular characteristics and varying complexity, making intense and specialised zones that effected the condition of interiority.

    I wish to consider the network as it has appeared within our experience of the public interior. Although our experience of networks within urbanised realms is deeply familiar, there is no single image or figure that articulates them, with the exception of the street. A network suggests a connective realm that is commonly understood, yet is grasped primarily through one's movement through it or through those maps that describe it as a whole, allowing one to appreciate its extensive totality as 'a group or system of interconnected people or things'. In public interiors derived from or assembled around the framework of networks, one's apprehension of spaces is reinforced by the connections that run through them, wherein one space leads to or adjoins another, either similar or completely different in character. The accumulation of the experience of the sequence of spaces, and the flows and pauses that make these spaces work in a continuum becomes the prevalent and characteristic experience of the network. A network may be a trace, or a web of connected interiors; a network may be linear or diffuse. In cities, networks have been used to resolve complex demands for the management of complementary and incongruous components and the activity, movement and distribution of many individuals within them and their interconnectivity. Networks in cities are consequences of agreements made over time that have yielded *ad hoc* environments that make informal relationships concrete; and networks in cities have been built all at once as attempts to both reconcile complex relationships and anticipate future conditions, connections and extensions, as systems whose forms have been defined that have been implemented in order to capture the 'freedom' of naturally emergent patterns and phenomena. Networks have assumed the form of paths and lanes, streets and motorways, souks and bazaars, monasteries and colleges, arcades and gallerias, stations, shopping malls and airports.   (vi) 01

    Many of the public interiors characteristic of our time (among those which one might not even consider to be either public or interiors) are networks or parts of larger networks, legible and navigable at least as much through their network characteristics as through those offered by their appearances. There are networks that offer themselves as natural, in the manner of ecological systems, and those that are made in the manner of circuitry. The latter have been often inspired by the former, whether they have been assembled over time, or implemented all at once, systematically.

    I propose that networks are deeply known in the way that topography is deeply known, deriving from precedents and patterns deeply embedded in the origins of settlements, the connections between them, and the experience of movement across and through them, related to our nomadic roots.

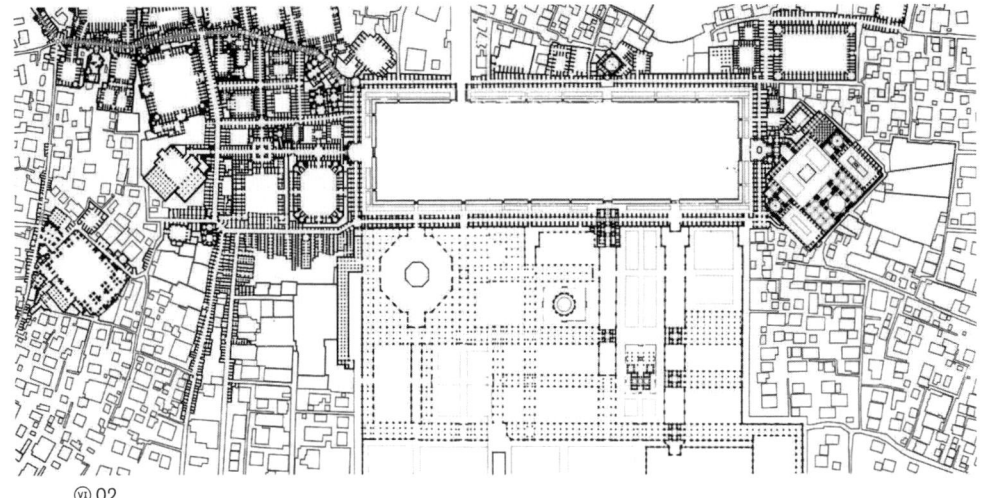

ⓥ 02

BAZAAR, SOUK

The public interior formed or informed by the network first appeared in the midst of settlements of Asia Minor, producing models that have been emulated in contexts far removed from their origins throughout history. In the period of modernity, the network became perhaps the most potent device available for the design of the public interior. The network has featured prominently in the architecture of the twentieth century, particularly in the context of the re-appraisal of Modernism by the Team Ten group of architects that emerged within CIAM (*Congrès internationale d'architecture moderne*) and questioned its orthodoxies in the 1950s. For some thirty years after the Second World War, the *souk* and the *bazaar*, in the natural authenticity of their otherness, offered organisational and spatial prototypes that, portrayed as anti-hierarchical by a new group of architects, seemed by inference to be democratic and unburdened by the outward signs of authoritarian or bureaucratic power.

ⓥ 02–04

The *bazaar* (Persian for 'market' or 'place of prices'),[1] which Johann Friedrich Geist cited as the model from which the building type of the arcades of the late eighteenth and then nineteenth centuries sprang, was a complex of interior streets interwoven within the fabric of the city, a more intense version of that fabric and a dedicated environment for merchant activity. In towns such as Isfahan and Tabriz, the grand bazaar (from the eleventh and tenth centuries, respectively) was the centrepiece of their cities' and regions' economies, and their quotidian lives. The bazaar's characteristic forms emerged there, typically consisting of streets with shops to either side that were covered with vaulted brick roofs punctuated at special junctures by crossings with elaborate domes and clerestory and zenithal light, and wrapped around open-air courtyards. Streets of the bazaar were furthermore integrated within the pattern of alleyways, lanes and streets of the settlements' fabric. The bazaar as a type appeared widely: variations in the designs of bazaars from city to city were those of scale or expression of the structure of the enclosing roofs. Its characteristic pattern was evident in Istanbul's Grand Bazaar (from 1455), whose figure in the midst of the city plan resembled that of another, walled city, with a grid of streets and gates that opened out into the surrounding network of those of the city and were effectively continuous with them. Within, the bazaar's streets were vaulted, and crossings offered the opportunity for elaborations of light and

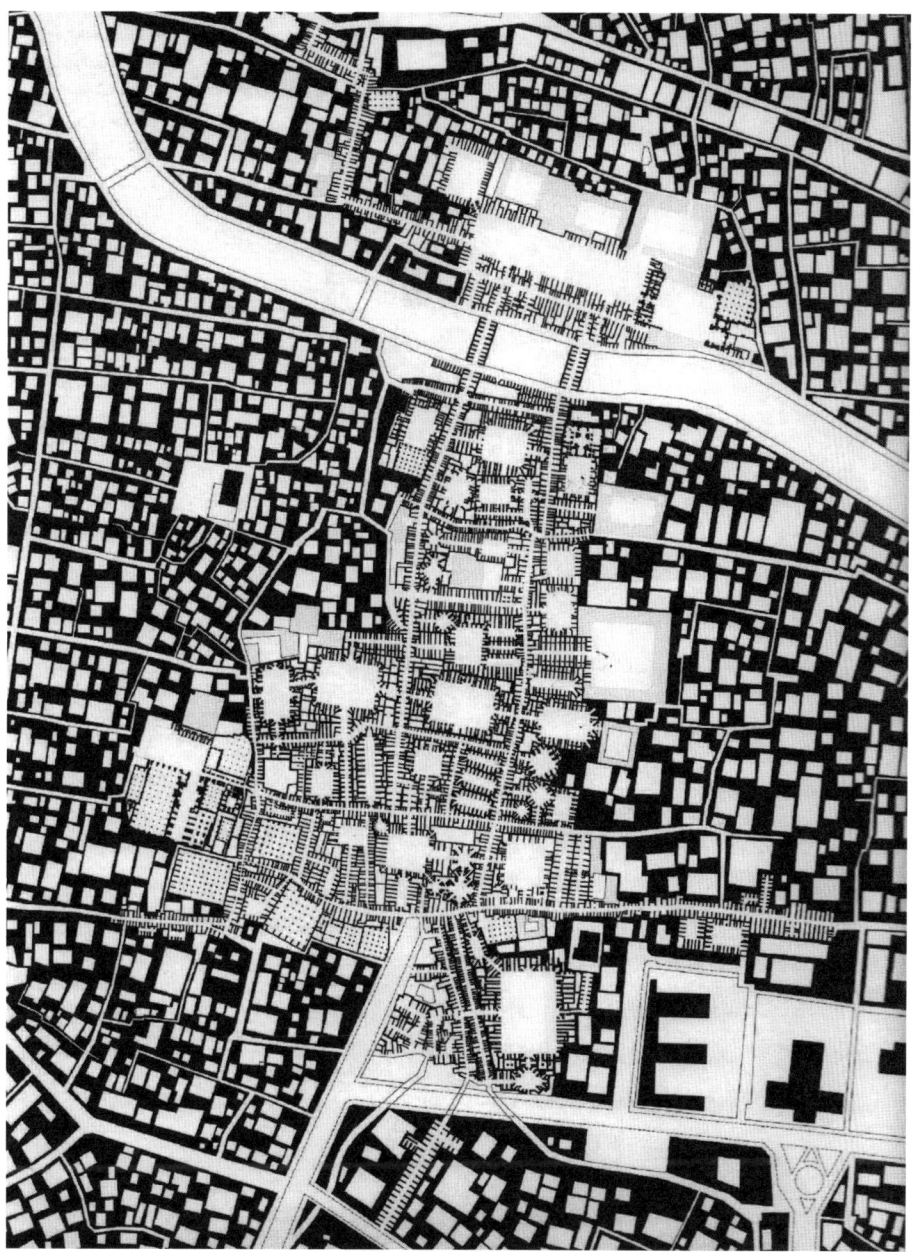

VI 04

space, altogether giving the visitor an impression of being in an interiorised urban district. The very intense space was a concrete image of the patterns of movement and exchange that ran through the city centre.

Interiorised realms indebted to the idea of the bazaar were widespread and applied internationally. Their environments were mimicked in the eighteenth- and nineteenth-century arcades of Paris, the 'bazaars' of London in the nineteenth century[2] (which might be regarded as interiorised districts incorporating shops, galleries and diverse entertainments), echoed in the mat-buildings of post-CIAM Team Ten architects, and unconsciously reiterated in twentieth- and twenty-first-century interior shopping malls and airports.

The *souk* was an open-air variety of the bazaar, and like it, essentially a commercial quarter whose streets were entirely dedicated to commercial activity, and whose character assumed, despite being outdoors, the quality of an interiorised environment. Souks existed throughout the Middle East and North Africa around the Mediterranean Sea, and though their origins were associated with temporary sites outside cities at the convergence of trade routes, they later moved to city centres, taking advantage of the benefits of their concentrated populations and the constructions that were offered to both accommodate and isolate their activities. These districts' streets could be either regular or labyrinthine, their intensity reinforcing their atmosphere of interiority. Clearings in their patterns such as courtyards acted as spatial outlets, allowing for open air trading, and places of rest. In the case of the *médina* of Marrakech, its greatest clearing or outlet, Jemaa el-Fna, was also the city's representative space. Souks' lanes and alleyways were typically filled with goods, people, and places for refreshment, and would inevitably adjoin the ordinary routes of the district in which they were embedded. The souk was a specialised zone of high connectivity that, through its congestion, increased the density of connectivity within the city. In Damascus,

VI 05–07

Ⓥ 05–06

ⓥ 07

ⓥ 08

(VI) 09–10

(VI) 11

Sequences

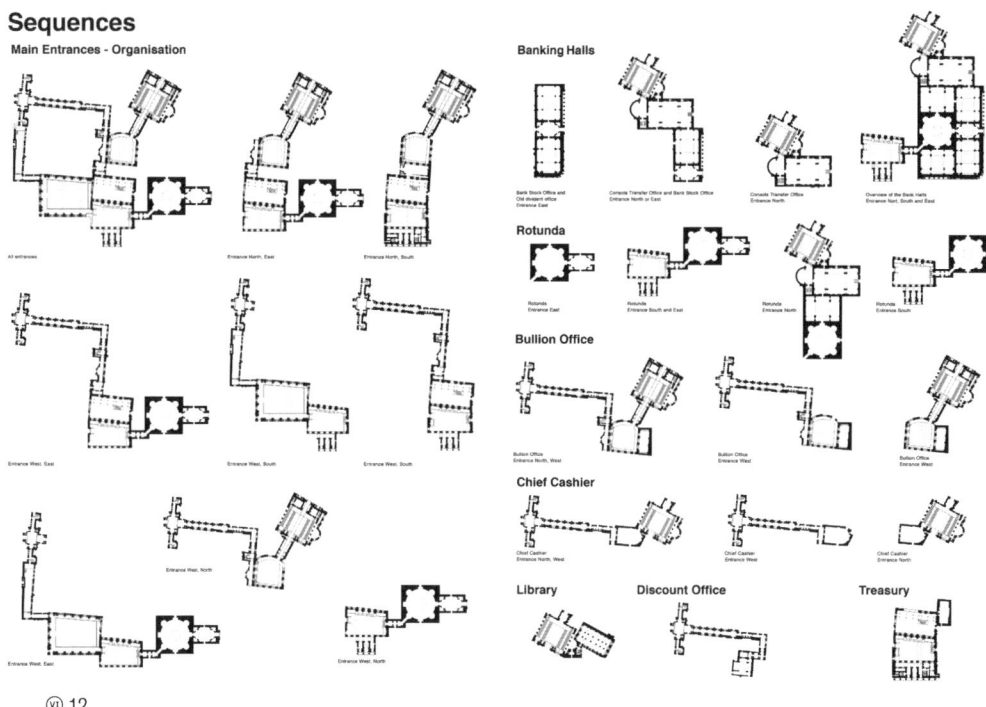

(VI) 12

the *souk* assumed a different form, a sheltered network of streets more closely resembling a nineteenth-century arcade. Its regularly articulated streets were covered with great vaults of corrugated tin (full of holes and evocative of a starry night sky), exclusively dedicated to commercial activity, and linked to the other streets of the district around it.

Such zones flourished in centres of trade elsewhere. The Rialto market in Venice, established at the end of the eleventh century, occupied a substantial and key part of the city. Its current buildings, dating from the mid-sixteenth century, were arranged around a set of open courtyards, some completely contained, others open on one side to the Grand Canal. Connected to the city on the east by the Ponte Rialto (1591), a bridge supporting two rows of shops[3] and all around by a network of small streets and passages that blended with the passages of its own buildings,[4] the market 'disappeared' into the urban fabric. Its buildings—the Fabbriche Vecchie, Antonio Abbondi (1520–1522) and Fabbriche Nuove, Jacopo Sansovino (1533–1555)— enclosed the courtyards, with the quality of *piazze* (or in the Venetian form, *campi*, the plural of the Latin *campus*, or field). Some of these buildings contained shops and *bàcari* (small bars for food and drink), but one, for fish, contained two empty, tenebrous, monumental shelters (Mercato del Pesce al Minuto, 1907), public halls whose column-delineated spaces merged with those of the streets and courtyards around. The surrounding streets were continuous with the network of the market and extended the facilities within the market itself, making it difficult to determine, in some instances, where the market ended and where local streets began. In these indeterminate zones, people gathered to meet, eat and drink, particularly at its edges, alleys, arcaded passages, and in their small, illuminated *bàcari*, and have done so for centuries.

ABBEYS AND COLLEGES

The morphology of Rialto, especially its passages and courtyards, evoked the arrangements of medieval monasteries and convents, which, although isolated from the world, contained elaborate internal networks. A model of these was the Cistercian abbey of Le Thoronet (c1200) in Provence: a complex of buildings and spatial elements abutting each other and bound by an arcaded cloister. The cloister, a figure central to the life of a monastery, was itself one sign among several for the enactment of the collective and spiritual life of the community.[5] The cloister was at once a passage, a route between various parts of the complex, and a place for thought, infinite in its continuous unfolding. Le Corbusier sought to re-shape this form in his design of the 'couvent' of Sainte-Marie de la Tourette, near Lyon (1959),[6] renaming the cloister an *ambulatoire* or 'walking-place', and casting it as a singular, recognisable figure of the central crossing of a quasi-urban street network—a *cardo* and *decumanus* of large 'stones' marked by the shifting shadows of the verticals of *fenêtres ondulatoire*—that connected all the elements of the monastery.

A constant model for the public interior proposed as an implicit and explicit network was represented by the patterns of colleges of the universities of Oxford and Cambridge, established in the eleventh century. At Oxford, these featured sets of buildings were grouped around courtyards or quads that were connected through covered gates and passages and were integrated with the pattern of streets of the town.

The arrangements of the colleges resembled those of the cloistered courtyards of abbeys and monasteries, and indeed it was the arrival of various religious orders in Oxford in the thirteenth century that influenced them. This model was used in various ways in other colleges in the town, many of which were packed together tightly, their walled enclosures bound by narrow lanes between them. Each college was an interior, urbane complex for the communication of scholars. The colleges featured heterogeneous compositions of singular buildings and regular constructions built around courtyard figures, whose lawns could be regarded as commons for each of their scholarly communities. The interiority of their arrangements was central to their experience, and reinforced their environments of academic community and contact—networking—essential to the cultivation of 'knowledge societies'.

Although we have referred earlier to the ruin, and to Giambattista Piranesi's speculations regarding ancient Rome's Campo Marzio as but one source for John Soane's designs for the Bank of England, it is plausible that the colleges' patterns of contact also inspired the design of the Bank's resolutely non-academic complex of buildings, courtyards and passages. Its sequences of connected courtyards and vaulted, top-lit rooms, were places of communication and commerce, and suggested not only the deep history of Rome and Greece, whose ruined imagery and authority through association we have discussed; they also suggested the walled, yet connected networks of the college and the monastery. All of these are models with which Soane would have been familiar. The interconnectedness of the Bank's plan and the forms of its interiors suggests that its scenography was experienced very much like the unfolding of a network, inferring the whole in each of its spatial episodes.

In all these cases, the character of spaces tended towards those of interiors regardless of whether literal interiors were encountered or not. The routes and spaces and experiences that reinforced the 'structures' of the Abbey, college, Bank, *bazaar* and *souk* affected conditions of interiority.

NETWORK AS URBAN PLAN

The networked spaces of the Grand Bazaar of Istanbul, the monasteries of the south of France, the colleges of Oxford and Cambridge and the Bank of England were all walled enclosures, in which specialised activities were reinforced largely to the exclusion of their contexts, their internal traces connected to the world or city without only at key points. The network has also been employed to realise urban zones with sophisticated and complex orders of connections to contexts, altering their uses, readings and meanings entirely. The Gallerie degli Uffizi in Florence (1560) designed by Giorgio Vasari[7]—a writer, painter and accomplished urban architect—were offices for the administration of Prince Cosimo I de Medici, who established Florence as an especially powerful republic among the many city-states of *cinquecento* Italy. The Gallerie were built among and attached to existing constructions, necessitating the appropriation and demolition of a band of properties standing between the Palazzo Vecchio—the seat of the city's government—and the River Arno. A competition was held that yielded a series of interesting freestanding designs, but Vasari's quite different design, both adjoining to and precisely cut into the existing fabric, was chosen; the economies of its

(VI) 13–14

(VI) 15–16

(vi) 15–16

reduced programme for demolitions and its clear urban gesture were among its many advantages. Its singular attribute was its integration with existing structures and its profound statement on the image of the Medici republic as represented by the modification to the urban fabric embodied in one exceptional urban space. Through this space—very much like an interior—an image of the state's power was carried from the Palazzo Vecchio right to the river, thereby claiming the city on its southern bank and the hills beyond as part of the city's world, and an image, furthermore, of Cosimo I de Medici's expansion and consolidation of power.

The building, wrapping around this space over four floors, contained administrative offices, the law courts (Tribunale di Stato) and the city archives (Archivio di Stato). It eventually came to accommodate the Medici art collection in a series of gallery rooms. The Gallerie degli Uffizi denote the corridors that bound Vasari's new urban space: an extremely elongated courtyard—effectively a street with identical façades and a powerful sense of enclosure known as the *Piazzale*—that stretched between the Piazza della Signoria and the Arno. The façades surrounding the courtyard, forming the image of the *Piazzale*, presented the building's organisational principle and its architectural image to itself (as in a mirror) and the city (as in an urban theatre); an ideal street that served as a theatrical frontage to a more complex arrangement of rooms behind. The space of this ideal street was terminated at the Arno by what may be described as a triumphal arch framing the views of the river, its southern bank and the hills beyond. The motif, to which the entirety of the *Piazzale* conformed, was common to the arrangements of the *frons scenae* of ancient Roman theatre, consisting of a fixed construction of arches from which characters might emerge, as though from streets and passages. In this case, the whole landscape of Florence served as a backcloth to the theatre of Florentine civic life.

The plan of the Uffizi hardly seems like a plan of any substance, so dominant is its continuous three-armed corridor connecting all its suites of rooms. This corridor, represented in the courtyard façade then facilitated a secret network that branched off it: in the southwest corner of the third floor gallery, another corridor led off and away from the Uffizi to continue its path in a specialised and contained route constructed for the isolated and safe conduct of Cosimo I de Medici to his residence across the Arno in the Palazzo Pitti.[8] The *Corridorio Vasariano* followed the northern bank of the river, dropping a couple of levels and appearing as a discreet structure on vaulted supports; it turned perpendicular to this to become integral to the Ponte Vecchio. Once across the river, it alternately concealed and exposed itself to the city's urban fabric, forming a gateway to the Via de' Bardi; disappearing into a building; emerging briefly in the Piazza di Santa Felicità, where it popped inside to provide a balcony for the Prince to worship privately, before disappearing again; reappearing as part of the wall to the Giardini Boboli, and settling at last within the safety of the monumentally rusticated Palazzo Pitti. The network that served the various facilities of the Uffizi was echoed in the building's service as an urban structure, implicitly connecting the city's main piazza with the river; and amplified by a private network, for one citizen and his retinue, that connected the seat of State with its ruler's home. The Vasari-designed network embodied the power of its sponsor, oscillating between brilliant, representative clarity, and obscured omnipresence.

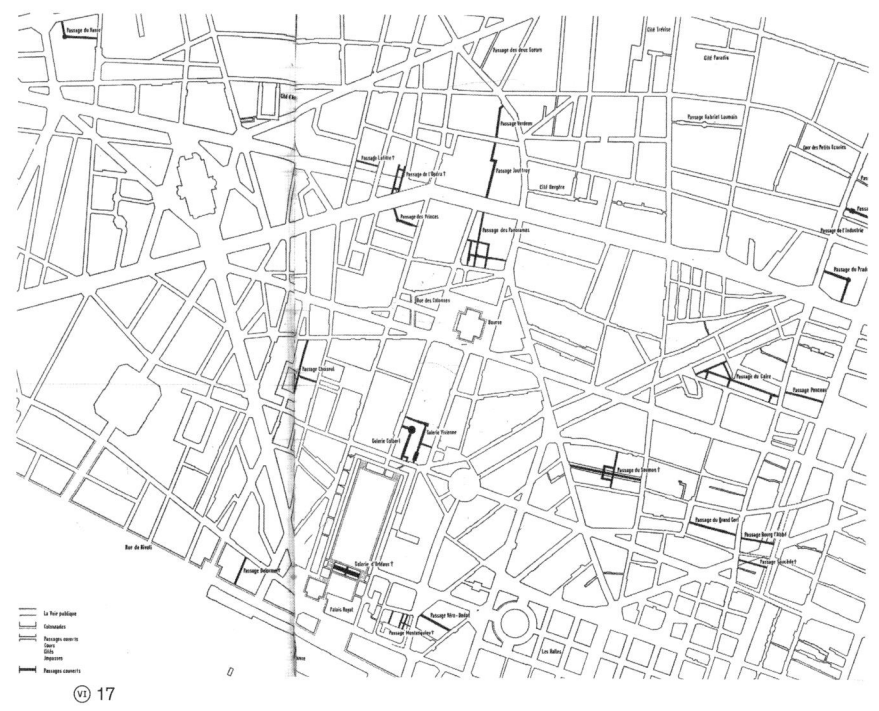

VI 17

VI 18

THE ARCADES

Connectivity reveals and enables relations in the structures of cities and between people; articulates power and its relations and provide profits for its sponsors. High degrees of connectivity are essential for the operation of urban complexes, for the movement of people and goods, and for the realisation of value of property for landowners. This complex of benefits has been germane to the making of urban networks, and has revealed itself in public interiors that have deployed a variety of inventions, that cut across and through existing urban structures in order to realise complex objectives.

In late eighteenth- and early nineteenth-century Paris, a new building type emerged—the arcade or *passage*—that ran through the dense grain of the city's fabric to create distinct interior environments that were at once additions and alternatives to its streets. We have encountered the arcades on several occasions already, and have noted the exemplary study by Johann Friedrich Geist, to which any consideration of the public interior has found itself indebted.[9] The urban blocks of pre-Haussmannian Paris were dense, with multi-storey properties forming their perimeters and a ragged collection of other buildings filling them. The values of properties on the outside of these city blocks or *îlots* were high, while their interiors were economically relatively 'unproductive'. The values of these hidden internal properties were transformed by the creation of interior shopping streets or arcades that connected the valuable perimeters. This approach to connectivity could be thought of anticipating the changes to Paris that were to follow under the direction of Georges-Eugène Haussmann, in which great connecting streets and boulevards were cut through the city's medieval fabric, finally eliminating the dark interiors of the city's *îlots* entirely.[10] Regarding the appearance of these arcades, we have noted their perfectly unified architecture, their materials, their particular quality of light, the phenomenon of reflections within, the fact that they were completely dedicated to the pedestrian, and how they ultimately acted as the repository for the residue of material culture of the nineteenth-century bourgeois city.[11] The arcades both short-circuited and extended the city's street system, contributed their own specific aura to it, and all together constituted an additional and complementary system that could be perceived and experienced as a network. As covered interior streets that wound through complex sections of the metropolitan fabric, their 'nature' (recall Laugier's characterisation of the city as a forested park[12]) was suited to the wandering, meandering pedestrian. Most were rather narrow, such as the Passage Choiseul (1827); some were rather grand, like the Passage Véro-Dodat (1826); and some were of a significant scale, such as the Galérie Colbert (1826) and Galérie d'Orléans (1830). Yet they were all paved, clean, and relatively quiet, unlike the city's streets in that period (the early to mid-nineteenth century), and ideal for the contemplation of artefacts, others and reflections oneself in myriad windows and displays. The arcades were the territory of the *flâneur*, that passerby who idled, walked and watched the phantasmagoria of the arcades and their denizens without feeling obliged to do anything: the temporarily emancipated individual of the city. The Parisian *passage* network was very extensive, and one could follow an itinerary quite without reliance on the network of streets. The *passages* were largely located in the *Rive droite* in the district to the north and east of Palais-Royal, that space

ⓥ 22

wherein the first arcade, the Galérie des Bois appeared at the end of the eighteenth century, and replaced, at the end of the first great construction period of the arcades, by the Galérie d'Orléans.[13]

GALLERIA

This first wave of *passages* built in Paris inspired the creation of arcades first in London (the first was the Royal Opera Arcade, between Pall Mall and Charles II Street, designed by John Nash in 1806) and then—given impetus by the transformation of Paris and their new, metropolitan scale—throughout Europe, the United States, Russia and even Australia at a variety of scales. England embraced the arcades (Royal Opera Arcade (1818); Burlington Arcade (1819)), and a form of the bazaar, in London (Soho Bazaar (1816); Queen's Bazaar (1828); Pantheon Bazaar (1834)).[14] They were taken up all over the country, notably in manufacturing cities of the North, such as Leeds, Leicester and Newcastle. In the Netherlands, the Passage in The Hague (1885) was representative of that large-scale arcade that had by that time become a standard type within European metropolitan centres. We have written in several instances about the role played by the Crystal Palace in establishing the possibility of a monumental glazed public interior, and its influence was most potently asserted in Giuseppe Mengoni's design for the Galleria Vittorio Emanuele II in Milan (1874). Here, the arcade appeared at a scale far greater than had been established in Paris, if not in its extensiveness. While the Parisian *passages* transformed the street network into a complex system—one that seized the full potential of exploitation by property owners and pedestrians (ultimately transcended by the highly connective Haussmannian programme of cutting streets and boulevards)—the Galleria in Milan established a metropolitan condition almost entirely on its own. Milan became a metropolis through the gesture of its plan, its representational character, and the fact that it connected two particularly charged

ⓥ 23–24

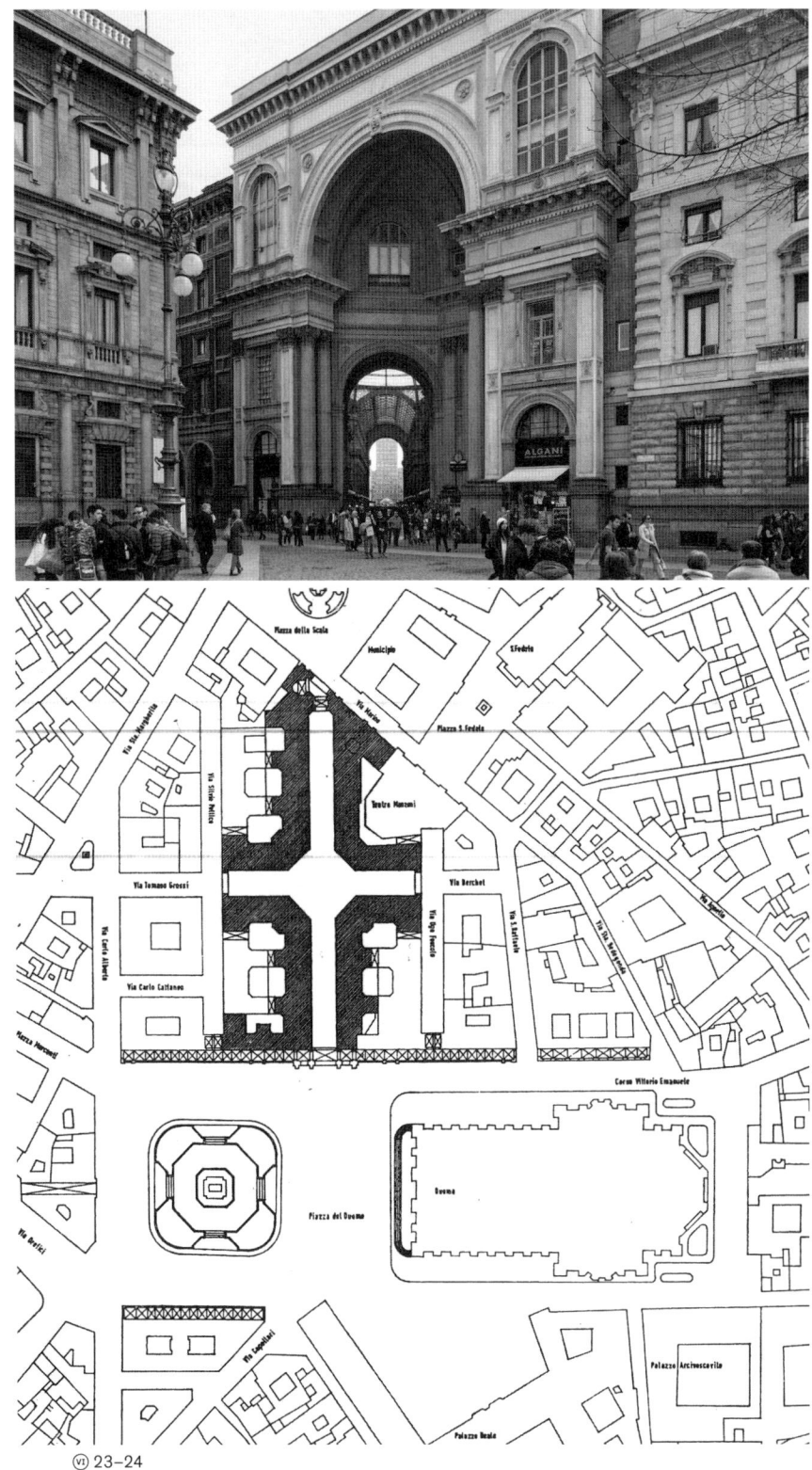

Ⅵ 23-24

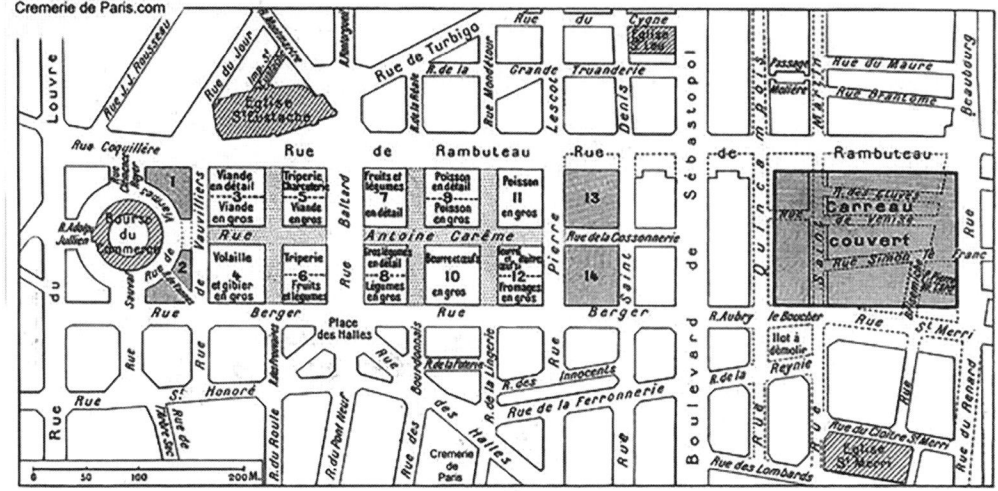

Projet d'agrandissement des Halles centrales de Paris soumis au conseil municipal par le préfet de la Seine.

Le pointillé foncé représente les pavillons et le carreau couvert à construire ; le pointillé clair indique les portions de rues couvertes. On a figuré en trait interrompu d'une part les rues appelées à disparaître, d'autre part la limite actuelle de certaines rues ou parties de rues dont on prévoit l'élargissement.

open public spaces in the city: its spiritual centre, the Piazza del Duomo, and its representative centre of contemporary culture, the Piazza Scala. The city was 'networked' by the Galleria's presence; through it, the complex of urban spaces in the historical centre were more directly linked. It changed the perception of the historical centre from within, and unlike the effect of the Parisian arcades, which added to the existing network while short-circuiting it, it rendered the historical centre of Milan simpler and less complex (certainly due in part to its extensive demolitions of its fabric). It transformed the image of a mysterious medieval centre into one of a highly visible and rational metropolitan centre, tying it to the international idea of the metropolis. This idea was underlined by the painted roundels crowning each of the four buildings at the Galleria's crossing, depicting figures representing the continents, ultimately portraying Milan and its citizens as at the centre of the world. The construction of the Galleria was as dramatic a gesture as the development of the telephone for communication. The network here, and in other monumental arcades such as those in The Hague, Berlin and Moscow, represented modernity, and a system with global dimensions.

URBAN NETWORKS

The project of the metropolis was multivalent, but key aspects of that project were efforts to overcome the burden of its size—both real and perceived—and the multiplication of its possible avenues for communication. The whole Haussmannian project for Paris, which we have looked at in terms of its operation as a machine, was also a project about communication and unification, through its creation of urban network systems that cut through its slow and 'dark' operations and favoured fast and highly visible operations. This was amply apparent in the overall plan, and dramatically illustrated by those plans that singled out the streets that were cut through the city; it was realised, furthermore, in individual buildings that were part of and linked to the metropolitan infrastructure, which contained networks within themselves and were connected to existing and new networks. We have previously considered the urban market Les Halles Centrales in Paris (Victor Balthard (1874))

(VI) 26

(VI) 25

in relation to the theme of the shed. Les Halles was a network building connected to a city thought of or conceived as a network. Each of the market buildings was a component of a system, in which every part worked in relation to the next and to the whole, efficiently. The network of streets that served and enabled the market buildings was as significant as them, and furthermore, bound them to the working patterns of the city in which they were set. Despite the market's isolation as a specialised 'structure of structures', infrastructure and highly organised operation, the perceived boundary of the market was porous; its covered interior streets and their arcade-influenced spaces were both integrated and continuous with the local surrounding street network, which itself was being worked to a condition of maximum efficiency by Haussmann's systemic transformations.

THREE-DIMENSIONAL URBAN NETWORKS

(VI) 26

The station complex of Grand Central Terminal in New York, designed by Warren and Wetmore (1910), was an elaborate network structure that commanded the concentration of a broad complex of local and regional rail networks. The terminal building was positioned over the termination of lines coming in both from New York's extended suburbs and the entire continent. The terminal project, known as Grand Central City, used the air space of several city blocks over these lines in its immense property development project. In the beginning of this development, the great yard of train rails was visible under the grid of roads and pavements. Eventually, these voids were built upon to become regular city blocks. The station itself managed several discrete systems of movement for passengers and trains that were separated and connected as necessity required, and was therefore the central figure in a much greater network complex both below and above ground. Cutaway sections through the terminal building indicated the Gordian knot of passages and tunnels that served the different train levels, subways, and pedestrians, and illustrated a fascination with the various and disparate paths of movement and their destinations. The drawings seemed to celebrate the networks at work both above and below the ground.

UNDERGROUND CONNECTING CONCOURSE – ROCKEFELLER CENTER AREA
AVENUE OF THE AMERICAS
ROCKEFELLER
PLAZA
RADIO CITY MUSIC HALL
FIFTH AVENUE
S= subway entrance
FIFTH AVENUE
UNDERGROUND CONCOURSE

ⓥ 27–28

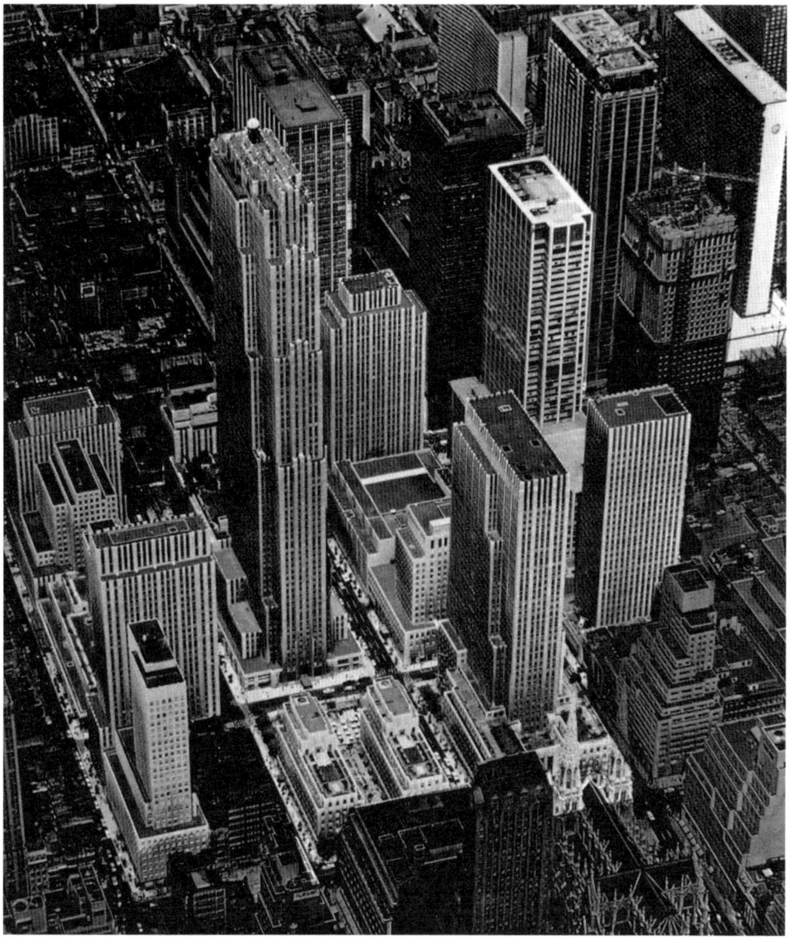

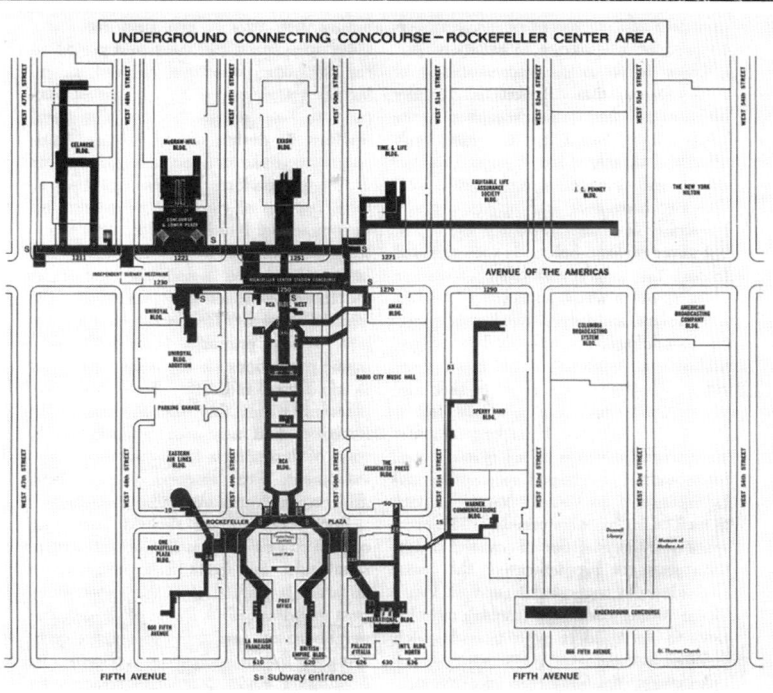

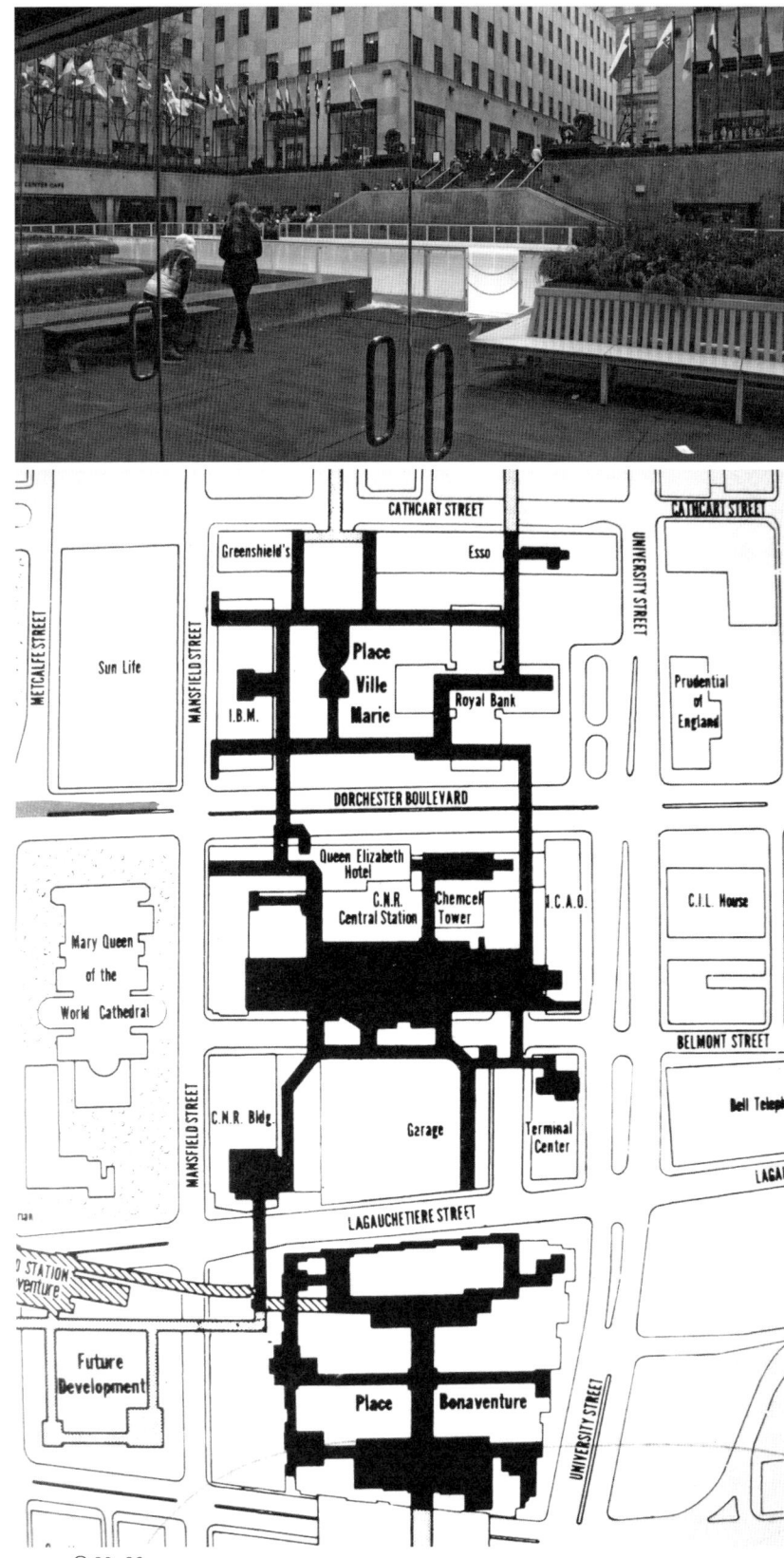

(vi) 31–32

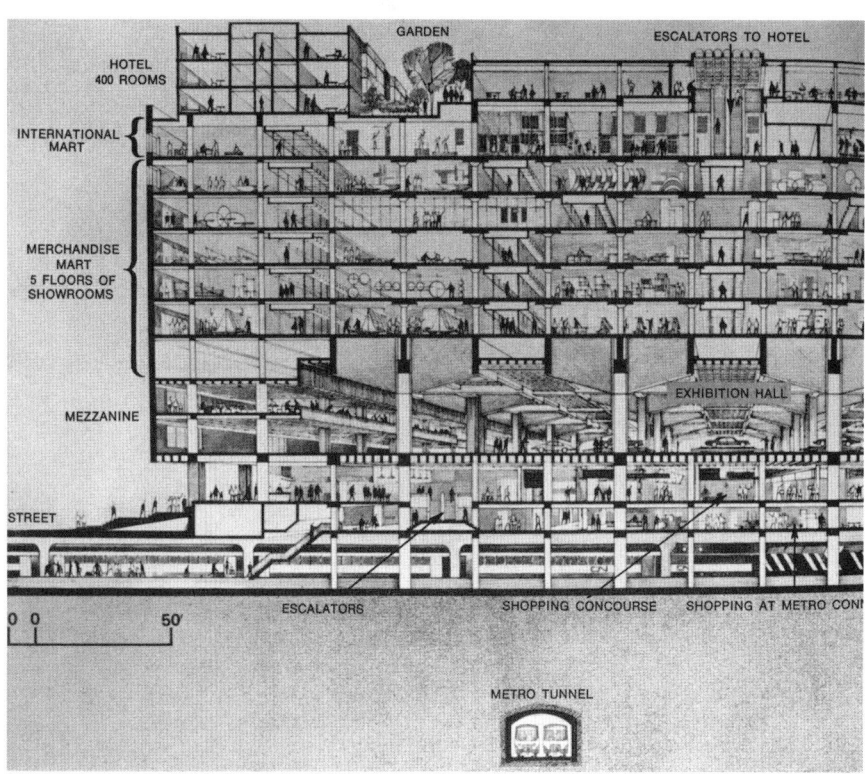

33

34

In that same city only twenty-five years later, the Rockefeller Center, designed by a grand consortium of corporate architects led by Raymond Hood (1935),[15] was the product of Nelson Rockefeller's initiative for a great complex of buildings in the midtown Manhattan, built in the depths of the Depression. Rockefeller took advantage of the economic conditions that stifled most development in the city at that time: property prices and construction costs were very low, due to the disappearance of capital and the correspondingly desperate labour situation (the project offered mass employment in a period of massive unemployment).[16] The result was a building complex that read—largely due to the harmonised character of its architectural design—as a coherent 'city within the city' consisting of several urban blocks of offices for corporations and smaller enterprises, a large variety theatre (Radio City Music Hall), luxury shops and agencies at ground level and shops and services within an extensive underground network that connected all the components of the complex under the city streets. These deep interiors were occasionally illuminated by light wells, the largest of which was the central courtyard, renowned for its transformation each winter into a public skating rink. The spaces underground were effectively decorated tunnels, but they represented the networked and rather exclusive quality of the Rockefeller Center to all its users and tenants. Furthermore, the treatment of buildings' materials and designs so that they appeared as variously and sympathetically sculpted masses, the public realm at street level and the extensive underground network rendered the whole complex a downtown urban realm that was set apart from the pattern of the rest of mid-town Manhattan, a district with a distinct character and an acute atmosphere of interiority.

 Both the Rockefeller Center and Grand Central Terminal directly inspired the plan for Place Ville-Marie (1962; 1966) and the master plan for adjacent blocks in downtown Montréal, designed by I. M. Pei, with Henry N. Cobb and planner Vincent Ponte, architects for the property developer William Zeckendorf. The project was a complex three-dimensional operation designed to exploit and integrate the maximum congestion of existing, new and projected infrastructures, with existing rail lines underground, and parking and a layer of pedestrian passageways—described as a promenade—just under street level. A cluster of office buildings, including a cruciform tower were set on open-air *place* raised slightly above street level on its southern side, and a full floor on the north. The low-ceilinged spaces of this promenade were similar to those in the Rockefeller Center, but more refined, and treated not like underground space but as a legitimate interior realm, one that aspired to the condition of the arcades of continental Europe.[17] The interior of the promenade was shortly thereafter connected to the south to a large hotel, the central train terminal, a 'megastructure'—Place Bonaventure (ARCOP, 1967)—and a new underground public transit station, Métro Bonaventure (Victor Prus, 1966), a core that represented what would was envisaged to be realised throughout the rest of the city centre, in accordance with the greater master plan developed by Vincent Ponte. Ponte's plan anticipated a complete interior city, or *ville intérieure*, that would connect urban blocks previously effectively isolated— like most North American urban blocks, by the dominance of the street and its traffic—and link them to the city's new subway or *Métro* system. This interior ran parallel to the 'normal' spaces of the city and offered an alternative system of movement to streets made

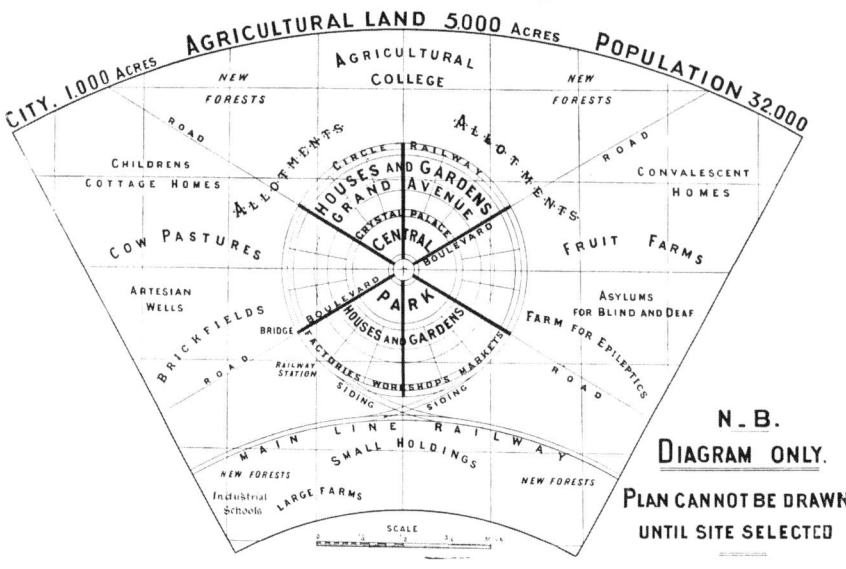

hostile by severe winter weather. The design of this core, and of the promenade of Place Ville-Marie in particular, was representative of an entirely different experience of the urban public realm proposed for the city's downtown zone: one that was new, interior, and artificial. The character of this alternative realm borrowed from the material and topographic characteristics of the streets above, evoking, particularly in its infrastructural nodes, the rough nature of the city's landscape. The 'complete' interior realm anticipated by Ponte grew, in accordance with his suggestions, in incremental developments on an *ad hoc* basis, given impetus by the regular incidence of Métro stations. Within the spaces of this extensive and continuous interior, a multitude of discrete environments and experiences were encountered sequentially, yielding an effect akin to collage, splicing together banal, infrastructural, commercial, civic and monumental episodes. The network extended itself by expanding around newly built infrastructural projects and then forging connections with new and established interior realms in proximity to them, gradually creating fully linked lines of disparate interiors. Its space has continued to expand over the last fifty years to create a loop of some 35km in length, merging with and influencing the character of public spaces above ground. Its latest developments in modifying original fragments of the network represent a fulfilment of the plan initiated by the architects, and the planner Ponte in particular, for an integrated, multi-level urban core.[18]

NETWORK AND TERRITORY

The rambling interior spaces of these North American examples may have also been familiar to the largely white-collar, suburb-based public that was using them. The pre-eminent daily routine included commuting in cars and trains from the comfort of mass-produced-as-unique tract houses throughout the regions, and at the weekend, visiting local shopping centres and indoor shopping malls. The condition

(vi) 36

of interiority in these suburban realms was the norm. Beyond the interior of the individual automobile, which offered freedom of mobility and access to the array of services connected to the motorways, the emblematic space was that of the first indoor shopping mall: the Southdale Center, designed by Victor Gruen. He recognised that regional shopping centres worked effectively as quasi-urban hubs for the suburban regions, and that the 'city' particular to the suburbs made was in fact a network binding dispersed or atomised components. Gruen addressed this condition in his 1964 book, *The Heart of Our Cities*[19] which suggested a diagrammatic, hierarchical and cellular organisation, reminiscent of Ebenezer Howard's prescriptions for a new kind of dispersed urban condition and its components—garden cities—in *Garden Cities of To-morrow* (1901). Howard projected, or anticipated, a system of urban development that would afford everyone the suburban ideal, through networks of planned settlements distributed across an entire country, in patterns that were then emulated by Gruen. The Garden Cities' public interiors, Howard suggested, would be Crystal Palaces, encircling Central Parks. In Gruen's ideal, those public interiors would be fully illuminated and air-conditioned quasi-civic malls. The Southdale Center provided the model of how such interiors should look: a language for the public interior of the dispersed city, with a character forged out of mediated versions of the everyday environment of suburban *everyman*. Such spaces became the representative public interiors of a city that was in fact distributed across a broad regional territory, and whose constituent elements—the home, the office and the mall—were connected by the automobile, the motorway network and the captive landscape within. All these elements had become constituent elements of an extensive interior realm; all were contributing elements to a condition of interiority.[20]

(v) 48–50

(vi) 35

267 THE NETWORK

(VI) 37

NETWORK AS MOTIF

In Europe, the architectural *avant-garde* had entertained the theme of the network for some time in their consideration of post-war reconstruction and the unanticipated shortcomings of Modernism. If the centric form of the city was representative of a European culture thoroughly discredited by two devastating wars and by the failures of the reconstruction and reordering that followed, architects asked what form the city should appropriately assume, and in particular, those environments in which people might live. Projects by the youngest generation of architects of the CIAM group, who formed Team Ten at CIAM's tenth congress as a reaction to the group's problematic orthodoxies, proposed other models, undertaking studies in urban conditions in Africa, England and Italy, inspired in part by vernacular constructions made 'without architects', and by a revived interest in scientific studies on natural forms.[21] Patterns of development drawn from natural, vernacular or non-western sources could claim a measure of authenticity, by their association with original or originating structures. These patterns were then proposed as alternative tissues stitched into the destroyed fabric of the European city, wherein their natural clarity could be seen as a remedy to the chaos born of defective planning and incendiary bombing. The image of Alison and Peter Smithson's competition project for the Golden Lane Housing estate in London (1952) was emblematic:[22] its layout of apartment blocks in root and branch forms, superimposed on the site by lines drawn over an aerial photograph, an homage to Le Corbusier's Plan Voisin (1927). The ruins were not just blasted buildings, but those of prevailing orthodoxies, constructed orders and hierarchies. The Golden Lane project's form, snaking across the site, was re-iterated in its internal circulation—elevated *passarelles*, gallery corridors, or 'streets in the air'. The project contained motifs the Smithsons used later, in their Haupstadt competition project for the reconstruction of central Berlin (1957, with Peter Sigmond), in which different modes of circulation occupied discrete levels of an elevated, citywide web. The public realms were found in the interstitial spaces of the project's all-over network.

Jaap Bakema, another architect of the Team Ten group, designed the Lijnbaan shopping district (1951–1953) for a neighbourhood of tall apartment blocks in a reconstructed Rotterdam dominated by automobile infrastructures. The design relied on a network motif inspired by the 'natural' and human scale of the archetypal *souk*, its low, interiorising spaces, and its pattern, which could be extended and woven through the urban pattern indefinitely. In this project—very un-Dutch, un-European—a character of otherness was central to its proposition. Its formal emphasis, giving priority to the space of communication, both of people and signs, encouraged horizontal perception and movement antithetical to the pre-war city, leaving the high-rise apartments around the site to be quite separate, even distant. Its appearance was shared with and assumed by outdoor shopping centres in North America of the same period, which operated like intimately scaled special pedestrian precincts (again, it was Victor Gruen who led in this area of design).

It was yet another Team Ten member—Shadrach Woods—who theorised about the patterns built into the plans of his colleagues, as a basis for the organisation of both form and movement, and as justification for his ongoing practice with George Candilis, Alexis Josic, and Manfred Schieldhelm. For their competition entry to reconstruct the centre of Frankfurt-Rödenburg (1963), the architects proposed a network of buildings, pathways and courtyards that were to be integrated with the remnants of the built fabric, a low-rise 'mat-building' (a description coined by Alison Smithson),[23] whose contrast with the iconic remains were startling. For their project for the Freie Universität in the western suburbs of West Berlin—won in competition in 1963 but only built in 1973 in altered form—the architects proposed a mat-building whose circulation systems were flattened out across the landscape, with contents caught amongst them, like fish caught in a net, or, more appropriately, like the binding of shops and circulation routes as found in a *souk*: a 'web', as described by Shadrach Woods,[24] and what the architects called a 'ground-scraper'. The ground-scraper achieved what it suggested: it 'disappeared' as an iconic or even linguistic figure on the landscape—the opposite of a skyscraper being the most obvious—and tended instead towards a condition of continuity with the urban fabric. Experience of the building would be turned entirely to the interior, and one could say that this interior emphasis and its correlative interiority were germane to the nature of the mat-building and, as its proponents would have it, central to the focus of Team Ten and the task of contemporary architecture. According to Alison Smithson, the 'interior' of the circulation routes of urban networks were those spaces in which Man moved and lived; as Man was the central 'building block' of architecture (as far as Team Ten were concerned), the network was at once architecture's central figure and its representative realm. The interior was considered an architectural space[25] and therefore subject to architectural methods and expression.

(vi) 38–41

 Within the Freie Universität's subtly hierarchical circulation system—consisting of major lines or *tracés* traversing the site and minor lines crossing them, providing internal access to the offices, classes and green spaces and formed its 'structural web'[26]—there was to be greater communication and interaction between students. The 'web' was to be a structuring device that would allow and encourage growth and change. Growth was intended to be realised in extensions of its main *tracés* to the streets and paths of the suburban district around it, which would at once connect the campus to the city and reinforce all the elements caught in the net: the city around would be fortified by the completion of the network. The consequences for the day-to-day character of the Universität's interior were uncertain, but anticipated that space we have encountered earlier—a continuous interior—and its condition of interiority. (The strategy informing the Freie Universität building stood as ideologically opposite to strategies used in the reconstruction of East Berlin; the fact that the building stood in the American sector, financed through American initiatives, may account for aspects of its spatial and urban morphology.) The mat-building's circulation routes were 'three-dimensional': service vehicles used a level below the ground open to courtyards, while university lecture rooms, classrooms and offices were arranged over two floors. Four major 'servicing spines' held main spaces, while secondary routes held smaller activities. Green spaces provided 'natural' figures in the plan for visual and physical rest, as well as daylight to the mat-building's very deep interior. All functions held within the web of circulation, both major and minor, could be imagined as being able to continue and connect with the part of the city in which was the university was set, very much in the manner of the *souk*.

(vi) 37

Ⓥ 38–39

Ⅵ 40–41

Although the competition project anticipated these connections with the suburban surroundings, the realised project was significantly smaller, and these connections were not possible. Without external connectivity, the building became an internal system, isolated and self-referential. Without the narrative of urban life upon which it was premised, its spaces suffered for their lack of visible qualities, save for the internal, green courtyards that became oases in warmer weather. As a purely architectural interior, it gave privilege to its systemic character, which was reflected in its construction, itself broken into a hierarchical system of prefabricated structural elements, developed with Jean Prouvé, who had designed the cladding of the Maison du Peuple at Clichy (1936): its intended flexibility of form, in which elements could be replaced according to desire, decreased over time. On their own, the skein of walkways, corridors and connecting ramps could not generate urbanism; rather, it created a stultifying, remote interior.

The use of the mat-building—as a type suggesting a rationalised *souk*—was not limited to Team Ten architects, but was embraced by both *avant-garde* and established or 'commercial' architects throughout the 1960s and 1970s. The idea of the mat-building was not lost on the older generation of architects that Team Ten architects were trying to separate themselves from, either: Le Corbusier's design for a hospital in Venice (1964), was a composition of a network of streets and little squares in the air—an interpretation of the city's *calli e campi*—that served treatment rooms on its uppermost floor. Administrative and medical services were fitted below these rooms (open to the sky only) amidst *piloti*, and set above the pavement and lagoon at the western end of Canareggio. The arrangement constituted a system that could potentially expand: yet Le Corbusier's project, despite its desired association with Venice's 'network nature', and because of it being a hospital rather than a truly connective urban feature, would have been as isolated as Berlin's Freie Universität.

UNDERGROUND NETWORKS

The most successful network-based public interiors of the city in the post-war period were those that made themselves integral to the workings of the city, tending to concede to the condition of infrastructure. However, rather than disappearing into a Futurist-styled, alienating maelstrom, network-based interiors were built whose images and atmospheres were constructed around their capacity to provide essential, haptic experiences associated with movement and topography, connected to the idea of the city's scale, which addressed fundamental issues of orientation and identification within the metropolis.

We have seen that Montréal was able to build a continuous realm of public interiors based on the notion that the network was a natural counterpoint and extension of the city above ground. In Milan, Franco Albini and Franca Helg, with the graphic designer Bob Noorda, designed an interior system for the city's new underground railway—the *Metropolitana Milanese* (1964)—that embraced the systematised network as its essential logic. The designers developed an experiential and visual identity, based on ubiquity, repetitiveness and the network's status as necessary urban equipment or infrastructure at the scale of the city, to propose a complete language that addressed and merged structural design, material identity,

(vi) 42–45

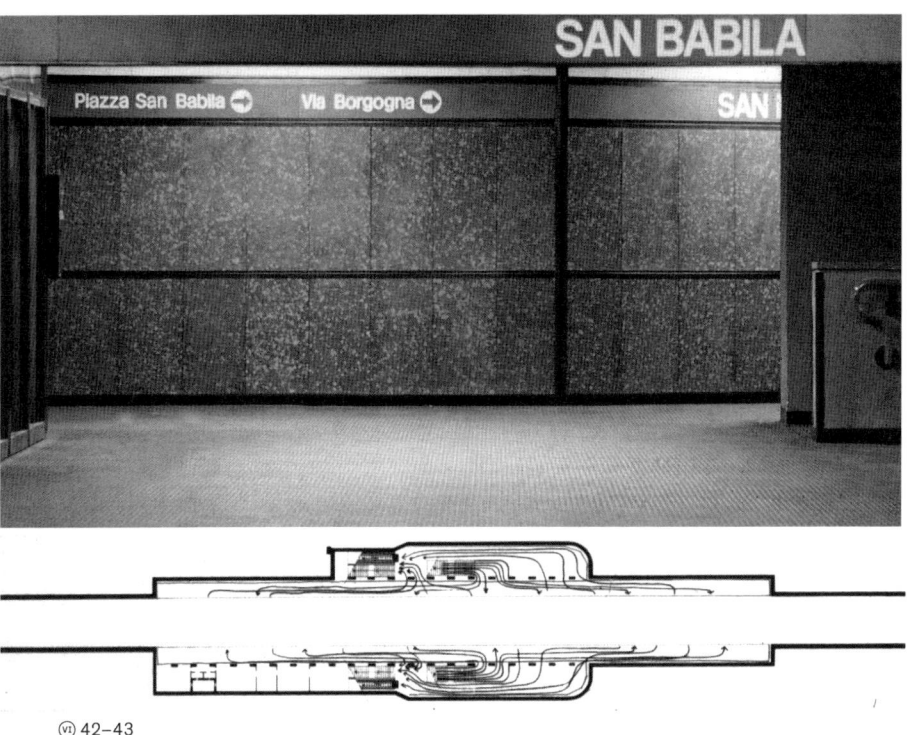

(VI) 42–43

dimensional and spatial regularity and graphic design. The Metropolitana Milanese constituted an architectural interior consistent with the aims of mat-building; yet it was an interior that relied on its relation to the city which it served, which played as its inspiration, its companion and its foil, whether its context was the historical centre, the suburbs, or the industrial areas. It was originally built to connect workers who lived in the centre to factories at the city's peripheries. The system announced itself as part of the city's industrial nature, and its interiors tied the whole metropolitan entity together, acting as the sign for the metropolis and its public interior by default: entering each station meant entering the public interior of the metropolitan body, which one could understand as an entity with material and atmospheric qualities, in its entirety. Thus, it was unnecessary for stations to cultivate anything more than a modest presence on the street, nor offer elaborate representative interiors, such as in the case of the metro systems of Moscow or St. Petersburg. Instead, they were designed like sturdy, utilitarian industrial equipment (of considerable elegance). The 'partnership' forged between the Milanese metropolis and the Metropolitana Milanese rendered the station interior urbane and correct. The design of all aspects of all stations on the first line of the network (M2 saw variations on the themes of the first) followed a narrow and precise regime of materials that started from the appearance of stair wells at pavement level and continued in the design of walls, floors and ceilings, signage and information design from the street to the mezzanine access level, and through to the level of train platforms. The use of local shell-figured granite, *sierizzo giandone*, for the stairwell walls and steps from the street, and Pirelli rubber tiles for the mezzanine level and platform level floors was consistent throughout the system, as were the stations' lining of 'Silipol' grit panels framed with brown painted steel brackets, sprayed very dark brown concrete soffits above them, enamelled steel station identity signage panels that ran above head height in

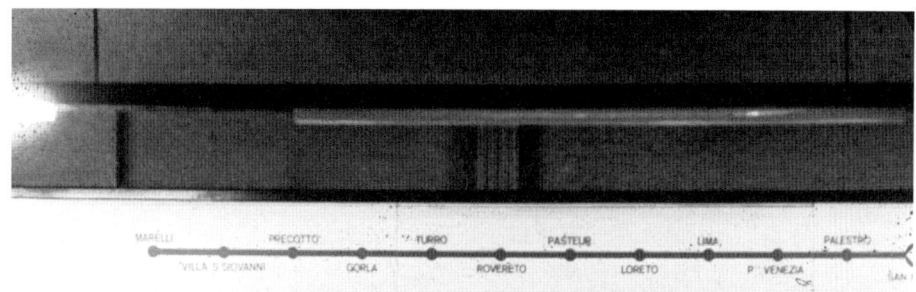

bright red, with directional panels in white, and the distinctive red lacquered steel handrail and its brown-painted steel supports that snaked through all levels and was contrasted with all other materials. The handrail was itself a 'sign' throughout the interior, orienting users both underground and on the street. The handrail and signage were parts of an information system that reinforced visual comprehension: signs and lighting were placed so to guide the user through the spaces, while the typeface designed for the system was intended to be read both obliquely and at speed. Other elements of equipment that populated this interior realm were treated with similar care, such as the clocks and benches that spoke of both industrialisation and domesticity, and further bound the interior to the city's fabric, regardless of whether the urban context was monumental or banal. The network interior had a specific character that communicated the idea of the metropolis, and in this, the Metropolitana Milanese shared an essential characteristic with the Paris Métro, and its consistent lining of white bevelled ceramic 'bricks'.

In such examples, the network was the motif that rendered the public interior logical, legible and familiar. Given our habituation with spaces of transit, airports, malls, concourses and hubs, the coherence of design of the network became ever more important. The interior of the Grand Louvre in Paris (1989), designed by Ieoh Ming Pei—the space inside and beneath the once infamous and now completely accepted glass pyramid—was designed to affect clear connections between the distant and isolated wings of the Palace for its huge number of daily visitors. Entrance to the various parts of the museum was onerous, and the facilities most museums expect to provide were woefully inadequate. Pei's design bound these wings together with a grand concourse, to which was attached a car park, a bus station, a shopping mall, restaurants and cafés, auditoria, visitor facilities, box offices, new exhibition halls and much needed staging and storage areas for the museum. Much of the enlargement of the Louvre's facilities went unseen, but its image was that of a great lobby, to which people descended on a sweeping spiral staircase, or a carefully managed bank of escalators. Visitors moved from the lobby either into the depths of the museum or the plethora of consumer pleasures—shops and restaurants—that supported it. A visitor could also watch people walking across the great concourse, or moving up and down on escalators or on a little hydraulic lift that rose and fell like a piston in the void of the spiral stair. The space had visible and palpable qualities: it was a monumental hall or atrium in its oldest sense, a sepulchral space, a significant catacomb. This was particularly clear as one went down into the interior: the view through the glass pyramid, operating as a huge window, revealed a panorama of the Palais du Louvre, while the act of descent itself assumed the character of entering an archaeological pit, an impression reinforced by an underground gallery later in the sequence that displayed the foundations of the original fortified Louvre palace. At the bottom of the atrium, people passed in various directions, and one could imagine oneself at the centre of a metropolis with a deep and noble history, perpetually in motion.

(VI) 46–47

In the publication *Cities Without Ground: A Hong Kong Guidebook* (2013), sets of complex diagrams guide the reader through Hong Kong's elevated pedestrian system of *ad hoc* passages,[27] which seem to exist and thrive independently of streets and buildings, yet are intimately related to and integrated with them, apparently

Ⅵ 46–47

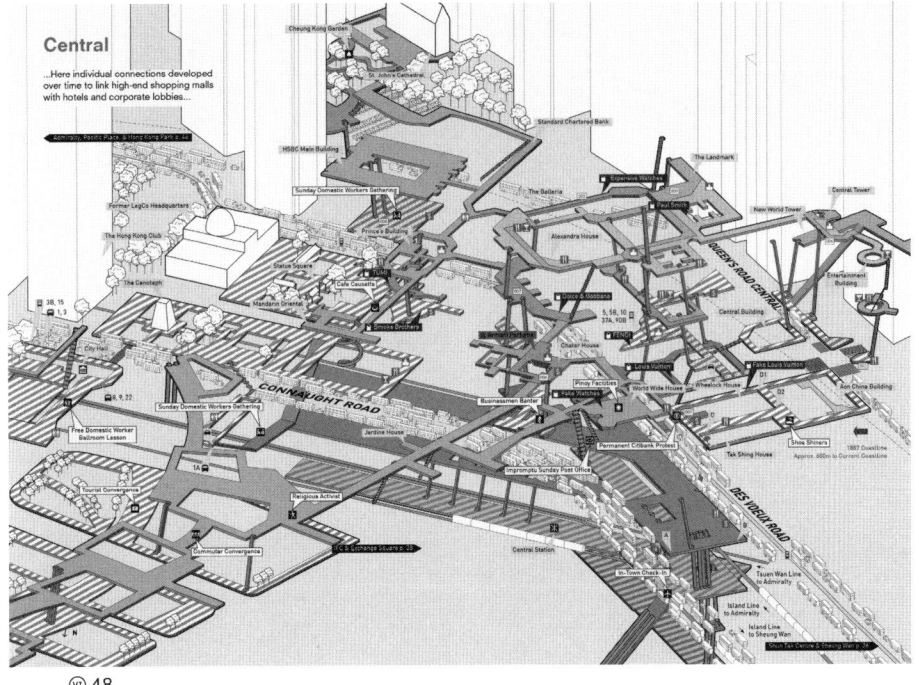

(VI) 48

supporting an array of informal and semi-formalised uses, from social gathering to political demonstrations. These pedestrian 'streets in the air' are of interest as they represent, in an unexpected way, a condition of all cities that has been present since their emergence, and essential to their inception. The metropolis, that product of modernity and industrialisation, tends to the condition of the network by nature and effort: the complex networks as it has been served by and the complex networks it has generated continue to be subjects of fascination for its citizens. The spectacle of the choreographed movement germane to these networks has been a central theme for the metropolitan public interior, and a great, inescapable visual theme of our epoch.

CONCLUSION

I have described a series of public interiors whose network characteristics have led to their immersion and occasionally seamless integration with the attention-demanding representations of the metropolis. More often than not, these interiors have been essential to the metropolis's workings and experience, fusing utility with an appropriate measure of significant experience for the body, the eye and the mind that can be sensed and appreciated. The object of the public interior is to make the city a home in the world for its citizens. As the city becomes ever more dense and yet ever more fragmented, harsh and inequitable in both fact and experience, this condition becomes more acute, and the case for a true public interior becomes more urgent. There is a persistent and increasing disparity between the means of international cities' ever-wealthier inhabitants—who often do not even reside in them, but invest in and distort the values of its properties—and those who support the city through their labour; and between developments that serve an investment market of pension and hedge funds and international financial institutions—that force real residents out of the centres and the inner peripheries, close small businesses,

(VI) 49

(VI) 49

and leave the public interiors of the city barren or transformed into thoroughly inaccessible, private, secure, surveilled enclaves—and places to work and live for the resident population.[28] These centres become instead the reserve of the occasionally resident wealthy investor, while the working class, the middle class and the underclass—that builds, serves and sustains the mirage of the new international metropolis—is pushed out to distant peripheral areas.[29] Tourists observe the spectacle and unwittingly perpetuate the mirage's shimmering yet ultimately phantasmagorical effects. Public spaces increasingly fall into private ownership or sponsorship, tying access to behaviour acceptable to their owners, inevitably obliging consumption; monetising all activities at the expense of wandering or rest; suffocating *flânerie*.

In such contexts, network interiors often become marketing runs; the *souk* of the present day is no longer the domain of the wanderer and the individual trader, but one in which the wanderer is a consumer, confronting the competing forces of international retailing concerns and their aggressive and omnipresent marketing campaigns, stoked by the demands of their shareholders for always improving profit performance. These demands contrive to privatise space, and diminish the public interior's capacity to accommodate and represent all.[30] In such spaces, the individual—who we would rather regard as the citizen—is meant to consume, to respect private property, to behave as instructed, to refrain from assuming any kind of freedom of either action or association. A far more desirable situation would be one in which one might come to depend on the public interior—as one has throughout the history of the city in modernity—and reflect on that condition of control, and propose a new public interior that is an antidote to omnipresent control; as an idea and as an environment that provides succour; as a place for everyone that stimulates the eye, the body, and the mind, and is, somehow, generous. The public interior might continue to reach back to draw from the well-spring of ideas that have moved us and have taken us out of ourselves—as we have seen, for centuries—so that we might delight in its play. The public interior might place us in profound contact with our own material culture, with what we have made in the world, with the natural world, and with each other. The element of contact between people seems to persist in that interior that is most difficult to grasp as a single entity: the network, that enables or structures connections in cities, their extensions and their outposts that hold their citizens together. The character of the network is bound to its experience: its dimensions and proportions, its qualities under one's feet and hands, its accommodation of the bodies and minds and lives of many, its ways of making those bodies and minds conscious of each other, as sensuous, sentient beings, free to move, to associate, to act, to be together, to be alone, to be.

(vi) 01
Paths, Łódź, Poland, 1994. Photo © and source: Mark Pimlott

(vi) 02
Plan of the Maidan and surrounding buildings, Isfahan, Iran. Photo Klaus Herdeg. © Rizzoli International Publications, Inc Source: http://archnet.org/sites/2717/media_contents/40361

(vi) 03
Rehabilitation of Tabriz Bazaar: General plan. ICHTO East Azerbaijan Office, Tabriz, Iran. Source: http://www.archdaily.com/426544/five-projects-win-aga-khan-award-for-architecture/522e0d28e8e44e92b600004c-five-projects-win-aga-khan-award-for-architecture-photo

(vi) 04
Carpet Bazaar of Tabriz, Iran (2008). Wikimedia user: Vathlu. © Public domain. Source: https://commons.wikimedia.org/wiki/File:Carpet_Bazaar_of_Tabriz.JPG

(vi) 05–06
Medina, Marrakech. Photo © and source: Mark Pimlott

(vi) 07
Djemaa El-Fnaa, Marrakech. Photo © and source: Mark Pimlott

(vi) 08
Al-Hamidiyah Souq, market in Damascus, Syria. Photo © and source: Mark Pimlott

(vi) 09
Rialto, Mercato, Fabbriche Nuove, Venice. Jacopo Sansovino, 1533–1555. Photo © and source: Mark Pimlott

(vi) 10
Rialto, Mercato del Pesce al Minuto, 1907. Photo © and source: Mark Pimlott

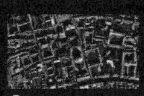
(vi) 11
Aerial view of Oxford city centre, showing a network of colleges. Google Earth, June 2015

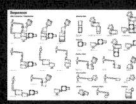
(vi) 12
Bank of England, Sequences, Main entrances– Organisation. Studio Adam Caruso, ETH Zürich. Courtesy Caruso St John Architects

(vi) 13
Palazzo Vecchio and Galleria degli Uffizi, plan *Piano nobile*, Florence. Giorgio Vasari, 1560. Michael Dennis © and source: Michael Dennis. Originally published in *Perspecta 16* (MIT Press, 1980)

(vi) 14
Corridorio di Vasari, plan from Palazzo Vecchio to Galerie degli Uffizi to Palazzo Pitti, Florence. Giorgio Vasari, 1560. Michael Dennis © and source: Michael Dennis. Originally published in *Perspecta 16* (MIT Press, 1980)

(vi) 15
Galerie degli Uffizi, Piazzale. Giorgio Vasari, 1560. View toward Palazzo Vecchio. (photograph Giacomo Brogi (1822–1881)). From *Perspecta 16* (MIT Press, 1980)

(vi) 16
Galerie degli Uffizi, Piazzale. Giorgio Vasari, 1560. View toward River Arno. (photograph Giacomo Brogi (1822–1881)). From *Perspecta 16* (MIT Press, 1980)

(vi) 17
Existing arcades, or *passages couverts* in Paris. Scan from Johann Friedrich Geist, *Passagen, ein Bautyp des 19. Jahrhunderts* (1969)

(vi) 18
Plan of Passage du Grand Cerf, Paris. Scan from Johann Friedrich Geist, *Passagen, ein Bautyp des 19. Jahrhunderts* (1969)

(vi) 19–20
Passage du Grand Cerf, Paris. Photo © and source: Marius Grootveld

(vi) 21
Arcades, or *passages*, Paris. Photo © and source: Marius Grootveld

(vi) 22
Passage du Palais Royale, Paris. Photo © and source: Mark Pimlott

(vi) 23
Galleria Vittorio Emanuele II, Milan. View from Piazza della Scala. Photo © and source: Marius Grootveld

(vi) 24
Galleria Vittorio Emanuele II, Milan. Plan in urban context. Source: Scan from Johann Friedrich Geist, *Passagen, ein Bautyp des 19. Jahrhunderts* (1969)

(vi) 25
Les Halles Centrales, Paris. Plan. Victor Balthard, 1875. Source: http://cremeriede-paris.com/baltard/plan-des-halles-de-paris.jpg

(vi) 26
Grand Central Station, Showing Concourses Connecting Subways With The Station. 1911. Delineator unknown. © The New York Public Library, 2016. Source: The New York Public Library Digital Collections

(vi) 27
Rockefeller Center, New York. Raymond Hood, et al, 1936. Aerial View. Photo Thomas Airviews. Source: http://wwwyoungwizards.com/ErrantryWiki/index.php/Rockefeller_Center

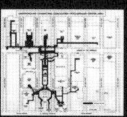
(vi) 28
Underground tunnel layout Rockefeller Center, New York. Author unknown. Source: http://wwwyoungwizards.com/ErrantryWiki/index.php/Rockefeller_Center

(vi) 29
Rockefeller Center, New York. Interior of underground network, looking toward skating rink. Photo © and source: Mark Pimlott

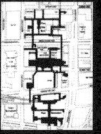
(vi) 30
Place Ville Marie, Montréal. Plan of underground pedestrian concourse. I M Pei and partners, Vincent Ponte, 1962. Source: Mark Pimlott

(VI) 31–32
Place Ville Marie, Montréal. Interior of pedestrian concourse, shopping promenade. I M Pei and partners, 1962. Photo George Cserna © and source: Pei Cobb Freed

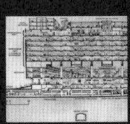

(VI) 33
Place Bonaventure, Montréal. Perspective section. ARCOP, 1967. Scan from *Horizon*, Spring 1970

(VI) 34
Métro station Bonaventure, Montréal. Victor Prus, 1966. Photo © and source: Mark Pimlott

(VI) 35
'Ward and Centre'. Plate No. 3 from *Garden Cities of To-morrow*, Ebenezer Howard, 1902. © Public domain. Source: https://commons.wikimedia.org/wiki/File:Garden_Cities_of_Tomorrow,_No._3.jpg

(VI) 36
View on the Lijnbaan in the centre of Rotterdam, the Netherlands. Van den Broek en Bakema, 1964. ANP 10280559 © ANP Foto. Source: ANP Historisch Archief

(VI) 37
'Stem', Candilis Josic Woods. © Shadrach Woods Archive. Source: Fine Arts Library at Columbia University

(VI) 38–41
Freie Universität Berlin. Candilis Josic Woods, 1978. Photo © and source: George Tashima

(VI) 42
Metropolitana Milanese, Milan. Mezzanine level San Babila station (1964). Franco Albini, Franca Helg, Bob Noorda, 1962. © and source: Fondazione Franco Albini

(VI) 43
Metropolitana Milanese, Milan. Movement studies (*Studio dei flussi*, Bob Noorda). Franco Albini, Franca Helg, Bob Noorda, 1962. © and source: Fondazione Franco Albini

(VI) 44
Metropolitana Milanese, Milan. Benches, San Babila station. Franco Albini, Franca Helg, Bob Noorda, 1962. © and source: Fondazione Franco Albini

(VI) 45
Metropolitana Milanese, Milan. Mezzanine level clock. Franco Albini, Franca Helg, Bob Noorda, 1962. © and source: Fondazione Franco Albini

(VI) 46–47
Grand Louvre, Paris. I M Pei, Pei Cobb Freed, 1989. Photo © and source: Mark Pimlott

(VI) 48
Hong Kong elevated pedestrian network. Area around Central Station. Jonathan B Solomon, Adam Frampton, Clara Wong. © the authors. Source: Only-if architects

(VI) 49
Aeroport Charles-de-Gaulle, Paris. An indoor mall. Photo © and source: Mark Pimlott

Notes

INTRODUCTION

1. Manuel de Solà-Morales, 'Openbaar en collectieve ruimte: De verstedelijking van he privédomein als nieuw uitdaging' *Oase* 33 (Rotterdam: NAi publishers, 1992): 3-8; 'Public Spaces, Collective Spaces' (1992), in Tom Avermaete, Klaske Havik, Hans Teerds (eds.), *Architectural Positions: Architecture, Modernity, and the Public Sphere* (Amsterdam: SUN, 2009), originally published in *La Vanguardia*, Barcelona.
2. Lois Weinthal (ed.), *Toward a New Interior: An Anthology of Interior Design theory* (Princeton: Princeton Architectural Press, 2012).

I THE GARDEN

1. I am indebted to Mohammed Sedighi, whose PhD dissertation at TU Delft concerns the Iranian dwelling, and its roots in the wall that surrounds Paradise and separates it from the world without: the inhabitable walls of Paradise; he also notes that Paradise constituted the theme of many Persian carpets, their borders representing its enclosure.
2. Bruce Barker-Benfield, curator of medieval manuscripts, Bodleian Library Oxford, in consultation process for a permanent artwork for the library extension by Wilkinson Eyre architects, July 2013: 'One of biblical Eden's most important aspects was knowledge, language and names: in particular, God assigned to Adam the task of naming the beasts.'
3. Joseph Rykwert, *The Idea of a Town: The Anthropology of Urban Form in Rome, Italy and the Ancient World* (Princeton: Princeton University Press 1976).
4. Claude Perrault (ed.), *Les dix livres d'architecture de Vitruve: corrigez et traduits nouvellement en françois, avec des notes & des figures* (1684).
5. 'Laugier's call to naturalism is an appeal to the original purity of the act of designing the environment, and at the same time shows an understanding of the preeminently anti-organic quality of the city.' From Manfredo Tafuri, *Architecture and Utopia: Design and Capitalist Development* (1973) (Cambridge MA: MIT Press 1976): 4.
6. The whole saga and trauma evoked in John Milton's epic poem 'Paradise Lost' (1667).
7. Simon Schama, *Landscape and Memory* (London: Harper Perennial 1995).
8. Oxford English Dictionary: From the Greek *panikos*.
9. (1627, at Chatsworth House; and 1637–38, at Musée du Louvre, Paris) 'Even in Arcadia, here am I (Death)'.
10. Andrea Mantegna, *Agony in the Garden* (of Gethsemene) (1455) National Gallery, London.
11. Georg Simmel, 'The Ruin' (1911); Brian Dillon *Ruin Lust: Artists' fascination with Ruins, from Turner, to the present Day* (2014). Georg Simmel, 'The Ruin' (1911); Brian Dillon Ruin Lust: *Artists' Fascination with Ruins, From Turner, to the Rresent Day* (London: Tate Gallery Publishing 2014).
12. Baroque, reflecting the order of Nature either in idealised and often contrapuntal compositions, or inspired by its sinuous forms and reflecting them; and Mannerist, embracing the attenuated, distended, distorted and grotesque. See John Shearman, *Mannerism: Style and Civilization* (London: Penguin 1967).
13. Leonard Benevolo, *The Architecture of the Renaissance* (1968) vol. 2 (London: Routledge & Kegan Paul 1973).
14. Built for the pleasure of the Elector of Bavaria Albert Wittelsbach, (later Holy Roman Emperor Charles VII) and his wife, Maria Amalia of Austria.
15. Kenneth Clark, *Civilisation* episode 9, director Peter Montagnon 'The Pursuit of Happiness' (BBC television: London, broadcast 20 April 1969); with regard to alchemy, see Dan Graham, 'Two adjacent pavilions' in Gary Dufour (ed.), *Dan Graham* (Perth: Art Gallery of Western Australia 1985).
16. Thomas Gainsborough, 'Portrait of Mr and Mrs Robert Andrews' (c 1748–1750).
17. House of Confucius (1749) demolished, Frederick, Prince of Wales Mausoleum (unexecuted), Gallery of Antiquities (1757) demolished, Orangery (1757–61), Temple of Pan (1758) demolished, Temple of Arethusa (1758) demolished, Alhambra (1758) demolished, Garden Seat (1758) demolished, Porter's Lodge (1758) demolished, Stables (1758) demolished, Temple of Victory (1759) demolished, Ruined Arch (1759), Theatre of Augusta (1760) demolished, Temple of Bellona (1760), Menagerie (1760) demolished, Exotic Garden (1760) demolished, Mosque (1761) demolished, Temple of the Sun (1761) demolished, Pagoda (1761–62), Temple of Peace (1763) demolished, Temple of Aeolus (1763), Temple of Solitude (1763) demolished, Palladian Bridge (1763) demolished, Dairy (1773) demolished and alterations to Kew House (demolished). From wikipedia.org/wiki/William Chambers_(architect) consulted 16 November 2013.
18. Jean-Jacques Rousseau, 'Du contrat social, principe du droit politique' (1763).
19. 'I went to the woods because I wished to live deliberately, to front only the essential facts of life, and see if I could not learn what it had to teach, and not, when I came to die, discover that I had not lived.' Introduction to Henry Thoreau, *Walden, or a life in the woods* (1854).
20. Alex Sowa, Jules Schoonman *Design by Choice: the Origin of Mass Customization in Europe* (Maastricht: Bureau Europa/NAi 2015)
21. John Hix, *The Glasshouse* (London: Phaeton 1996).
22. Georg Kohlmaier, Barna von Sartory, *Houses of Glass: A Nineteenth-Century Building Type* (1981) (Cambridge MA: MIT Press 1986).
23. Sigfried Giedion *Space, Time and Architecture: the Growth of a New Tradition* (1941) (Cambridge MA: Harvard University Press 1970).
24. Johann Friedrich Geist, *Passagen: ein Bautyp des 19. Jahrhunderts* (1969).
25. Eve Blau, *Ruskinian Gothic: the Architecture of Deane and Woodward* 1845–1861 (New York: Princeton University Press 1982)
26. Christoph Grunenburg, 'Wonderland: Spectacles of Display from the Bon Marché to Prada' in Christoph Grunenburg, Max Hollein (eds.), *Shopping: A century of Art and Consumer Culture* (Ostfildern-Ruit: Hatje Cantz 2002).
27. Émile Zola, *Au Bonheur des Dames* (1883), translation F. Belmont, *The Ladies' Paradise* (1883).
28. Gavin Stamp (ed.), 'London 1900', in *Architectural Design Profiles* 13 (London: May-June 1978).
29. Steen Eiler Rasmussen, *London: the Unique City* (1934) (London: Penguin Books 1960).
30. Rem Koolhaas, *Delirious New York* (New York: Oxford University Press 1978).

31 Phyllis Lambert (ed.), *Viewing Olmsted: Photographs by Robert Burley, Lee Friedlander and Geoffrey James* (Montreal: Canadian Centre for Architecture 1996); Lee Friedlander, *Lee Friedlander Photographs Frederick Law Olmsted Landscapes* (New York: D.A.P. 2007).

32 Weston Naef (ed.), *In Focus: Carleton Watkins. Photographs from the J. Paul Getty Museum* (Los Angeles: J. Paul Getty Museum 1997).

33 Even before Olmsted's appearance (Yosemite was officially protected in 1864, and designated a National Park in 1890), the suburb had been identified with the rural, arcadian idyll. Llewellen Park, in Orange, New Jersey (1853) was one such place: a settlement apparently without the infrastructure of a settlement, and houses set apart from each other in a contrived, sylvan scene. The settlement's missing infrastructure was, in fact, provided by the nearby town's centre. In the case of Olmsted's design for Riverside, it was Chicago that provided the urban features, and a rail connection between the suburb and the convulsively expanding city ensured the working of a ruralised dormitory dependence. Riverside's streets of hidden houses were arranged in gentle, winding arcs that followed the local, managed topography, their character far removed from those predominantly gridded settlements west of the Appalachian Mountains (the first American frontier). The inhabitant found rest and leisure in a bucolic setting, and then commuted to and from the comparatively chaotic city in a comfortable train carriage. Olmsted's project was important for Chicago, and all American cities, as it provided a model for how a dream of engagement with unspoiled nature (ideologically bound to the Creation) could be maintained by burgeoning and unpredictable urban centres; and furthermore, provided their close and distant suburbs, both in the nineteenth and twentieth centuries with a sustaining myth.

34 Mark Pimlott *Without and Within: Essays on Territory and the Interior* (Rotterdam: episode publishers 2007).

35 A process of regional urbanisation was given new impetus and reinforced by the coordinated efforts of government, financial institutions, industry and publicity to transform a war-based industrial economy into a consumer-based economy. Individual home ownership and mobility were central to the policy; the pre-war Roosevelt administration New Deal, designed to raise the country out of the Great Depression had already begun the process, concentrating on regional infrastructural development. The network of motorways—known as parkways—was to cross regions, connecting urban centres and provide bases for establishing a dispersed urban condition and correlated suburban development.

36 Joseph Rykwert, *The Seduction of Place: the History and Future of Cities* (New York: Vintage: 2000).

37 Dan Graham, *Rock My Religion: Writings and Projects 1965–1990* (Cambridge MA: MIT Press 1993).

38 Rosten Woo, Meredith Ten Hoor, Damon Rich (eds.), *Street Value: Shopping, Planning and Politics at Fulton Mall* (New York: Inventory Books 2010).

39 Francesco dal Co, *Kevin Roche* (New York: Rizzoli 1986).

40 The office was also considered a public interior alongside many, including lobbies to social housing blocks in literature of the period. See Misha Black *Public Interiors: an International Survey* (London: Batsford 1960).

41 Martine Duijvis, Julia Hegenwald, Giulia Principi, from a study made of Bürolandschaft and the Willis Faber Dumas Building for a research workshop in the graduation design studio 'The Place of Work' directed by the author and Laura Alvarez, at Delft University of Technology, Chair of the Architecture of the Interior, Autumn 2014.

II THE PALACE

1 Robin Evans, 'Figures, Doors and Passages' (1978), in *Translations from Drawing to Building and Other Essays* (London: Architectural Association 1997).

2 *Russian Ark*, directed by Aleksandr Sokurov (Russia: 2002).

3 Arata Isozaki, 'The Diagonal Strategy: Katsura as Envisioned by "Enshu's taste"'; Bruno Taut, 'Reflections on Katsura'; Walter Gropius, 'Architecture in Japan'; Kenzo Tange, 'Tradition and Creation in Japanese Architecture', in Virginia Ponciroli (ed.), *Katsura Imperial Villa* (Milan: Electa 2004); Kenzo Tange, Walter Gropius, photographs Yasuhiro Ishimoto, *Katsura: Tradition and Creation in Japanese Architecture* (1960); Arata Isozaki, photographs Yasuhiro Ishimoto, *Katsura Villa: Space and Form* (1983).

4 A *Shoin* is a type: a room at heart of aristocratic residences in Momoyama and Edo periods; originally a reading room in a temple that was also used as a reception room.

5 This insight, arising from Inez Tan and Eke Wondaal's analysis of Katsura Imperial Villa (2014) was augmented by several perceptive readings of the Villa's interior and its landscape by students in the course Fundamentals I at TU Delft, from September 2014-January 2016, to whom, throughout this book, I am indebted.

6 Isozaki, op. cit.

7 Isozaki, ibid. Bruno Taut, 'Houses and People of Japan' (1937).

8 Giulia Foscari, *Elements of Venice* (Zurich: Lars Müller Publishers 2014).

9 Kenneth Clark, *Civilisation* episode 9, director Peter Montagnon 'The Pursuit of Happiness' (BBC television: London: broadcast 20 April 1969).

10 Dan Graham, 'Two adjacent pavilions' in Gary Dufour (ed.), *Dan Graham* (Perth: Art Gallery of Western Australia 1985).

11 Nikolaus Pevsner, *A History of Building Types* (1970: A. W. Mellon Lectures in the Fine Arts, National Gallery of Art, Washington DC) (Princeton: Princeton University Press 1976).

12 Kurt W. Forster, 'Schinkel's Panoramic Planning of Central Berlin' in *Modulus* 16 (1983); Dirk Somers 'A kind of picturesque' in Heinz Wirz (ed.), *Sergison Bates Architects: Buildings* (Lucerne: Quart 2012).

13 Kurt W. Forster, lecture at the Canadian Centre for Architecture, Montreal, autumn 1982, attended by the author

14 Kurt W. Forster, 'A Day at the Office, A Night at the Opera', Mellon lecture, Canadian Centre for Architecture Study Centre, 30 March 2006.

15 The clubs included the Athenaeum, designed by Decimus Burton, co-designer of the Palm House, Kew (1824) and the Royal Automobile Club, designed by Mewès and Davis, designers of the Ritz, in Piccadilly (1911), marking the beginning and end of such constructions.

16 Georg Kohlmaier, Barna von Sartory, *Houses of Glass: a nineteenth-century building type* (Cambridge MA: MIT Press: Cambridge MA, 1986) (1981).

17 Field instituted an atmosphere of service, in which, in his one words, 'the customer was always right.' This was part of

the 'machinery' of the department store or grand magasin, an elaborate mechanism, an aspect and theme that will be explored in a later chapter. See Christoph Grunenburg, 'Wonderland: Spectacles of Display from the Bon Marché to Prada', in Christoph Grunenburg, Max Hollein (eds.), *Shopping: A century of Art and Consumer Culture* (Ostfildern-Ruit: Hatje Cantz 2002).
18. Christoph Grafe, 'People's Palaces: Architecture, Culture and Democracy in Two European Post-war Cultural Centres' PhD dissertation, TU Delft, 2010.
19. Frederick Starr, *Melnikov: solo architect in a mass society* (Princeton NJ: Princeton University Press 1978); Richard Pare, *The Lost Vanguard: Russian Modernist Architecture 1922–1932* (New York: Monacelli Press 2007)
20. Cedric Price, *Cedric Price: Works* II (London: Architectural Association 1984).
21. Cedric Price, Hans Ulrich Obrist (eds.), *Re: CP* (Basel: Birkhäuser 2003); Stanley Mathews, *From Agit-Prop to Free Space: the Architecture of Cedric Price* (London: Black Dog Publishing 2007).
22. For an extensive discussion of 'People's Palaces' in Stockholm and London, see Christoph Grafe, *People's Palaces: Architecture, Culture and Democracy in Post-war Western Europe* (Amsterdam: Architectura & Natura 2014).
23. Aspects of transformations of the Centre Pompidou discussed by Wouter Davidts in a lecture, 'Triple Bound: Art, Architecture and the Museum' at Delft University of Technology on 3 March 2016.
24. See Christoph Grafe, op. cit.
25. David Bennett, *Metro: the story of the underground railway* (London: Michell Beazley 2004).
26. The proliferations of these lights—glass globes caught within a Constructivist spatial grid of brass—led to the nickname for the Palast as 'Erich's Lamp Shop' (after Erich Honecker, chancellor of the German Democratic Republic, 1965–1989); a room with these lights was displayed at the German Pavilion in the Giardini at the 13. Biennale internazionale di Architettura di Venezia, 2012.
27. Andreas Ulrich, *Palast der Republik: ein Rückblick/a retrospective* (Munich: Prestel 2006).

III   THE RUIN

1. Walter Benjamin, *The Arcades Project*, Rolf Teidemann (ed.), transl. Howard Eiland, Kevin McLaughlin; Walter Benjamin *Das Passagen-werk* (Berlin: Sührkamp Verlag 1982) (Cambridge MA: Bellknap/Harvard University Press 1999).
2. Georg Simmel, 'The Ruin' from 'Two essays: 'The Handle' and 'The Ruin" *Hudson Review* (Autumn, 1958): 371–378, originally published as 'Die Ruine' in *Philosophische Kultur* (1911), second edition (Leipzig: Alfred Kröner 1919): 116–124, and in English translation in ed. Kurt H.Wolff (ed.) *Georg Simmel 1858–1918* (Columbus OH: Ohio State University Press, 1958): 259–266.
3. Brian Dillon *Ruin Lust: Artists' Fascination with Ruins, from Turner, to the Present Day* (London: Tate Gallery Publishing 2014).
4. W. G. Sebald, transl., Anthea Bell, *On the Natural History of Destruction* (London: Modern Library Paperbacks 2003); originally published as *Luftkrieg und Literatur* (Munich: Carl Hanser Verlag 1999).

5. Those of Greece did not figure in the architectural imagination until the eighteenth century, and the civilisations of Asia minor, the beginnings of civilisation itself, did not emerge for use until the end of the nineteenth or beginning of the twentieth century.
6. Peter Murray, *Renaissance Architecture* (Milan: Electa 1978). Vitruvius's Latin text had been known across Europe through the Middle Ages, but it was difficult and obscure with missing passages, and descriptions of architecture that were not evident in the ruins that Alberti studied directly in the 1430s when he was, as later, at the service of the Papal court (as the best buildings of Rome were largely built after Vitruvius's death).
7. Published in 1485 in Latin, first Italian version 1546, common version 1550.
8. Jan Pieper, *Pienza: il progetto di una vision umanistica del mondo* (Stuttgart: Axel Menges 2000).
9. 'Città ideale' Luciano Laurana, although possibly attributable to Piero della Francesca or Francesco di Giorgio Martini (1480–90); Piero della Francesca 'The Flagellation of Christ' (c1470) both in the collection of the Galleria Nazionale delle Marche, Palazzo Ducale, Urbino.
10. Murray, op. cit.
11. Edwin Lutyens, still starstruck with Palladio in the 1930s, referred to this manipulation of classical architecture as 'The Great Game'. Christopher Hussey, *The Life of Sir Edwin Lutyens* (1950) (Woodbridge: Antique Collectors' Club 1984).
12. Many of these are displayed in il Museo Teatrale, Teatro alla Scala in Milan.
13. Giambattista Piranesi, *Vedute, o Antichità Romane de' tempo della prima repubblica e dei primi imperatori* (1743; 1745; 1748–1774).
14. Giambattista Piranesi, *Invenzioni Capric di Carceri* (1745; 1761).
15. Abraham Thomas, *Diverse Maniere: Piranesi, Fantasy and Excess* (Madrid: Factum Arte 2014).
16. In Germany, similar work was pursued by Johan Joachim Winckelmann (1717–1768): his publication *Gedanken über die Nachahmung der griechischen Werke in der Malerei und Bildhauerkunst* (1755) considered discoveries of Greek painting and sculpture; his works were the foundations of the German archaeological tradition. More broadly, Winckelmann established scientific bases for archaeology, and art history as a discipline.
17. Dorothy Stroud, *Sir John Soane, Architect* (1984) (London: De La Mar 1996); John Summerson, David Watkin *John Soane* (London: Academy Editions/St Martin's Press 1983); John Summerson, *A New Description of Sir John Soane's Museum* (1955) (London: Trustees of Sir John Soane's Museum 1991).
18. Joseph Gandy was an architect of prodigious talent in his own right, whose visionary work had no place in commercial, Georgian London. See Christopher Woodward, 'Let there be light' in *The Guardian*, 1 April 2006, consulted 2016/04/02 in review of Brian Lukacher *Joseph Gandy: an Architectural Visionary in Georgian England* (London: Thames and Hudson 2006).
19. Hubert Robert spent 11 years in Rome (1754–1765) painting its ruins. His paintings often featured fantastic arrangements of ruins in landscapes; he famously depicted the picture galleries of the Louvre in a state, which both Gandy and Soane must have been aware of.

20 Le Roy was a rival to Stuart and Revett, who published their work partly as a critique of Le Roy's.
21 Loed Stolte and Thomas Broos's study of Bank of England revealed unexpected readings of the Bank of England's scenographic effects. November 2013.
22 'I met a traveller from an antique land/Who said—Two vast and trunkless legs of stone/Stand in the desert. Near them, on the sand,/Half sunk, a shattered visage lies, whose frown,/And wrinkled lip, and sneer of cold command,/Tell that its sculptor well those passions read/Which yet survive, stamped on these lifeless things,/The hand that mocked them and the heart that fed:/And on the pedestal these words appear:/"My name is Ozymandias, king of kings:/Look on my Works, ye Mighty, and despair!"/Nothing beside remains. Round the decay/Of that colossal Wreck, boundless and bare/The lone and level sands stretch far away.' Percy Bysshe Shelley, 'Ozymandias' Margaret Ferguson, Mary Jo Salter, John Stallworthy (eds.), *The Norton Anthology of Poetry* (fifth edition) (New York: W. W. Norton 2004): 870.
23 Dominique de Ménil, J-C LeMagny, Louis I. Kahn, *Visionary Architects: Boullée, Ledoux, Lequeu* (Houston: University of St Thomas 1968).
24 Wolfgang Schäche 'Nazi architecture and its approach to antiquity: a criticism of the 'Neoclassical' argument, with reference to the Berlin museum plans', in Doug Clelland (ed.), 'Berlin: an Architectural History', *Architectural Design* 53 (London: 11/12, 1983): 81–88.
25 Rolf Bothe, *Friedrich Gilly 1772–1800, und die Privatgesellschaft junger Architecten* (Berlin:Verlag Willmuth Arenhövel 1987).
26 Brian Dillon, *Ruin Lust: Artists' Fascination with Ruins, from Turner, to the Present Day* (London: Tate Gallery Publishing 2014).
27 Yehuda Saffran, Wilfried Wang (eds.), *The Architecture of Adolf Loos* (London: Arts Council of Great Britain 1988).
28 Joseph Rykwert *On Adam's House in Paradise* (1971) (Cambridge MA: MIT Press 1981).
29 Stuart Wrede, *The Architecture of Gunnar Asplund* (Cambridge MA: MIT Press 1980).
30 This was characteristic of Swedish architects since the time of Nicodemus Tessin the Elder (1615–1681) and Nicodemus Tessin the Younger (1654–1728). See Haig Beck (ed.), *International Architect* 8 (London: 1981).
31 Hakon Ahlberg, *Gunnar Asplund Architect,* 1885–1940 (Stockholm: Byggmästaren 1950).
32 Janne Ahlin, *Sigurd Lewerentz, Architect* (1985) (Cambridge MA: MIT Press 1987).
33 Giuliano Gresleri (ed.), *Le Corbusier: Il viaggio in Toscana,* 1907 (Venice: Cataloghi Marsilio 1987).
34 Le Corbusier, transl., Frederick Etchells, *Towards a New Architecture* (New York: Holt, Rinehart and Winston 1960); facsimile version of Architectural Press publication of 1927, London.
35 Jean Petit, *Un couvent de Le Corbusier* (Paris: Editions de minuit 1961).
36 Heinz Ronner, Sharad Jhaveri, Alessandro Vasalla, *Louis I. Kahn: Complete Works 1935–1974* (Boulder: Westview Press 1977).
37 Erich Altenhöfer, 'Hans Döllgast and the Alte Pinakothek: Designs, Projects and Reconstructions 1946–1973), in Rosamund Diamond, Wilfried Wang (eds.), *9H, no. 9 'On continuity'* (Cambridge MA/Oxford: 9H 1995): 61–105.
38 Franca Helg (ed.), *Franco Albini 1930–1970* (1979) (New York: Rizzoli 1981).
39 The British artists Graham Ellard and Stephen Johnstone described this in a lecture at Stroom Den Haag 'Franco Albini, Carlo Scarpa and the Museum of Floating Objects' 2016/03/23 in research conducted for their film on the displays in Palazzi Rosso and Bianco, *Neue Museen* (2011). The title of the film derived from the title of Michael Brawne's monograph on new museum constructions, highlighting the emerging Italian approaches to display, *Neue Museen: Planung und Einrichthung* (Stuttgart: Verlag Gerd Hatje: 1965); see also Gio Ponti (ed.), *Milano oggi* (Novara: Edizione Milano moderna 1957).
40 Licisco Magagnato (ed.), *Carlo Scarpa a Castelvecchio* (Milan: Edizione di Comunità 1982).
41 Such as 'Freeze' (1988), 'Modern Medicine' (1990) and 'Gambler' (1990) assembled by Damien Hirst in East and South London, as a riposte to and attraction of the attention of collectors like Charles Saatchi, dealers like Jay Jopling and major art funding bodies and institutions.
42 Lina Bo Bardi, SESC-*Fábrica da Pompéia* (Lisbon: Blau 1996).
43 Michael Asher, Benjamin H.D. Buchloh; Benjamin H. D. Buchloh (ed.), *Michael Asher Writings* 1973–1983 *on Works* 1969–1979 (Halifax/Los Angeles: Nova Scotia College of Art and Design; Museum of Contemporary Art Los Angeles 1983).
44 Nicolas Bourriaud, *Relational Aesthetics* (Paris: Presses du réel 2002). A practice consistent with this notion was exemplified by the work of Rikrit Tiravanija, who, among other gestures, cooked for his audience.
45 Rem Koolhaas, Bruce Mau; Jennifer Sigler (ed.), *S, M, L,* XL (Rotterdam: 010 Publishers: 1995).

IV   THE SHED

1 Oxford English Dictionary: Origin, Old English: hall, heall (originally denoting a roofed space, located centrally, for the communal use of a tribal chief and his people); of Germanic origin and related to German Halle, Dutch hall, also to Norwegian and Swedish hall.
2 Sigfried Giedion *Space, Time and Architecture: the Growth of a New Tradition* (1941) (Cambridge MA: Harvard University Press 1970).; Georg Kohlmaier, Barna von Sartory, *Houses of Glass: a Nineteenth-Century Building Type* (1981) (Cambridge MA: MIT Press1986).
3 For example, Jon Jerde's Mall of America: the shed that accommodates the democracy of consumption.
4 Fritz Neumeyer (transl. Mark Jarzombek), *The Artless Word: Mies van der Rohe on the Building Art* (Cambridge MA: MIT Press 1991).
5 Peter Carter, *Mies van der Rohe at Work* (1974) (London: Phaidon 1999).
6 Nikolaus Pevsner, *A History of Building Types* (Princeton: Princeton University Press 1979).
7 Pevsner, op. cit.
8 Alban Janson; Thorsten Bürklin, *Auftritte/Scenes: Interaktionen mit dem architektonishen Raum: die Campi Venedigs/Interaction with Architectural Space* (Basel: Birkhäuser 2002).
9 Sigfried Giedion, *Space, Time and Architecture: the Growth of a New Tradition* (Cambridge MA: Harvard University Press 1941).

10 Their demolition made room for the multi-storey underground complex that included the huge Métro and RER transit hub Châtelet-Les Halles, and an indoor shopping mall and sports complex, surmounted by a park. Never loved, and fraught with problems of crime and other anti-social behaviour, it was demolished to make way for a new Les Halles, featuring the largest single-span roof in Paris—another shed—open in 2016, designed by Patrick Berger and Jacques Anziutti, to accommodate transit hub, shopping, sports facilities and a hip-hop centre. Recognised as a centre of Paris life, the new Les Halles is proposed to a public beyond the confines of the *Périphérique*, appealing to the city's much more cosmopolitan constituency.

11 Emile Zola *Le Ventre de Paris* (1873); first English translation Henry Vizetelly,*The Fat and the Thin* (1888); transl. Brian Nelson *The Belly of Paris* (London: Oxford World's Classics 2005).

12 Christopher Curtis Mead 'Le pratique urbain de l'architecture: Victor Balthard et les Halles centrales de Paris' www.musee-orsay.fr/fr/evenements/conferences/conferences-en-ligne/vicotr-balthard-et-les-halles-centrales-de-paris.html; Christopher Curtis Mead, *Making Modern Paris: Victor Balthard's Central Markets and the Urban Practice of Architecture* (Philadelphia PA: Penn State University Press 2012).

13 Oxford English Dictionary.

14 Pevsner, op. cit.: Expositions of 1798, 1801, 1802, 1806, 1819, 1823, 1827, 1834, 1839, 1844.

15 R. Buckminster Fuller, *Operating Manual for Spaceship Earth* (1969) (Zurich: Lars Müller Publishers 2008); R. Buckminster Fuller, *Utopia or Oblivion: the Prospects for Humanity* (1969) (Zurich: Lars Müller Publishers 2008).

16 The exhibition setting was designed by Cambridge Seven Associates: originally Lou Bakanowski, Ivan Chermayeff, Peter Chermayeff, Alden Christie, Paul Dietrich, Tom Geisman and Terry Radkine.

17 Penelope Curtis, *Patio and Pavilion: the Place of Sculpture in Modern Architecture* (London: Ridinghouse 2007).

18 Phyllis Lambert (ed.), *Mies in America* (New York: Harry N. Abrams 2001).

19 Robin Evans 'Mies's Paradoxical Symmetries' AA*files* 19 (London: Spring 1990).

20 Alison Sky, Michelle Stone, *Unbuilt America: Forgotten Architecture in the United States from Thomas Jefferson to the Space Age* (New York: McGraw Hill 1976).

21 Werner Blaser (ed.), *Myron Goldsmith: Buildings and Concepts* (New York: Rizzoli 1987).

22 Marina van den Bergen, Piet Vollaard, *Hinder en ontklontering: architectuur en maatschappij in het werk van Frank van Klingeren* (Rotterdam: 010 Publishers 2003).

23 Lina Bo Bardi, SESC-*Fábrica da Pompéia* (Lisbon: Blau 1996); Olivia de Oliveira *Lina Bo Bardi: obra construida/Built work* (Barcelona: Editorial Gustavo Gili 2002).

24 Chihua Judy Chung, Jeffrey Inaba, Rem Koolhaas, Sze Tsung Leong, *Harvard Design School Guide to Shopping/Harvard Design School Project on the City* 2 (Cologne: Taschen 2002).

25 Peter Cook, Warren Chalk, Dennis Crompton, Ron Herron, Mike Webb, *Archigram* (1972) (New York: Princeton Architectural Press 1999).

26 Ian Lambot (ed.), *Norman Foster: Buildings and Projects, vol.* 2 1971-1978 (Hong Kong: Watermark 1989).

27 Georg Kohlmaier, Barna von Sartory, Houses of Glass: a Nineteenth-Century Building Type (Cambridge MA: MIT Press 1986) (1981).

28 Anne Lacaton and Jean-Philippe Vassal, text (English transl.) for FRAC-Dunkerque, from website Lacaton Vassal, consulted 13 December 2015: http://www.lacatonvassal.com/index.php?idp=61#.

29 Iwona Blazwick, Marc Dubois, William Mann, Paul Robbrecht, *Robbrecht en Daem, 2G no.* 55 (Barcelona: Editorial Gustavo Gili 2010).

V   THE MACHINE

1 Susan Buck-Morss, 'Aesthetics and Anaesthetics: Walter Benjamin's Artwork Essay Reconsidered' *October* 62 (New York: 1992).

2 Henry Russell Hitchcock, Philip Johnson, *The International Style* (New York: W. W. Norton & Company 1932).

3 Mari Hvattum, *Gottfried Semper and the Problem of Historicism* (Cambridge: Cambridge University Press, 2004): 39-42.

4 One might consider them as architectural reflections of the Encyclopédie (1751-72) as edited by Denis Diderot and Jean le Rond d'Alembert, which showed, through texts and illustrations, what the world of arts and sciences and the knowledge of every branch therein consisted of.

5 Such as St Bartholomew's, St Thomas's and St Mary of Bethlehem (Bedlam), all in London.

6 Michel Foucault, *Discipline and Punish* (1977). Michel Foucault, 'Discipline and Punish, Panopticism', transl. Alan Sheridan, *Discipline & Punish: The Birth of the Prison (*New York: Vintage Books, 1977): 195–228.

7 Augustus Northmore Welby Pugin, *Contrasts: or a Parallel Between the Noble Edifices of the Middle Ages, and Corresponding Buildings of the Present day; Shewing the Present Decay of Taste. Accompanied by appropriate text* (London: Charles Dolman 1836): '...where the poor were beaten, half starved and sent off after death for dissection. Each structure was the built expression of a particular view of humanity: Christianity versus Utilitarianism.'

8 Manfredo Tafuri, Francesco Dal Co, *Modern Architecture* (Milan: Electa 1978).

9 Stanley Buder, *Pullman: an experiment in industrial order and community planning 1880–1920* (New York: Oxford University Press 1967).

10 Peter Wolf, 'The First Modern Urbanist: Eugène Hénard', *Architectural Forum* (10/1967): 50–55.

11 Reyner Banham, *Megastructures: Urban Futures of the Recent Past* (New York: Harper & Row 1976).

12 Paul Rudolph, *The Lower Manhattan Expressway* (New York: The Drawing Centre 2010).

13 From the Japanese Metabolists (see Fumihiko Maki, 'Investigations in Collective Form' (1964)) through German, French, Italian, British and American examples, the longevity of the Megastructure was brief. See description in Rayner Banham, *Megastructures: Urban Futures of the Recent Past* (1976).

14 Marshall Berman, *All That Is Solid Melts Into Air: the Experience of Modernity* (1982) (London: Verso 1983).

15 Christoph Grunenburg, Max Holbein (eds.), *Shopping: a Century of Art and Consumer Culture* (Ostfildern-Ruit: Hatje Cantz 2002).

16 Charles Garnier *Le Théâtre* (Paris: Hachette et cie. 1871).

17 Rem Koolhaas, *Delirious New York: A Retroactive Manifesto for Manhattan* (London: Oxford University Press 1978).
18 Owen Williams was noted for his designs for factories and production halls, such as those for Boots in Nottingham, and Express Newspapers in Manchester and London.
19 Tim Benton, 'The Biologist's Lens: The Pioneer Health Centre' in Gavin Stamp (ed.), *Britain in the Thirties: Architectural Design Profiles* 24 (London: Academy editions 1980): 56–59.
20 Jurjen Zeinstra (ed.), *Interiors on Display/Stijlkamers* DASH: *Delft Architectural Studies on Housing* (Rotterdam: nai010 publishers 2014).
21 Mark Pimlott, *Without and Within: Essays on Territory and the Interior* (Rotterdam: episode publishers 2007).
22 See Dan Graham, *Homes for America* (1966).
23 Adam Curtis, *The Century of the Self* (documentary) (Manchester: BBC 2002).
24 Alex Wall, *Victor Gruen: from Urban Shop to New City* (Barcelona: Actar 2006).
25 Andy Logan, Brendan Gill, 'New City', *The New Yorker* (17 March 1956).
26 Michael Sorkin (ed.), *Variations on a Theme Park: the New American City and the End of Public Space* (New York: Noonday Press 1992).
27 Robert Venturi, Denise Scott Brown, Steven Izenor, *Learning from Las Vegas: the Forgotten Symbolism of Architectural Form* (Cambridge MA: MIT Press 1980).
28 Francesco Dal Co, *Kevin Roche* (New York: Rizzoli 1985).
29 *Norman Foster Buildings and Projects vol. 2 1971–1978* (Hong Kong: Watermark 1989).
30 Corin Hughes-Stanton, 'Schiphol puts passengers first', *Design* 240 (1968): 48–60.

VI THE NETWORK

1 Johan Friedrich Geist, *Arcades: a Nineteenth-Century Building Typology* (1976).
2 For a description of London arcades and bazaars, see Ian Mitchell, *Tradition and Innovation in English Retailing 1700 to 1850: narratives of consumption* (Farnham: Ashgate 2014).
3 The Ponte Rialto was designed by Giovanni da Ponte (1591) under the inspiration of Andrea Palladio's competition scheme.
4 Alban Janson, Thorsten Bürklin, *Scenes: Interaction with Architectural Space: the Campi of Venice* (Basel: Birkhäuser 2002).
5 Philip Gröning, director, *Into Great Silence* (2005).
6 Jean Petit (ed.), *Un couvent de Le Corbusier* (Paris: Éditions de Minuit 1961).
7 Giorgio Vasari (1511–1574) Architect, planner, painter, and the author of the 'Lives of the Artists' (1550) (or, 'Lives of the Most Excellent Painters, Sculptors and Architects').
8 Michael Dennis, 'The Uffizi: Museum as Urban Design', *Perspecta* 16 (Cambridge MA: MIT Press 1980).
9 Johan Friedrich Geist, *Passagen: ein Bautyp des 19. Jahrhunderts* (1969) (Munich: Prestel 1982). Not only did Geist catalogue the arcades of Europe and elsewhere; he set out their origins and their distinct characteristics while placing them in a very broad context of historical and contemporary developments and influences.
10 See Marshall Berman, *All That Is Solid Melts Into Air: the Experience of Modernity* (1982) (London: Verso, 1983).

11 Walter Benjamin (transl. Howard Eiland, Kevin McLaughlin), *The Arcades Project* (1935–1939) (Cambridge MA: Belknap/Harvard University Press 1999).
12 Manfredo Tafuri, *Architecture and Utopia: Design and Capitalist Development* (1973) (Cambridge MA: MIT Press 1976): 4.
13 Johann Friedrich Geist, op. cit.
14 Gerard M. Koot, 'Shops and Shopping in Britain: From Market Stalls to Chain Stores', History Department, University of Massachusetts Dartmouth (2011): 26–27.
15 Robert A. M. Stern, Thomas P. Catalano, *Raymond Hood: AUS Catalogue* 15, (New York: Rizzoli 1982).
16 Manfredo Tafuri, Francesco Dal Co, *Modern Architecture* (Milan: Electa 1976).
17 Henry N. Cobb, interview with Mark Pimlott, New York 23 February 2011.
18 Vincent Ponte, 'Montreal's Multi-level City Centre', *Traffic Engineering* (09/1971).
19 Victor Gruen, *The Heart of Our Cities* (1964) (London: Thames and Hudson, 1965); Ebenezer Howard, *Garden Cities of To-morrow* (1901).
20 Mark Pimlott, *Without and Within: Essays on Territory and the Interior* (Rotterdam: episode publishers 2007).
21 D'Arcy Wentworth, *Thompson On Growth and Form* (1916; 1941) (London: Cambridge University Press 1942).
22 Dirk van den Heuvel, *Alison and Peter Smithson: from the House of the Future to the House of Today* (Rotterdam: 010 Publishers: Rotterdam, 2004).
23 Debora Domingo Calabuig, Raúl Castellanos Gomez, Ana Abalos Ramos, 'The Strategies of Mat-building' *The Architectural Review* (08/2014).
24 Tom Avermaete, 'Stem and Web: A different Way of Analyzing, Conceiving and Understanding the Work of Candilis-Josic-Woods', from the conference 'Team Ten: Between Modernity and the Everyday', at TU Delft, 5–6 June 2003, section Sociology, Production and the City: 237–281 on http://www.team10online.org/research/papers/delft2/avermaete.pdf consulted 2016/01/06.
25 Tom Avermaete, 'Mat-building: Team 10's Reinvention of the Critical Capacity of Urban Tissue', in Max Risselada, Dirk van den Heuvel (eds.), *Team Ten 1953–1981: in Search for a Utopia of the Present* (Rotterdam: NAi Publishers 2005): 307–312.
26 Tom Avermaete, 'Mat-building' op. cit.
27 Adam Frampton, Jonathan D, Solomon, Clara Wong, *Cities Without Ground: A Hong Kong Guidebook* (Novato CA: ORO 2012).
28 Anna Minton, *Ground Control: Fear and Happiness in the Twenty-first-Century City* (London: Penguin 2012).
29 Ben Judah, *This is London* (London: Picador 2016).
30 Rowan Moore, *Slow Burn City* (London: Picador 2016).

Bibliography

Hakon Ahlberg, *Gunnar Asplund Architect, 1885–1940* (Stockholm: Byggmästaren, 1950)

Janne Ahlin, *Sigurd Lewerentz, Architect* (1985) (Cambridge MA: MIT Press, 1987)

Michael Asher, Benjamin H.D. Buchloh; Benjamin H. D. Buchloh (ed.), *Michael Asher Writings 1973–1983 on Works 1969–1979* (Halifax/Los Angeles: Nova Scotia College of Art and Design; Museum of Contemporary Art Los Angeles 1983)

Tom Avermaete, Klaske Havik, Hans Teerds (eds.), *Architectural Positions: Architecture, Modernity, and the Public Sphere* (Amsterdam: SUN, 2009)

Reyner Banham, *Megastructures: Urban Futures of the Recent Past* (New York: Harper & Row, 1976)

Leonardo Benevolo, *The Architecture of the Renaissance* (1968) vol. 2 (London: Routledge & Kegan Paul 1973)

Walter Benjamin, *The Arcades Project* (Rolf Teidemann (ed.), transl. Howard Eiland, Kevin McLaughlin; Walter Benjamin *Das Passagen-werk* (Berlin: Sührkamp Verlag 1982) (Cambridge MA: Bellknap/Harvard University Press 1999)

Marina van den Bergen, Piet Vollaard, *Hinder en ontklontering: architectuur en maatschappij in het werk van Frank van Klingeren* (Rotterdam: 010 Publishers, 2003)

Marshall Berman, *All That Is Solid Melts Into Air: the Experience of Modernity* (1982) (London: Verso, 1983)

Werner Blaser (ed.), *Myron Goldsmith: Buildings and Concepts* (New York: Rizzoli, 1987)

Eve Blau, *Ruskinian Gothic: the Architecture of Deane and Woodward 1845–1861* (New York: Princeton University Press 1982)

Misha Black, *Public Interiors: an International Survey* (London: Batsford 1960)

Iwona Blazwick, Marc Dubois, William Mann, Paul Robbrecht, *Robbrecht en Daem: 2G no. 55* (Barcelona: Editorial Gustavo Gili, 2010)

Lina Bo Bardi, *SESC-Fábrica da Pompéia* (Lisbon: Blau 1996)

Rolf Bothe, *Friedrich Gilly 1772–1800, und die Privat-gesellschaft junger Architecten* (Berlin: Verlag Willmuth Arenhövel, 1987)

Nicolas Bourriaud, *Relational Aesthetics* (Paris: Presses du reel, 2002)

Michael Brawne, *Neue Museen: Planung und Einrichtung* (Stuttgart: Verlag Gerd Hatje, 1965)

Stanley Buder, *Pullman: an experiment in industrial order and community planning 1880–1920* (New York: Oxford University Press, 1967)

Peter Carter, *Mies van der Rohe at Work* (1974) (London: Phaidon, 1999)

Chihua Judy Chung, Jeffrey Inaba, Rem Koolhaas, Sze Tsung Leong, *Harvard Design School Guide to Shopping/Harvard Design School Project on the City 2* (Cologne: Taschen, 2002)

Kenneth Clark, *Civilisation* episode 9, director Peter Montagnon 'The Pursuit of Happiness' (BBC television: London: broadcast 20 April 1969)

Doug Clelland (ed.), 'Berlin: an Architectural History', *Architectural Design 53* (London: 11/12, 1983)

Peter Cook, Warren Chalk, Dennis Crompton, Ron Herron, Mike Webb, *Archigram* (1972) (New York: Princeton Architectural Press, 1999)

Adam Curtis, *The Century of the Self* (documentary) (Manchester: BBC 2002)

Christopher Curtis Mead, *Making Modern Paris: Victor Balthard's Central Markets and the Urban Practice of Architecture* (Philadelphia PA: Penn State University Press 2012)

Penelope Curtis, *Patio and Pavilion: the Place of Sculpture in Modern Architecture* (London: Ridinghouse, 2007)

Francesco dal Co, *Kevin Roche* (New York: Rizzoli, 1986)

Rosamund Diamond, Wilfried Wang (eds.), *9H, no. 9 'On continuity'* (Cambridge MA/Oxford: 9H, 1995)

Brian Dillon, *Ruin Lust: Artists' fascination with Ruins, from Turner, to the present Day* (2014)

Gary Dufour (ed.), *Dan Graham* (Perth: Art Gallery of Western Australia, 1985)

Robin Evans, *Translations from Drawing to Building and Other Essays* (London: Architectural Association 1997)

Giulia Foscari, *Elements of Venice* (Lars Müller Publishers: Zurich, 2014)

Michel Foucault, transl. Alan Sheridan, *Discipline & Punish: The Birth of the Prison* (New York: Vintage Books, 1977)

Adam Frampton, Jonathan D, Solomon, Clara Wong, *Cities Without Ground: A Hong Kong Guidebook* (Novato CA: ORO 2012)

R. Buckminster Fuller, *Operating Manual for Spaceship Earth* (1969) (Zurich: Lars Müller Publishers 2008)

R. Buckminster Fuller, *Utopia or Oblivion: the Prospects for Humanity* (1969) (Zurich: Lars Müller 2008)

Charles Garnier, *Le Théâtre* (Paris: Hachette et cie., 1871)

Johann Friedrich Geist, *Passagen: ein Bautyp des 19. Jahrhunderts* (1969) (Munich: Prestel, 1982)

Sigfried Giedion, *Space, Time and Architecture: the Growth of a New Tradition* (1941) (Cambridge MA: Harvard University Press 1970)

Christoph Grafe, 'People's Palaces: Architecture, Culture and Democracy in Two European Post-war Cultural Centres' PhD dissertation, TU Delft, 2010

Christoph Grafe, *People's Palaces: Architecture, Culture and Democracy in Post-war Western Europe* (Amsterdam: Architectura & Natura, 2014)

Dan Graham, *Rock My Religion: Writings and Projects 1965–1990* (Cambridge MA: MIT Press 1993).

Giuliano Gresleri (ed.), *Le Corbusier: Il viaggio in Toscana, 1907* (Venice: Cataloghi Marsilio, 1987)

Victor Gruen, *The Heart of Our Cities* (1964) (London: Thames and Hudson, 1965)

Christoph Grunenburg, Max Hollein (eds.), *Shopping: A century of Art and Consumer Culture* (Ostfildern-Ruit: Hatje Cantz, 2002)

Franca Helg (ed.), *Franco Albini 1930–1970* (1979) (New York: Rizzoli, 1981)

Dirk van den Heuvel, *Alison and Peter Smithson: from the House of the Future to the House of Today* (Rotterdam: 010 Publishers, 2004)

Henry Russell Hitchcock, Philip Johnson, *The International Style* (New York: W. W. Norton & Company, 1932)

John Hix, *The Glasshouse* (London: Phaeton, 1996)

Mari Hvattum, *Gottfried Semper and the Problem of Historicism* (Cambridge: Cambridge University Press, 2004)

Alban Janson; Thorsten Bürklin, *Auftritte/Scenes: Interaktionen mit dem architektonishen Raum: die Campi Venedigs/Interaction with Architectural Space* (Basel: Birkhäuser, 2002)

Ben Judah, *This is London* (London: Picador 2016)

Georg Kohlmaier, Barna von Sartory, *Houses of Glass: A Nineteenth-Century Building Type* (1981) (Cambridge MA: MIT Press 1986)

Rem Koolhaas, *Delirious New York* (New York: Oxford University Press, 1978)

Rem Koolhaas, Bruce Mau; Jennifer Sigler (e.), *S, M, L, XL* (Rotterdam: 010 Publishers: 1995)

Phyllis Lambert (ed.), *Viewing Olmsted: Photographs by Robert Burley, Lee Friedlander and Geoffrey James* (Montreal: Canadian Centre for Architecture, 1996)

Phyllis Lambert (ed.), *Mies in America* (New York: Harry N. Abrams 2001)

Ian Lambot (ed.), *Norman Foster: Buildings and Projects, vol. 2 1971-1978* (Hong Kong: Watermark, 1989)

Le Corbusier, transl., Frederick Etchells, *Towards a New Architecture* (New York: Holt, Rinehart and Winston, 1960)

Licisco Magagnato (ed.), *Carlo Scarpa a Castelvecchio* (Milan: Edizione di Comunità, 1982)

Christopher Curtis Mead, *Making Modern Paris: Victor Balthard's Central Markets and the Urban Practice of Architecture* (Philadelphia PA: Penn State University Press, 2012)

Dominique de Ménil, J-C LeMagny, Louis I. Kahn, *Visionary Architects: Boullée, Ledoux, Lequeu* (Houston: University of St Thomas, 1968)

Anna Minton, *Ground Control: Fear and Happiness in the Twenty-First Century City* (London: Penguin, 2012)

Rowan Moore, *Slow Burn City* (London: Picador 2016)

Peter Murray, *Renaissance Architecture* (Milan: Electa, 1978)

Weston Naef (ed.), *In Focus: Carleton Watkins. Photographs from the J. Paul Getty Museum* (Los Angeles: J. Paul Getty Museum, 1997)

Fritz Neumeyer (transl. Mark Jarzombek), *The Artless Word: Mies van der Rohe on the Building Art* (Cambridge MA: MIT Press 1991)

Olivia de Oliveira, *Lina Bo Bardi: obra construida/Built work* (Barcelona: Editorial Gustavo Gili, 2002)

Richard Pare, *The Lost Vanguard: Russian Modernist Architecture 1922-1932* (New York: Monacelli Press, 2007)

Jean Petit, *Un couvent de Le Corbusier* (Paris: Editions de minuit, 1961)

Nikolaus Pevsner, *A History of Building Types* (1970: A. W. Mellon Lectures in the Fine Arts, National Gallery of Art, Washington DC) (Princeton: Princeton University Press, 1976)

Jan Pieper, *Pienza: il progetto di una vision umanistica del mondo* (Stuttgart: Axel Menges, 2000)

Mark Pimlott *Without and Within: Essays on Territory and the Interior* (Rotterdam: episode publishers, 2007)

Virginia Ponciroli (ed.), *Katsura Imperial Villa* (Milan: Electa 2004)

Gio Ponti (ed.), *Milano oggi* (Novara: Edizione Milano moderna 1957)

Cedric Price, *Cedric Price: Works II* (London: Architectural Association, 1984)

Cedric Price, Hans Ulrich Obrist (eds.), *Re: CP* (Basel: Birkhäuser 2003); Stanley Mathews, *From Agit-Prop to Free Space: the Architecture of Cedric Price* (London: Black Dog Publishing, 2007)

Steen Eiler Rasmussen, *London: the Unique City* (1934) (London: Penguin Books 1960)

Max Risselada, Dirk van den Heuvel (eds.), *Team Ten 1953-1981: in Search for a Utopia of the Present* (Rotterdam: NAi Publishers, 2005)

Heinz Ronner, Sharad Jhaveri, Alessandro Vasalla, *Louis I. Kahn: Complete Works 1935-1974* (Boulder: Westview Press, 1977)

Paul Rudolph, *The Lower Manhattan Expressway* (New York: The Drawing Centre 2010).

Joseph Rykwert, *The Idea of a Town: The Anthropology of Urban Form in Rome, Italy and the Ancient World* (Princeton: Princeton University Press, 1976)

Joseph Rykwert, *On Adam's House in Paradise* (1971) (Cambridge MA: MIT Press, 1981)

Joseph Rykwert, *The Seduction of Place: the History and Future of Cities* (New York: Vintage, 2000)

Yehuda Saffran, Wilfried Wang (eds.), *The Architecture of Adolf Loos* (London: Arts Council of Great Britain, 1988)

Simon Schama, *Landscape and Memory* (London: Harper Perennial, 1995)

W. G. Sebald, transl., Anthea Bell, *On the Natural History of Destruction* (London: Modern Library Paperbacks, 2003); originally published as *Luftkrieg und Literatur* (Munich: Carl Hanser Verlag, 1999)

John Shearman, *Mannerism: Style and Civilization* (London: Penguin 1967)

Georg Simmel, 'The Ruin' (1911)

Alex Sowa, Jules Schoonman *Design by Choice: the Origin of Mass Customization in Europe* (Maastricht: Bureau Europa/NAi Pulbishers, 2015)

Robert A. M. Stern, Thomas P. Catalano, *Raymond Hood: AUS Catalogue 15*, (New York: Rizzoli, 1982)

John Summerson, David Watkin *John Soane* (London: Academy Editions/St Martin's, Press 1983)

Frederick Starr, *Melnikov: solo architect in a mass society* (Princeton NJ: Princeton University Press, 1978)

Alison Sky, Michelle Stone, *Unbuilt America: Forgotten Architecture in the United States from Thomas Jefferson to the Space Age* (New York: McGraw Hill, 1976)

Michael Sorkin (ed.), *Variations on a Theme Park: the New American City and the End of Public Space* (New York: Noonday Press, 1992).

Dorothy Stroud, *Sir John Soane, Architect* (1984) (London: De La Mar, 1996)

John Summerson, *A New Description of Sir John Soane's Museum* (1955) (London: Trustees of Sir John Soane's Museum 1991)

Manfredo Tafuri, *Architecture and Utopia: Design and Capitalist Development* (1973) (Cambridge MA: MIT Press, 1976)

Manfredo Tafuri, Francesco Dal Co, *Modern Architecture* (Milan: Electa, 1978)

Abraham Thomas, *Diverse Maniere: Piranesi, Fantasy and Excess* (Madrid: Factum Arte, 2014)

D'Arcy Wentworth Thompson, *On Growth and Form* (1916; 1941) (London: Cambridge University Press, 1942)

Henry Thoreau, *Walden, or a life in the woods* (1854)

Andreas Ulrich, *Palast der Republik: ein Rückblick/a retrospective* (Munich: Prestel 2006)

Robert Venturi, Denise Scott Brown, Steven Izenor, *Learning from Las Vegas: the Forgotten Symbolism of Architectural Form* (Cambridge MA: MIT Press, 1980)
Robert Venturi, *Complexity and Contradiction in Architecture* (New York, Museum of Modern Art, 1977, reprint 1988)

Alex Wall, *Victor Gruen: from Urban Shop to New City* (Barcelona: Actar, 2006)
Lois Weinthal (ed.), *Toward a New Interior: An Anthology of Interior Design theory* (Princeton: Princeton Architectural Press, 2012)
Rosten Woo, Meredith Ten Hoor, Damon Rich (eds.), *Street Value: Shopping, Planning and Politics at Fulton Mall* (New York: Inventory Books 2010)
Stuart Wrede, *The Architecture of Gunnar Asplund* (Cambridge MA: MIT Press 1980)

Jurjen Zeinstra (ed.), *Interiors on Display/Stijlkamers DASH: Delft Architectural Studies on Housing* (Rotterdam: nai010 publishers, 2014)

Index

A
Abbondi, Antonio 249
Adam 18, 126, 285
Adler, Dankmar 218
Albert (Prince) 40
Alberti, Leon Baptista 101–102, 104, 112, 146, 288
Albini, Franco 132–133, 273, 283
Alphand, Jean-Charles 45
Andreu, Paul 236, 239
Antonioni, Michelangelo 133
Anziutti, Jacques 289
Archigram 182, 225
Ashbee W. N. 162
Asher, Michael 141
Asplund, Erik Gunnar 126, 147
Aulenti, Gae 87, 139, 147, 175

B
Bakema, Jaap 269, 283
Baker, (Sir) Herbert 114
Balthard, Victor 159–160, 186, 259, 282
Barry, Charles 75, 94
Bartolomeo, Maso di 67, 94
Beaudouin, Eugène 82, 94, 222
Benjamin, Walter 97
Bentham, Jeremy 200
Bentham, Jan (Benthem Crouwel Architects) 236, 239
Berger, John 13
Berger, Patrick 289
Berlage, Hendrik Petrus 153
Bo Bardi, Lina 138, 175–176
Boccione, Umberto 190
Boezem, Marinus 21, 154
Boileau, Louis Auguste 41–42, 94
Boucicault, Aristide 42, 78, 179
Boullée, Etienne-Louis 117, 119, 146, 195
Bourriaud, Nicolas 87, 141
Bouvard, J.-A. 166
Bramante, Donato 67
Branzi, Andrea 55, 57
Brody, Davis Associates 171, 187
Brown, Lancelot 'Capability' 29
Brown, Denise Scott 228, 239
Bruegel the Younger, Jan 18, 56
Bruegel the Elder, Jan 18
Brunelleschi, Filippo 101
Buckminster Fuller, R. 167, 186
Buonarotti, Michelangelo 75
Burnham, Daniel 80
Burton, Decimus 34, 287

C
Callimachus 21
Campbell, Colen 109
Candilis, George 269, 283
Carl of Prussia (Prince) 119
Carrà, Carlo 190
Celsing, Peter 84, 94
Chambers, William 21, 30, 56, 112
Chambliss, Edgar 205
Chanut, Ferdinand 78
Charles VII 71, 285
Chedanne, Georges 78, 94
Chipperfield, David 141, 147
Clark, Kenneth 12–13, 71
Cobb, Henry N. 136, 147, 182, 265, 283
Cockerell, Samual Pepys 30
Collet, Félix 159
Columbo, Joe 225
Considerant, Victor 202
Contamin, Victor 166
Cook, Peter 225
Corbett, Harvey Wiley 218
Crouwel, Mels (Benthem Crouwel Architects) 236, 239
Crompton, Dennis 225
Cuvilliés, François de 70
Cuypers, Pierre 75–77, 94, 218

D
Daem, Hilde 185, 187
Danforth, Charles 150, 186
Davis, Arthur Joseph 42, 76, 287
Deane, Thomas Newenham 40, 56–57, 123, 132
Dietrich, Joachim 70
Dinkeloo, John 51, 55, 57, 228, 239
Döllgast, Hans 132, 141
Duintjer, Marius 236, 239
Durand, Jean-Nicolas-Louis 192, 195, 238
Dutert, Ferdinand 124, 147, 166, 186

E
Eiffel, Gustave 42, 94
Eisenman, Peter 205
Enshu, Kobori 62, 287
Eugénie (Empress) 216
Eve 18, 126

F
Fehn, Sverre 133, 147
Foucault, Michel 200
Fourier, Charles 202
Foster, Norman 55, 57, 182, 187, 220, 230, 233, 239
Frederick the Great 72, 119
Freed, Ingo 136, 147, 182, 283
Friedrich Wilhelm III 72
Friedrich Wilhelm (Crown-Prince), later Friedrich IV of Prussia 123

G
Galli-Bibiena, Ferdinando 106, 146
Gandy, Joseph 112, 114, 117, 146, 288
Garnier, Charles 78, 213, 216, 218, 237, 239
Geist, Johann Friedrich 35, 242, 255, 282, 291

Gendt, A.L. van 77
Giedion, Sigfried 156
Gilly, Friedrich 117, 119
Ginzburg, Moisei 202
Giorgio Martini, di Francesco 67, 94, 288
Girardin, René de 30
God 18, 150, 285
Godin, Jean-Baptiste-André 202–203, 238
Goldsmith, Myron 173, 187
Gordon, Max 138
Graffunde, Heinz 90, 95
Graves, Michael 205
Greene, David 225
Gropius, Walter 62, 222, 287
Gruen, Victor 47, 51, 57, 226–227, 239, 267, 269

H
Händel, Georg Friedrich 26
Haussmann, (Baron) Georges-Eugène 39, 42, 44, 78, 139, 159–160, 189, 207–208, 213, 218, 238, 255, 257, 259–260
Hawksmoor, Nicholas 29
Helg, Franca 132–133, 273, 283
Hénard, Eugène 205, 216, 218, 238
Henry VIII 123, 195
Herron, Ron 225
Herzog & de Meuron 138, 144, 147, 185
Hines, Gerald D. 47
Hirt, Alois 72
Hitler, Adolf 119
Hogarth, William 117
Hood, Raymond 265, 282
Horta, Victor 82
Howard, Ebenezer 39–40, 56, 78, 267, 283
Hultén, Pontus 84, 87, 141, 175

I
Ishimoto, Yasuhiro 62, 64, 94, 287
Izenor, Steven 228, 239

J
Jerde, Jon Associates 179, 182, 187, 289
Johnson, Philip 182, 187
Jones, Inigo 106, 114
Josic, Alexis 269, 283

K
Kahn, Albert 150
Kahn, Louis I. 127, 131, 147
Kahn, Fazlur 173
Kiley, Dan 52
Klenze, Leo von 32
Klingeren, Frank van 147, 175, 187
Kolbe, Georg 150

Koolhaas, Rem (OMA)   144, 147, 220
Krupp, Alfred   203

L
La Pietra, Ugo   225
Labrouste, Henri   41, 57
Lacaton, Anne   87, 95, 139, 147, 182, 187
Lang, Fritz   144, 190, 220
Laugier, Abbé Marc-Antoine   21, 35, 40, 56, 255, 285
Laurana, Luciano   67, 94, 102, 288
Le Corbusier   88, 127, 145, 147, 190, 249, 269, 273
Le Nôtre, André   29
Le Play, Fréderic   166
Le Roy, Julien-David   114, 288
Ledoux, Claude Nicolas   117, 203
Leonidov, Ivan   205
Lewerentz, Sigurd   126–127
Lewis, James   196
Liang Ie, Kho   236, 239
Littlewood, Joan   82, 173, 225
Lods, Marcel   82, 94, 222
Loos, Adolf   125–126, 147
Loudon, John Claudius   34

M
Malcolmson, Reginald   172
Manet, Édouard   162
Martin, (Sir) Leslie   88, 95
Marinetti, Filippo Tomasso   190
McKim, Charles Follen   124, 147, 162, 191, 228
Mead, Willam Rutherford   124, 147, 162, 191, 228
Medici, (Prince) Cosimo I de   250, 253
Mengoni, Guiseppe   39, 56, 257
Mewès, Charles   42, 77, 287
Meyndier, Hippolyte   35
Mies van der Rohe, Ludwig   150, 153, 171–173, 176, 182, 185–187
Mitterrand, François   139
Monet, Claude   162
Montefeltro, Federico III da   67
Monville, François Racine de   25
Moretti, Luigi   132
Moro, Peter   88, 95

N
Napoléon III, Louis   39, 159, 162, 207, 216
Nervi, Pier Luigi   173, 205, 238
Neumann, Balthasar   69–70, 82, 94
Newton, (Sir) Isaac   117, 119, 146
Nightingale, Florence   196
Nishizawa, Ryue   55
Noorda, Bob   273

O
Olmsted, Frederick Law   45, 47, 52, 57, 286
Orsini, Pier Francesco   25, 56
O'Shea, James   40, 123
O'Shea, John   40
Otto, Frei   167, 171, 186
Outshoorn, Cornelis   77

P
Palladio, Andrea   104, 106, 109, 112, 114, 146, 288, 291
Pan   25
Pask, Gordon   83, 225
Paxton Joseph   34–35, 39, 56, 165, 173
Pearse, Innes Hope   225
Pecz, Samu   160
Pei, Ieoh Ming   136, 139, 147, 182, 265, 277, 282–283
Perrault, Claude   21, 56
Pevsner, Nikolaus   11
Piano, Renzo   84, 95, 173, 187, 225, 239
Pisano, Giovanni   133
Piranesi, Giambattista   106, 109, 112, 114, 117, 131, 144, 146–147, 236, 250
Ponte, Giovanni da   291
Ponte, Vincent   265–266, 282
Poussin, Nicolas   25, 29–30, 56, 127
Price, Cedric   26, 56, 82–83, 94, 173, 187, 225, 239
Prouvé, Jean   82, 94, 222, 273
Prus, Victor   265, 283
Pugin, Augustus Welby Northmore   200, 238
Pullman, George   203, 205, 238

Q
Quatremère de Quincy, Antoine-Chrysostome   192, 195

R
Rastrelli, Francesco Bartolomeo   50, 94
Rausmüller, Urs   138
Repton, Humphry   29–30
Revett, Nicholas   110, 112, 146, 288
Richardson, Henry Hobson   80
Robert, Hubert   112, 288
Robbrecht, Paul   185, 187
Roche, Kevin   51–55, 57, 228, 230, 239
Rogers, Richard   84, 95, 173, 187, 225, 239
Rousseau, Jean-Jacques   30, 32, 56
Rovira i Trias, Antoni   160, 186
Rudolph, Paul   205, 238
Ruskin, John   123

S
Saenredam, Pieter   150, 186

Sampson, George   112
Sangallo, da Antonio   75
Sans, Jérome   87, 141
Sansovino, Jacopo   249, 282
Sant'Elia, Antonio   190
Sauvage, Henri   222, 239
Scamozzi, Vincenzo   104, 146
Scarpa, Carlo   132–133, 147, 289
Schinkel, Karl Friedrich   72, 75, 94, 117, 119, 147
Schönborn, (Prince-Bishop) Johann Philipp Franz von   69–70
Schönbrunn (Archbishop)   70
Scott, George Gilbert   138, 225
Sejima, Kazuyo   55
Semper, Gottfried   126
Shakespeare, William   26
Shelley, Percy Bysshe   114, 288
Schieldhelm, Manfred   269
Shikubu, Murasaki   64
Sigmond, Peter   269
Smirke, Robert   196
Smithson, Alison   269, 270
Smithson, Peter   269
Soane, (Sir) John   112, 114, 117, 126, 132, 146, 250, 288
Soane, Mrs.   117
Soria y Mata, Alberto   205
Speer, Albert   119
Stalin, Josef   88, 90
Stuart, James   110, 112, 146, 288
Stubbins, Hugh   51, 57
Sutherland, Maurice   47
Sullivan, Louis   218

T
Tange, Kenzo   62, 64, 287
Taut, Bruno   62, 65, 287
Taylor, Frederick   190, 233
Taylor, (Sir) Robert   112
Team Ten   242, 244, 269–273
Thoreau, Henry   32, 56
Tiepolo, Giovanni Baptista   70
Turner, Joseph Mallard William   123, 147
Turner, Richard   34
Tyng, Anne   131

V
Van Hee, Marie-José   185, 187
Vanbrugh, John   29
Vasari, Giorgio   250, 253, 282
Vassal, Jean-Philippe   87, 95, 139, 147, 182, 187
Vaux, Calvert   45, 57
Velásquez Bosco, Ricardo   78
Venturi, Robert   12–13, 228
Vinci, Leonardo da   218
Viollet-le-Duc, Eugène   125
Vitruvius Pollio, Marcus   2, 101–104, 106, 109, 288

W
Wachsmann, Konrad   172
Warren, Whitney   218, 239, 260
Waterhouse, Alfred   40
Watkins, Carleton   45, 57
Webb, Michael   225
Weissmann, Adriaan Willem   77
Wetmore, Charles   218, 239, 260
Whelan, Edward   40
White, Stanford   124, 147, 162, 191, 228
Williams, Owen   222, 239, 290
Williamson, George Scott   225
Wilson, Edward   162
Winckelmann, Johan Joachim   119, 288
Woods, Shadrach   269–270, 283
Woodward, Benjamin   40, 56–57, 123, 132
Wright, Frank Lloyd   230, 233

X
Xenakis, Iannis   127

Z
Zeckendorf, William   265
Zeidler, Eberhard   47
Zimmermann, Joseph Baptist   70
Zola, Emile   42, 160

Image index

299 IMAGE INDEX

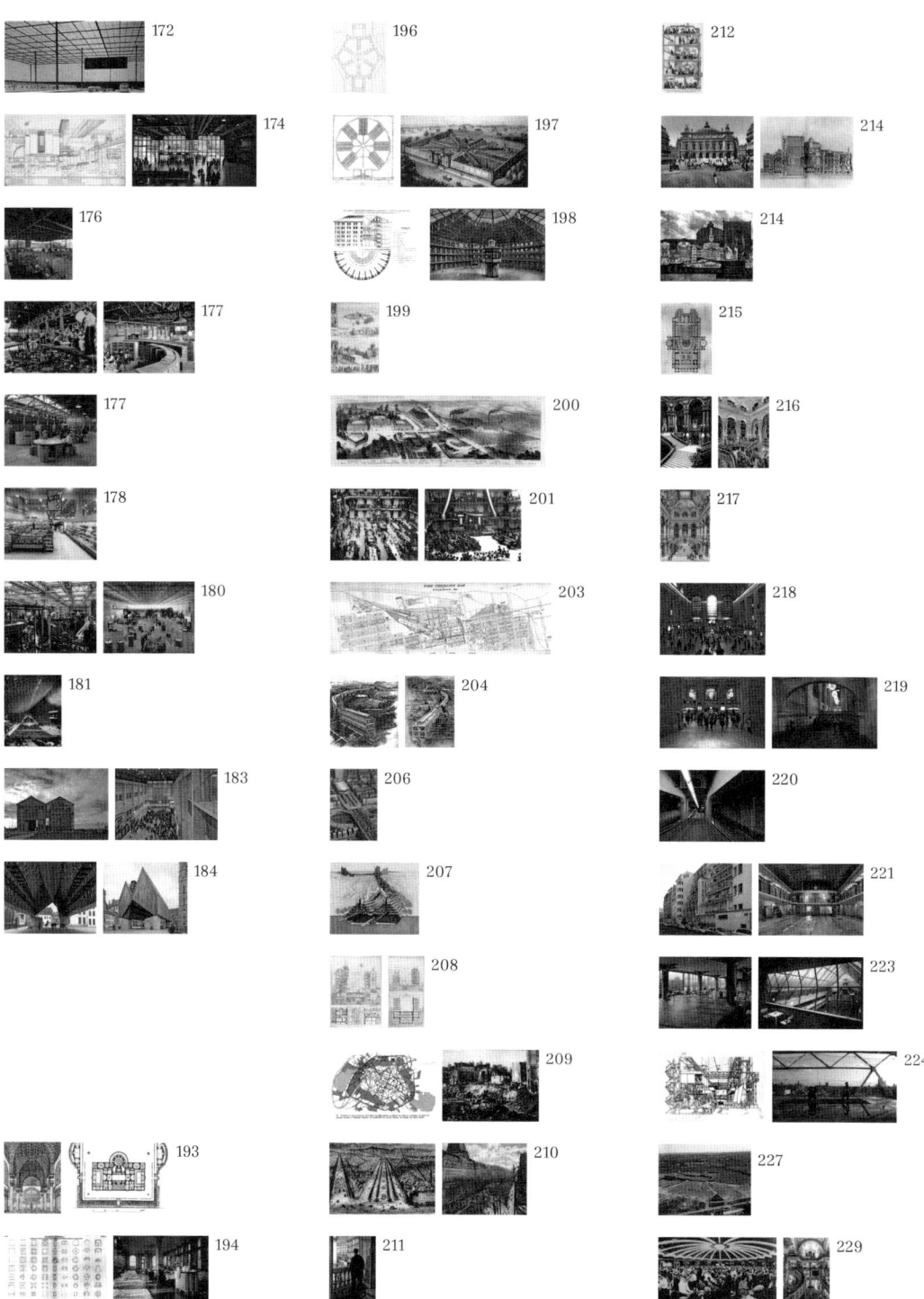

301 IMAGE INDEX

The Public Interior as Idea
and Project

AUTHOR
Mark Pimlott

GRAPHIC DESIGN
SJG/ Joost Grootens, Silke Koeck
Simon Ruaut

PRINTING, BINDING & LITHOGRAPHY
Oro Grafisch Projectmanagement

PUBLISHER & EDITOR
Eleonoor Jap Sam
Jap Sam Books, Prinsenbeek,
the Netherlands

The author and publisher gratefully
acknowledge the permission granted
to reproduce the copyright material
in this book.
Every effort has been made to trace
copyright holders and to obtain their
permission for the use of copyright
material.

All rights reserved. No part of this
publication may be reproduced in any
form by any electronic or mechanical
means without permission in writing
from the artist, authors and the
publisher.

www.japsambooks.nl

ISBN 978-94-90322-52-6

© 2022 Second edition /
© 2016 First edition Mark Pimlott,
the photographers, and Jap Sam Books

The first edition has been made
possible with the support of the
Creative Industries Funds NL and
the Delft University of Technology.